IMAGES
of America

MIDTOWN PHOENIX

Derek D. Horn

ARCADIA PUBLISHING

ISBN 978-1-4671-1555-1

Published by Arcadia Publishing
Charleston, South Carolina

Printed in the United States of America

Library of Congress Control Number: 2015948916

For all general information, please contact Arcadia Publishing:
Telephone 843-853-2070
Fax 843-853-0044
E-mail sales@arcadiapublishing.com
For customer service and orders:
Toll-Free 1-888-313-2665

Visit us on the Internet at www.arcadiapublishing.com

Contents

ACKNOWLEDGMENTS

During the preparation of this manuscript, I was very fortunate to receive the assistance and support from many individuals and organizations. First, thank you to G.G. George, Encanto Citizens Association, for both inspiring and encouraging this work, along with sharing photographs from her collection. I also thank the following archivists, librarians, and officials for generously sharing their time and providing access to their collections: Jean Barry, Arizona Room, Phoenix Public Library; Libby Coyner and Wendi Goen, Arizona State Library; Mario Klimades and Betty Murphy, Billie Jane Baguley Library and Archives, Heard Museum; David Rock, Arizona Science Center; Robert Spindler, Arizona State University Libraries; Morris Stein, FAIA, Trustee Varney Sexton Sydnor Architectural Records; Michelle Dodds, City of Phoenix Historic Preservation Office; Joshua Bednarek and Joél Carrasco, City of Phoenix Planning and Development Department; Serena Washington, Ryerson and Burnham Libraries, The Art Institute of Chicago; Jill Brownley, Greater Phoenix Chamber of Commerce; Julie Glass, Del Web Sun Cities Museum; Rebekah Tabah Percival, Arizona Historical Society; Leah Harrison, Salt River Project; Holly Aguilar, and the Regency House Association.

I would also like to thank the following individuals for generously sharing their photograph collections, stories, and their assistance: Missy Shackelford, Douglas Sydnor, FAIA, Timothy J. O'Malley, Ron Robinette, Webb Ellis, Marilyn Barrows, Richard Ely, Katherine Coles, Jean Switzer, Linda and Robert Russman, Betsey Bayless, Frank Barios, Len Huck, Travys Harvey, Glenda Walker, Lowell Adkins, Jim Johnson, Margaret Dietrich, and the team at Arcadia Publishing.

To all, I extend my sincerest gratitude.

INTRODUCTION

Midtown stretches north of downtown along the Central Avenue Corridor. Once an area of desert, farms, and ranches, it would, over the years, become home to many of the city's wealthiest and most influential citizens; a center of commerce, arts, and culture; a showcase for mid-century and modern architecture; and a destination for those seeking an urban lifestyle in a city known for its suburban culture and sprawl.

After its establishment on the original townsite north of the Salt River in 1870, the city grew and changed rapidly. Structures built of adobe gave way to wood and brick buildings as these materials became available through increased commerce and improved transportation. In time, concrete and steel would dominate modern construction in the Corridor.

Between 1900 and 1945, Midtown and the Central Corridor was established with the homes of the wealthy and middle class in pleasant, lushly landscaped neighborhoods supported by shops, stores, churches, and schools. Central Avenue itself was lined with houses constructed and occupied by the city's business and community leaders. It became known as Millionaires' Row. The center of commerce, accessed by a streetcar system, was downtown, south of Van Buren Street.

After 1945, the city grew rapidly in the postwar prosperity. Houses and small shops in the Corridor were replaced by bigger buildings, some of which would be demolished just a few years later for even bigger buildings. The 1950s and 1960s saw big changes as office and residential towers rose over a landscape recently occupied with farms, ranches, and houses.

By the 1980s, Midtown rivaled downtown as the city's center of commerce as growth in the Corridor continued. By the early 1990s, however, Midtown was no longer the growth center of the city, having been supplanted by a renewed interest in downtown and growth in other areas.

In the early 2000s, after a period of stagnation, residents and businesses attracted by an urban lifestyle, historic neighborhoods, cultural destinations, and easy access to downtown commerce and sporting events began flocking to Midtown. Today, Midtown is undergoing a renaissance with new housing units under construction and mid-century office towers being adapted for modern business needs.

Writing a history of Midtown is both a daunting and inspiring task. Fortunately, many citizens documented their lives and their city with photographs. Many of these photographs are preserved in archives, libraries, and private collections. These images, along with the written word, provide a rich treasure trove upon which the researcher can draw.

Because of the author's education and profession in building design, construction, and regulation, this story of Midtown Phoenix is told primarily through its buildings and physical development, with a focus on the Central Corridor and Central Avenue, the main thoroughfare that runs north from downtown. It was along Central Avenue, originally named Centre Street, where the character of the Midtown area was first shaped by the homes and estates of the business and community leaders that, over time, gave way to the museums, businesses, and towers that dominate the Corridor today.

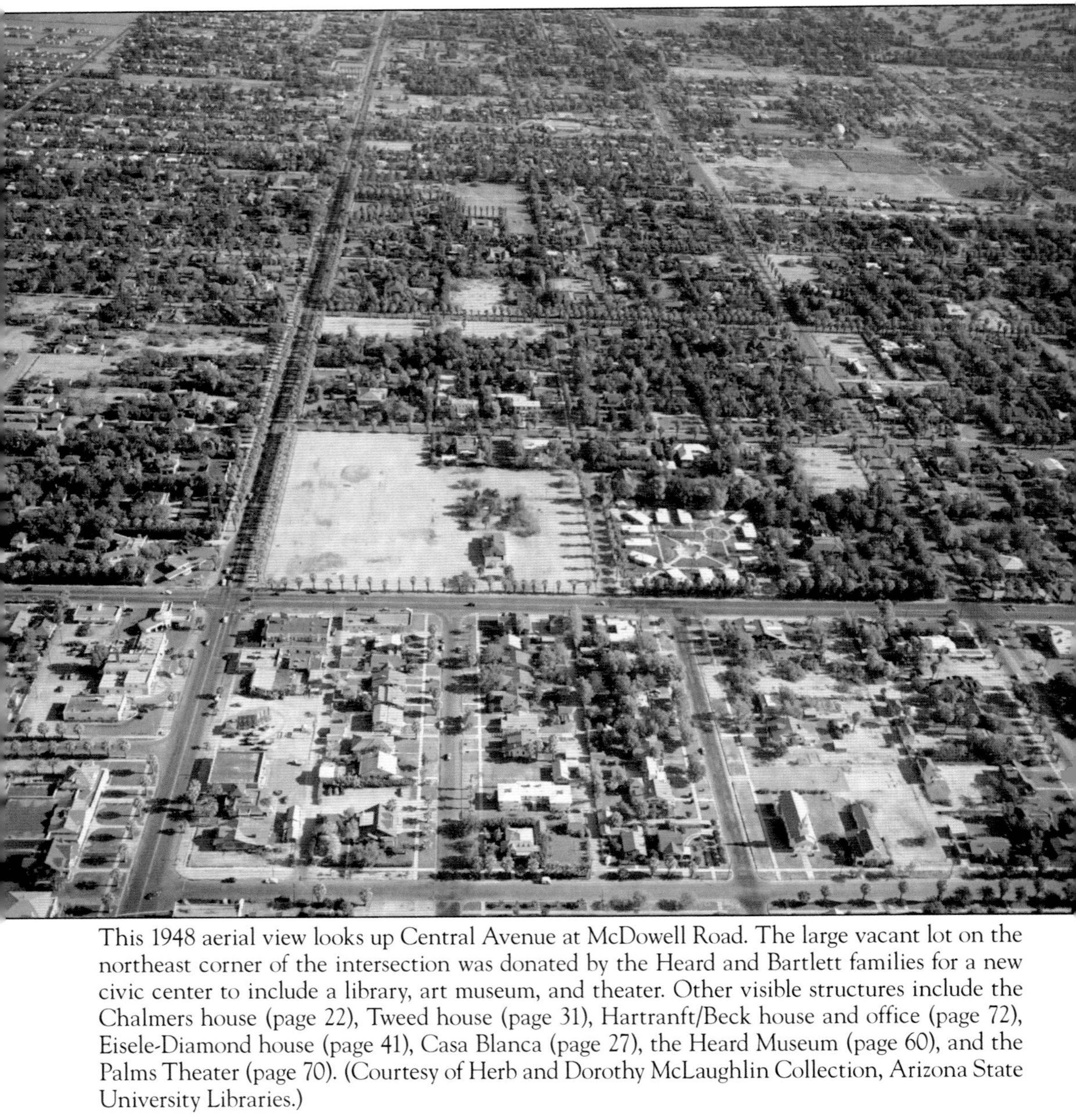

This 1948 aerial view looks up Central Avenue at McDowell Road. The large vacant lot on the northeast corner of the intersection was donated by the Heard and Bartlett families for a new civic center to include a library, art museum, and theater. Other visible structures include the Chalmers house (page 22), Tweed house (page 31), Hartranft/Beck house and office (page 72), Eisele-Diamond house (page 41), Casa Blanca (page 27), the Heard Museum (page 60), and the Palms Theater (page 70). (Courtesy of Herb and Dorothy McLaughlin Collection, Arizona State University Libraries.)

One

From the Hohokams to the Town Ditch 300–1900

It began with the Hohokams, the Native American peoples who settled in the Salt River Valley in the Sonoran Desert around 300 CE. In the decades and centuries that followed, they constructed villages, farmed the land, and developed an extensive system of canals that used the free-flowing Salt River to irrigate their crops. They lived at peace with each other, and their settlements thrived due to the rich soil and climate. Around 1400, their civilization disappeared for unknown reasons, perhaps as a result of extended drought, hostile invaders, disease, soil depletion, natural forces, or civil unrest. Regardless of the reasons for their disappearance, all that remains of the Hohokams, whose name means "those who have disappeared," are their artifacts and the remnants of their villages and canal system—clues of what life was like in the valley.

The site of the Hohokam civilization remained vacant for centuries. Spanish explorers might have passed through it, and some Native American tribes might have occupied the area intermittently but not permanently. The Spanish eventually settled in the southern areas of the region, and Anglo settlement began in the rest of the Arizona Territory in the mid-19th century. The valley remained unsettled, but that would soon change.

A need for food and fodder for the garrisons that protected the Arizona settlements led some to take a second look at the area. John William "Jack" Swilling—soldier, scout, prospector, farmer, and speculator—realized the potential of the rich soil and the ancient Hohokam irrigation system. He formed the Swilling Irrigation and Canal Company in 1867. Swilling and his colleagues restored some of the Hohokam ditches and constructed new ones. Soon, a network of canals fanned out from the river, and agriculture returned to the Salt River Valley.

To support the farms and businesses in the area, a small community sprung up beside its own "town ditch." The settlement needed a name, and either Swilling or Darrell Duppa, one of his associates, suggested naming it after the mythological bird that is consumed by fire and then rises anew from the ashes—the phoenix.

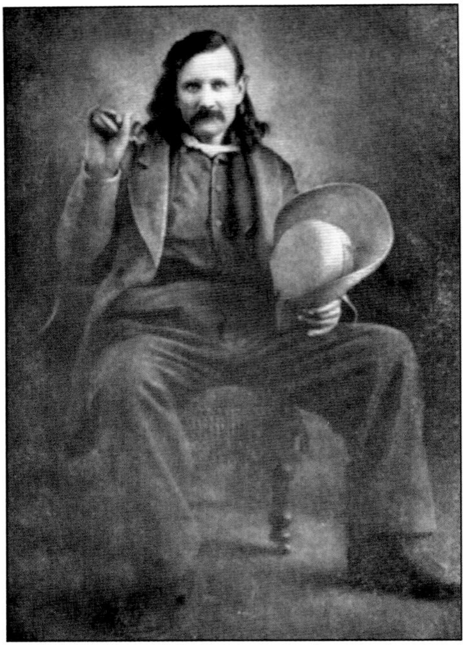

John W. "Jack" Swilling saw the agricultural and commercial potential of the Salt River Valley. After forming his irrigation company, he served the new Phoenix community as justice of the peace and the first postmaster. Despite his reputation as a kind and generous family man and visionary, Swilling was charged with a crime he did not commit and died in the Yuma County Jail. (Courtesy of Arizona Science Center.)

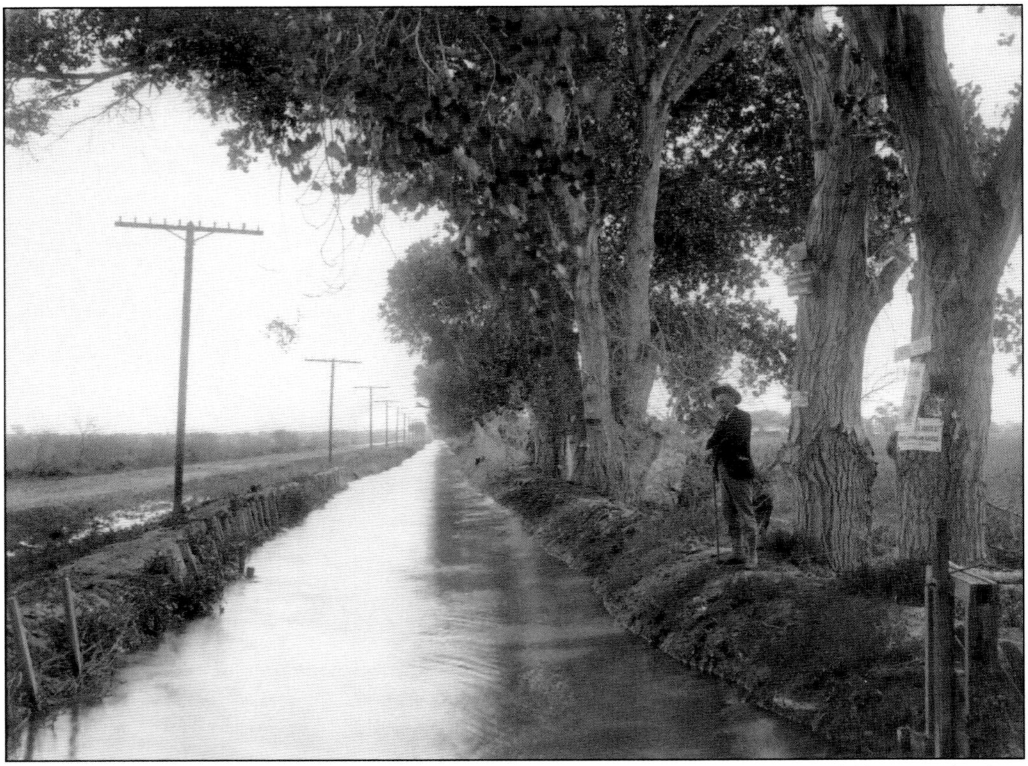

Swilling built his first canal, known as Swilling's Ditch, in 1868. In the years following the first settlements in the Salt River Valley, other irrigation canals sent water from the Salt and Verde Rivers to the farms and settlements in the region. The Salt River Valley Canal, sometimes known as the Town Ditch, shown here, flowed just north of Van Buren Street. (Courtesy of Salt River Project; photograph by Walter J. Lubken.)

In 1871, the territorial legislature created Maricopa County from Yavapai and Pima Counties. Constructed in 1884, this courthouse was located on the south side of Washington Street, between First and Second Avenues. It served the citizens of the county until about 1928, when it was demolished for a new county courthouse building shared with the City of Phoenix government. (Author's collection.)

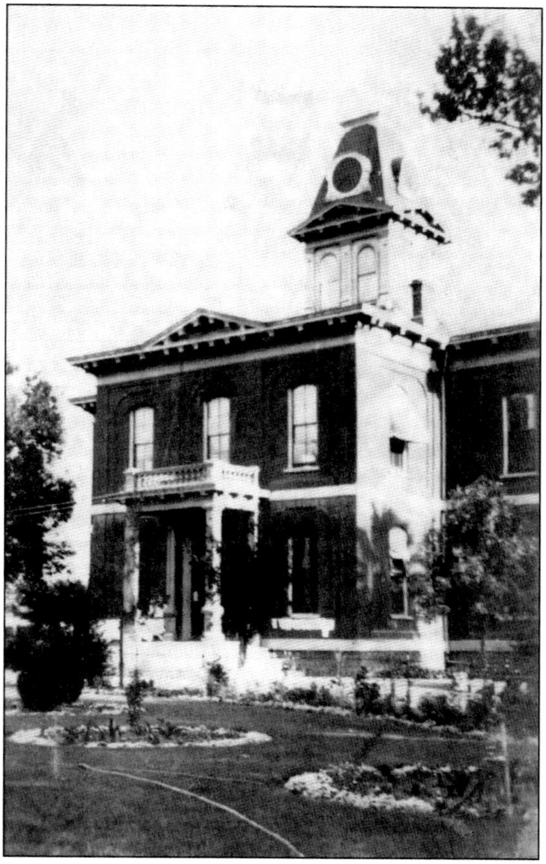

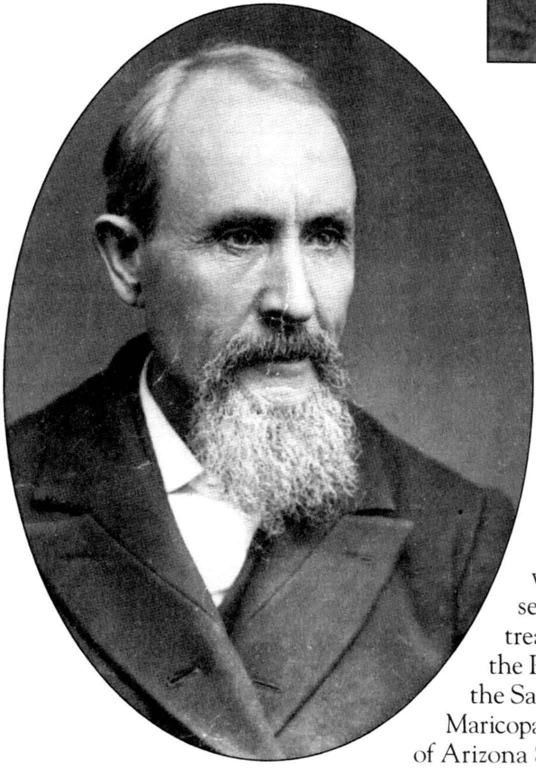

Phoenix incorporated in 1881, and John Alsap was elected as its first mayor. He had served several terms in the legislature and as the first treasurer of the Arizona Territory. He helped form the Phoenix Ditch Company and began farming in the Salt River Valley. He had a major role in creating Maricopa County and was also a probate judge. (Courtesy of Arizona Science Center.)

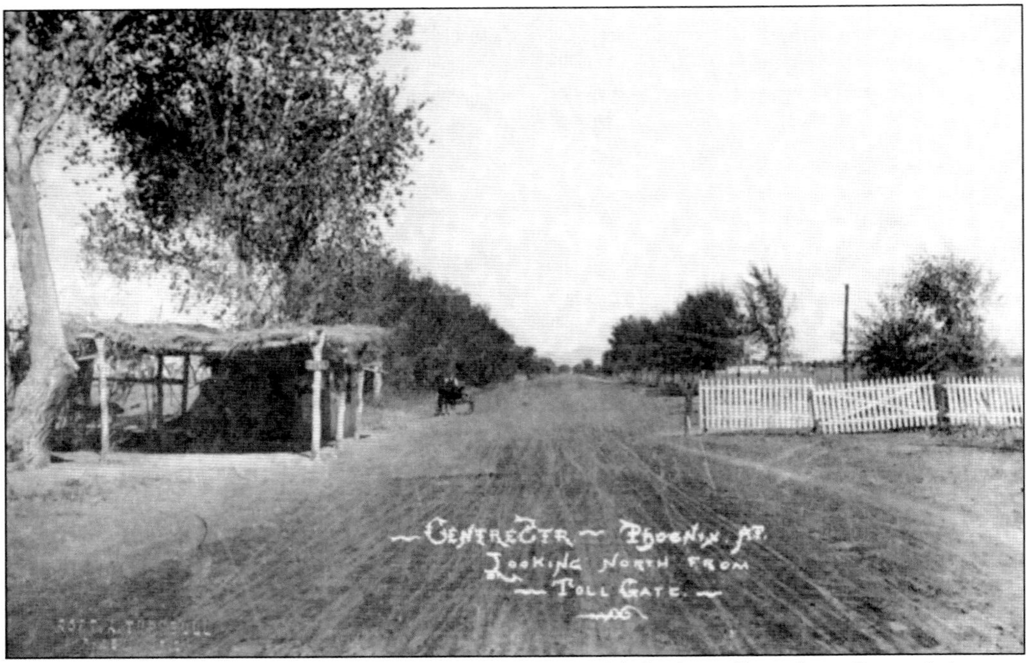

Starting in 1893, the Central Driving Association established a toll road on Central Avenue north of McDowell Road. Annual dues for members were $2, and one could walk or ride a horse, wagon, or bicycle north of McDowell for a toll that would be paid at the toll gate, shown here, at Central and McDowell. The Central Avenue Driveway, as it was known, extended to the Arizona Canal. The gate lasted as late as 1905. (Courtesy of Arizona Historical Society, Creighton Collection, 73-2-96.tif.)

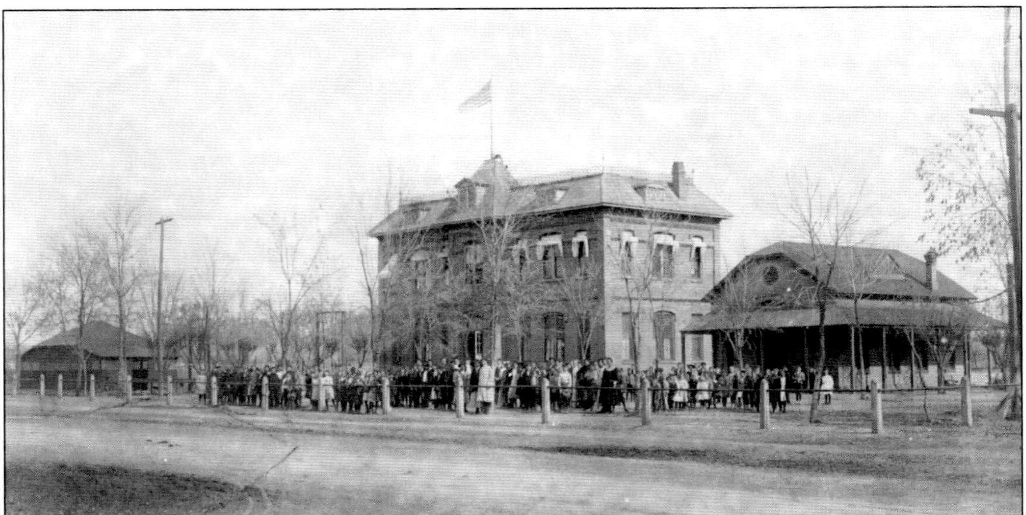

The Osborn School was established in 1879 at the corner of Seventh Street and Osborn Road to serve the farming areas north of Phoenix. During the next two decades, the school constructed buildings at the northeast corner of Central Avenue and Osborn Road. This 1890s photograph shows the school as seen from an unpaved Central Avenue. For many years, the school had hitching posts for those students who rode their horses to class. (Courtesy of Herb and Dorothy McLaughlin Collection, Arizona State University Libraries.)

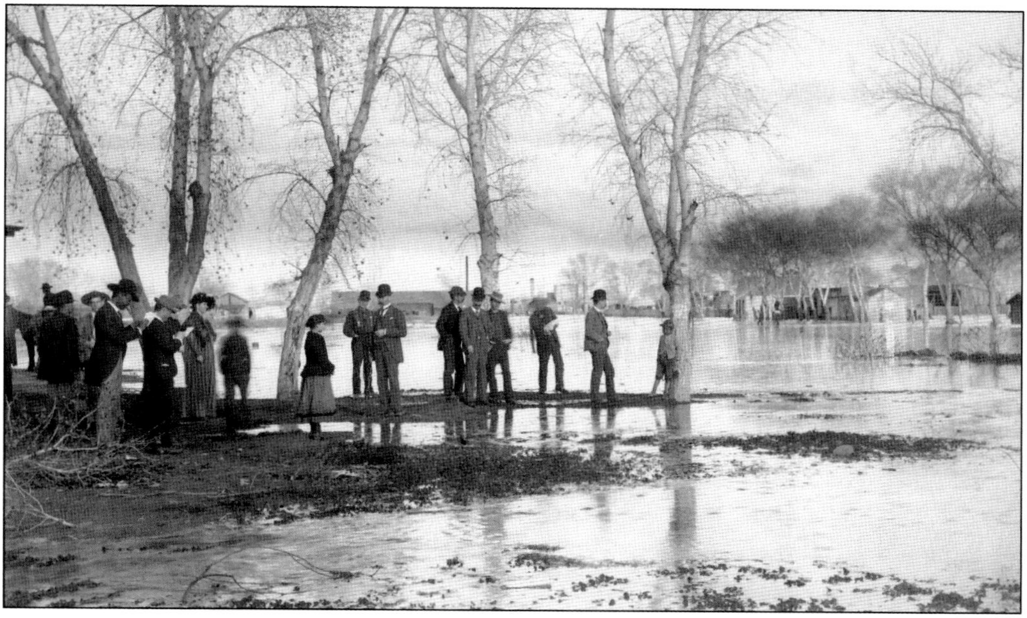

Even though the Salt River became the primary source of water for the valley's agriculture, it was still free flowing into the 20th century and subject to floods and droughts. In February 1891, during a severe flood, the river reached into downtown Phoenix. Here, the floodwaters lap along Jackson Street (above) and the depot for the Maricopa & Phoenix Railroad at the northwest corner of Harrison and Seventh Streets (below). The severity of this flood was a catalyst for later efforts to tame the Salt River. (Both, courtesy of Arizona Science Center.)

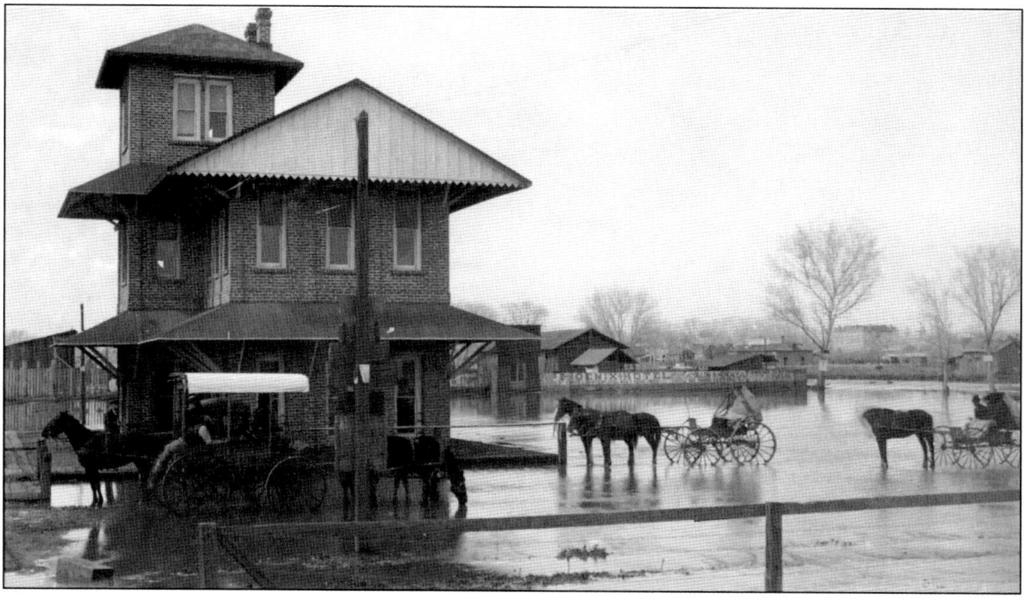

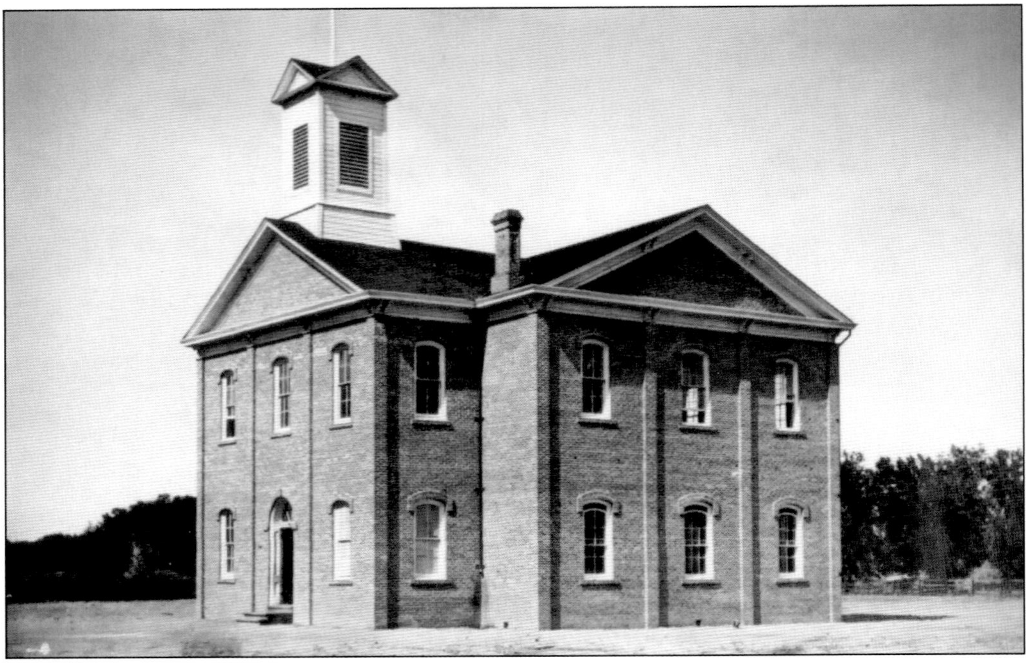

In 1879, the Central School at the northwest corner of Central Avenue and Monroe Street replaced the original one-room adobe schoolhouse that had served the community since 1874. Just north of the business district along Washington Street, its neighbors were residences and the Centre Street Methodist Church. (Courtesy of Arizona Science Center.)

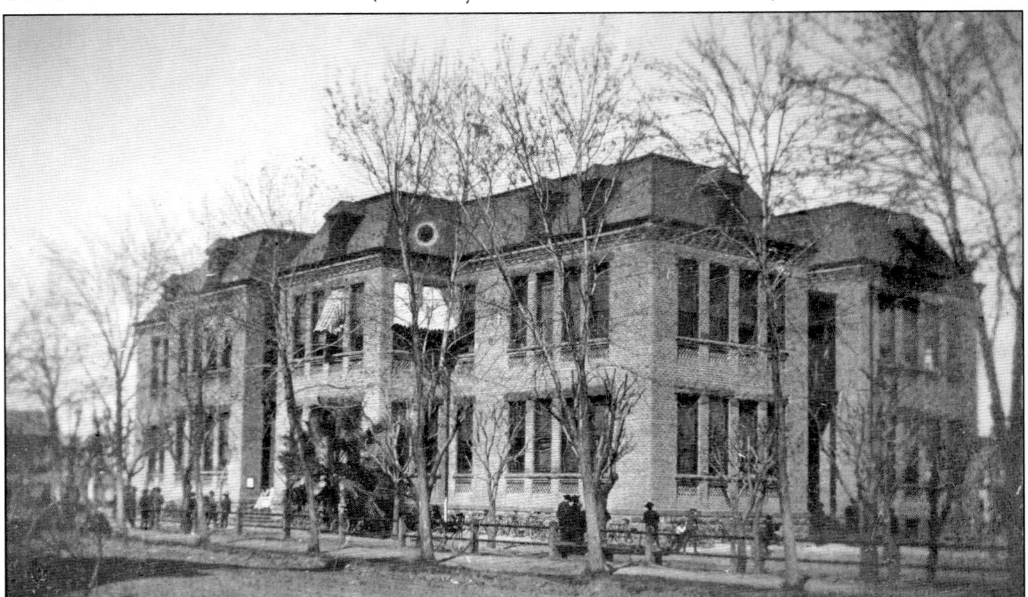

The Central School expanded in 1893 and 1899 to serve the growing population. It had both elementary and high school students. In 1895, the Phoenix Union High School was created at Fifth and Van Buren Streets. The Central School lost students and soon fell into disrepair. In 1919, it was condemned and eventually demolished. The Hotel San Carlos now occupies the site. (Courtesy of Arizona Science Center.)

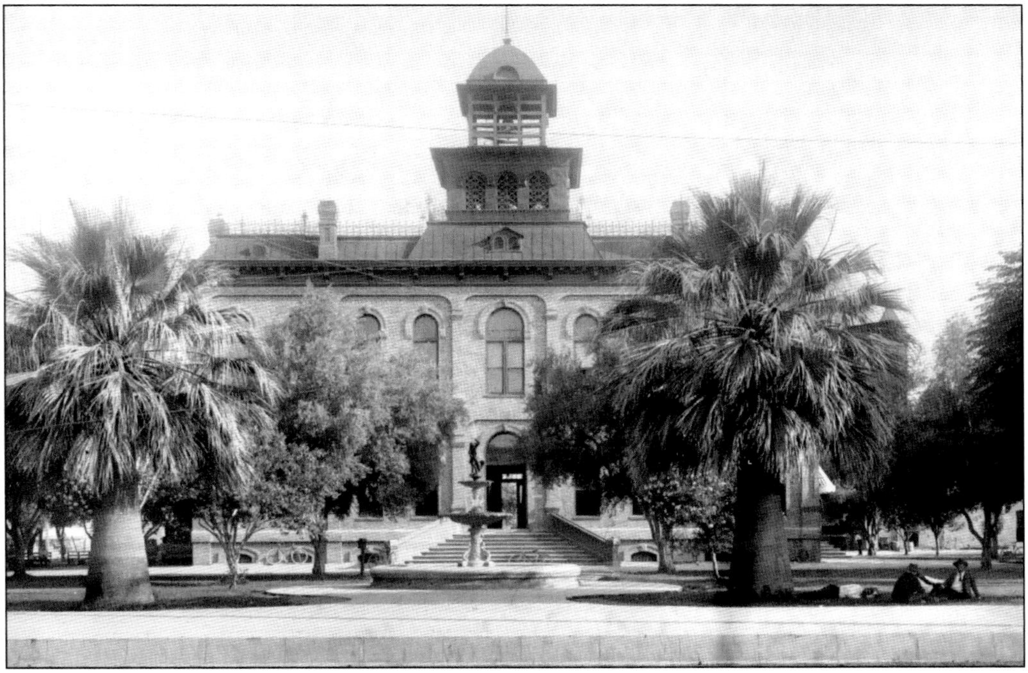

Constructed in 1889, the Phoenix City Hall occupied the south side of Washington Street, between First and Second Streets. When Phoenix became the territorial capital, the legislature and governor were offered use of the top floor until the new capitol building was completed. It remained the seat of city government until the new city/county building was completed in 1929. It was demolished shortly thereafter. (Author's collection.)

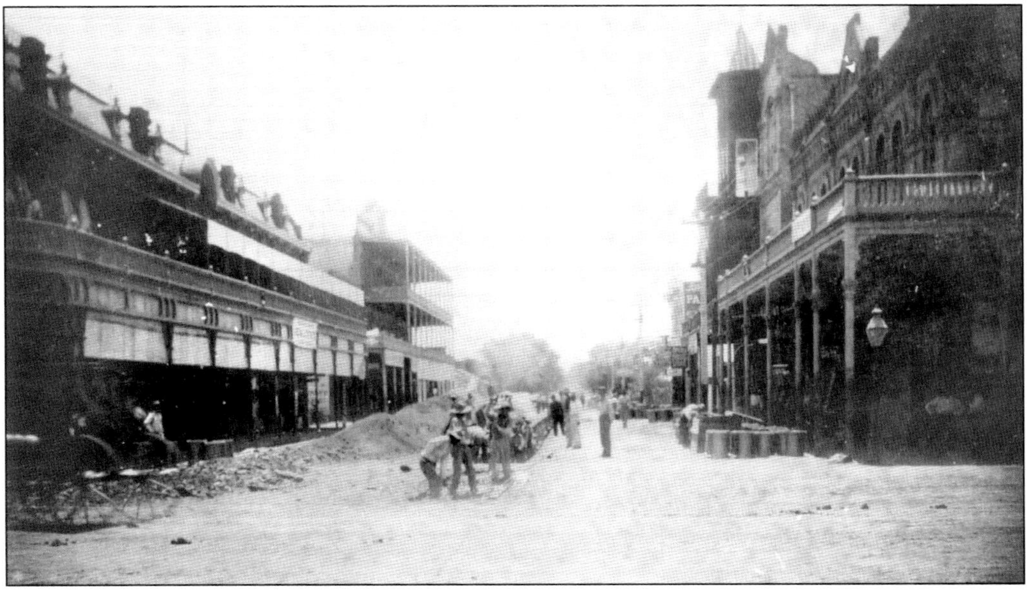

This is Central Avenue as viewed to the south from Washington Street in the 1890s. Here, a construction crew is installing a new water line. The Cotton Building occupies the left corner, and behind it is the Commercial Hotel. The Porter Block and the Phoenix Opera House behind it are on the right. (Courtesy of Arizona State Library, Archives and Public Records, History and Archives Division, Phoenix, No. 97-0979.)

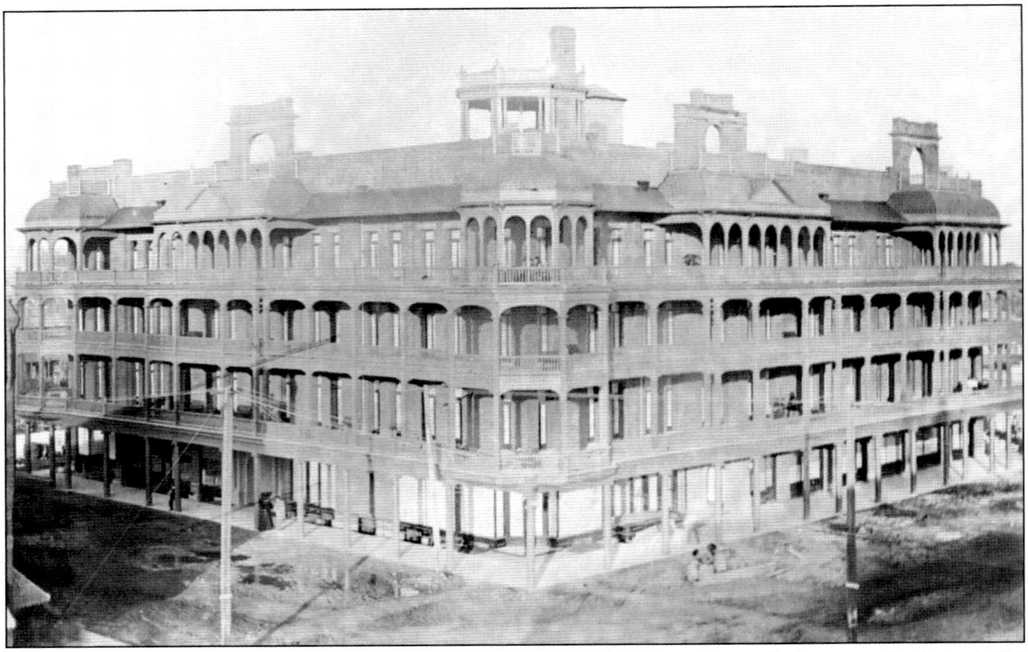

The Adams Hotel was one of the most prominent buildings on Central Avenue. Built in 1896 by John C. Adams, a leading local businessman and mayor between 1897 and 1899, the Adams gained a reputation as having the best food and drink in the area. It became a primary meeting spot for both local and national community, business, and political leaders. (Courtesy of Arizona Science Center.)

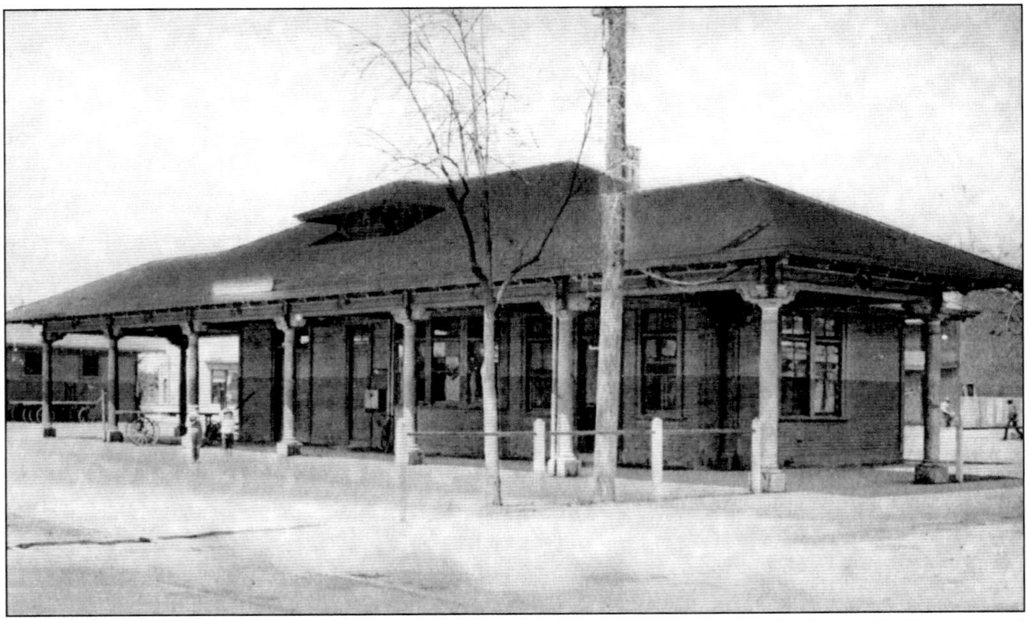

Two transcontinental rail lines ran across Arizona: the Southern Pacific through Tucson and the Atchison, Topeka & Santa Fe through Flagstaff. In 1887, a spur line connected Phoenix to the Southern Pacific, and in 1895, another line linked the city to the Santa Fe, thus connecting Phoenix to national markets and enabling tourism. This was the Southern Pacific depot at Central Avenue and Jackson Street. (Author's collection.)

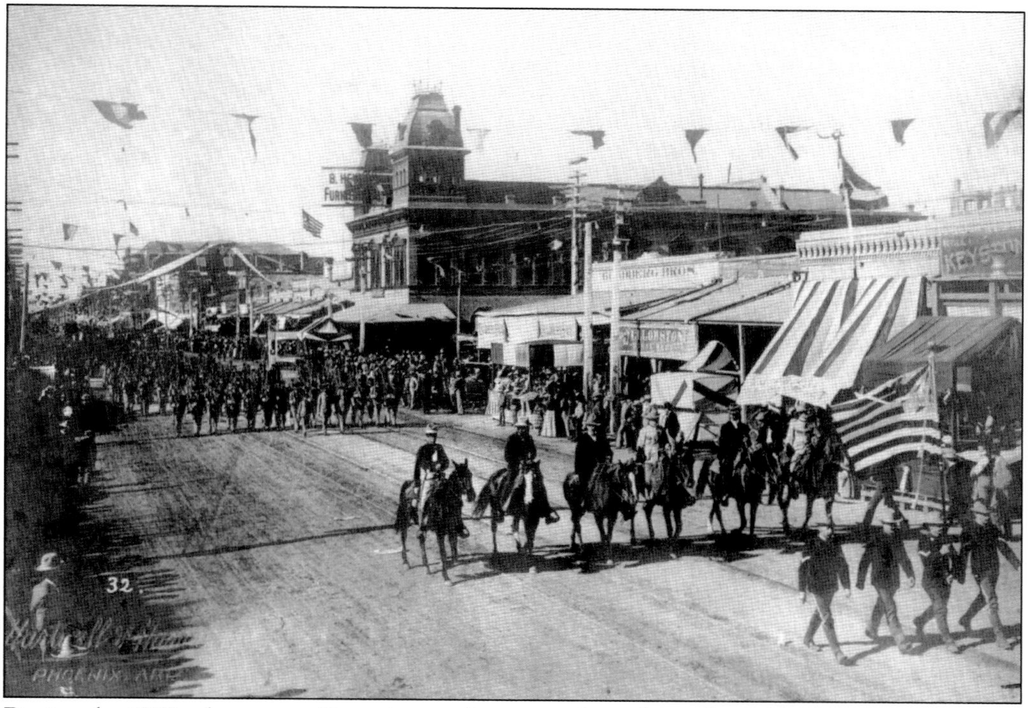

During the 1890s, downtown Phoenix was the scene of parades such as this one. This view looks west along Washington Street. On the right is B. Heyman Furniture in the Anderson Building at First Street. The Fleming Building can be seen farther up the street. (Author's collection.)

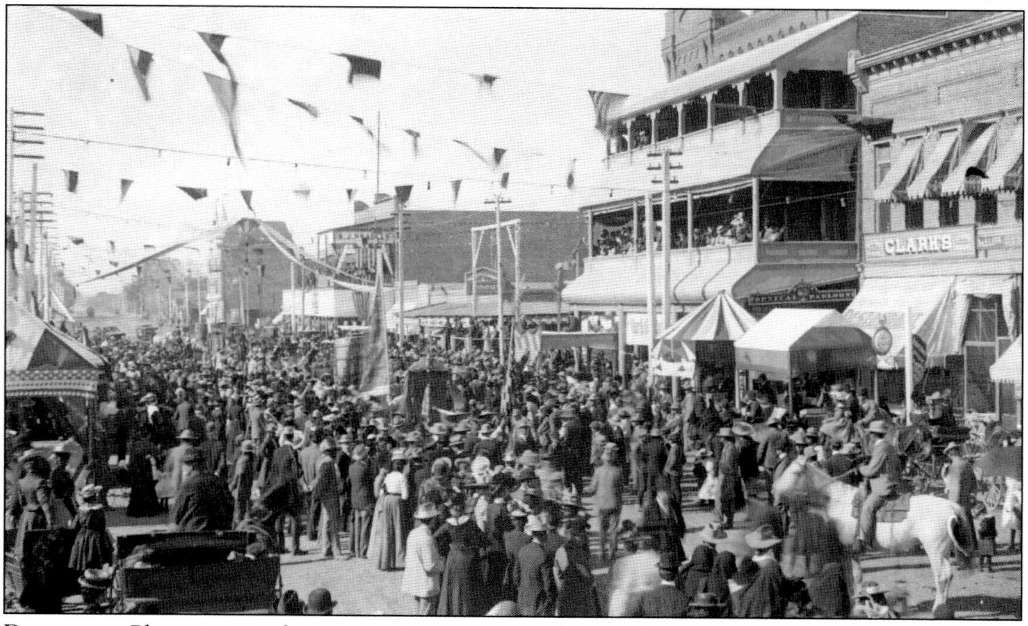

Downtown Phoenix was the scene of street carnivals as well. This crowded street fair occurred along Washington Street around 1899. The building with the covered porches on the immediate right side of the street is the Ford Hotel. The one farther up the street with the spires is the Patton Grand (later Dorris) Theater. It would soon figure prominently in Phoenix history. (Courtesy of Arizona Science Center.)

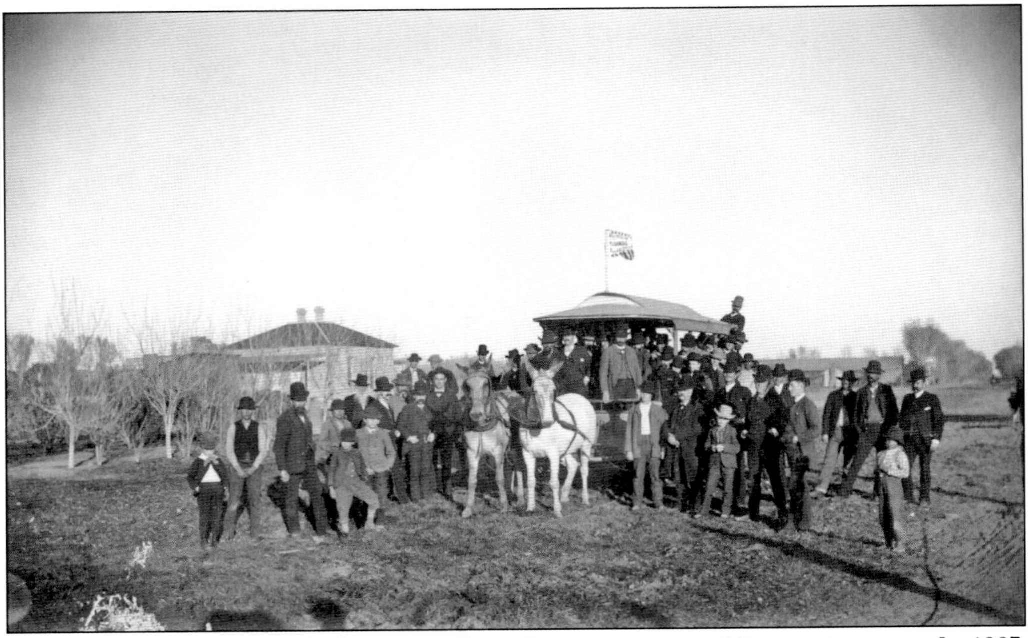

By the mid-1880s, the city had grown sufficiently to support a public transit system. In 1887, landowner and banker Moses Sherman started a streetcar service on a line that ran along Washington Street. This image shows the first streetcar at Seventh Avenue for its first eastbound run. The early streetcars were pulled by a team of horses, and the fare was a nickel. (Courtesy of Arizona Science Center.)

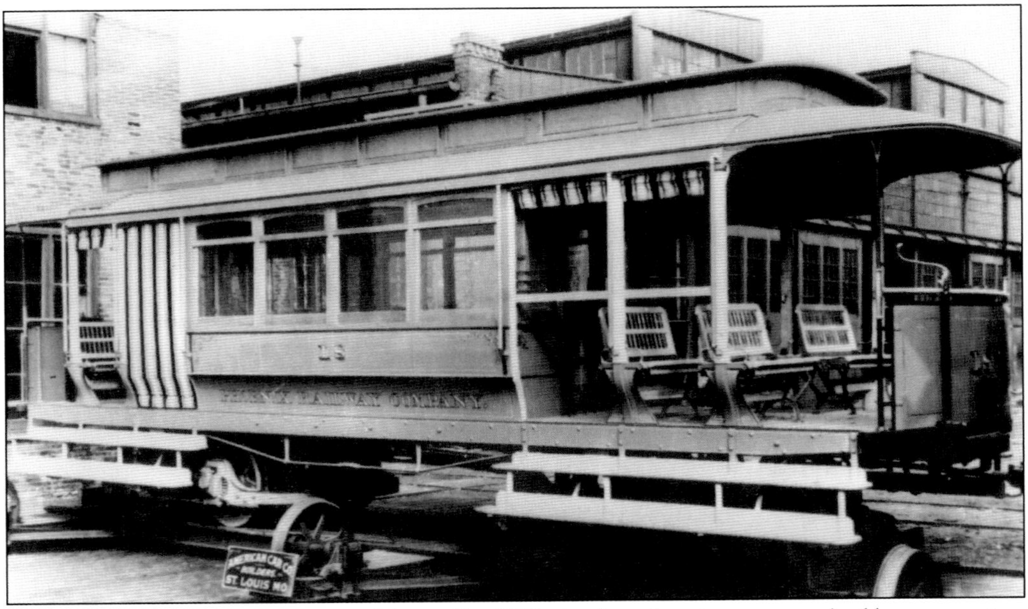

The street railway system grew quickly, and by 1893, the first electric streetcars had begun service. In 1895, the lines extended as far as McDowell Road and Tenth Street on the northeast and to the fairgrounds on the west though the system was a hybrid of both horse- and electric-powered cars. (Author's collection.)

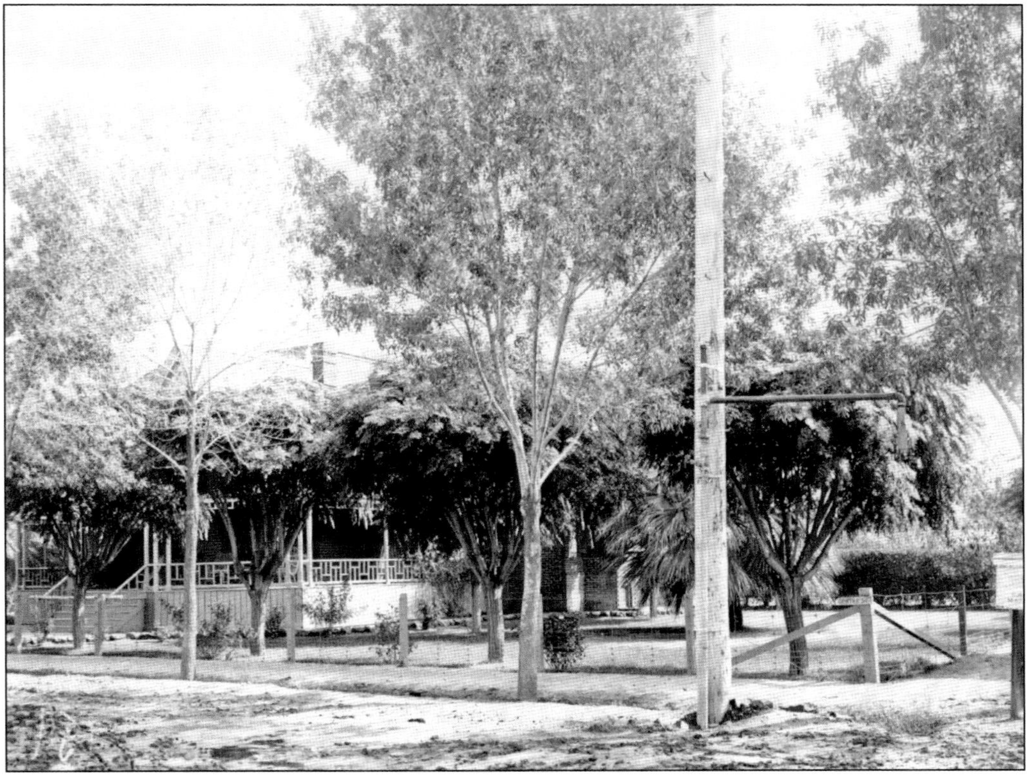

The Goldman House stood on the east side of Central Avenue, between Fillmore and Pierce Streets, and was one of the earliest examples of the residential migration north from downtown. The Goldman family ran an agricultural goods business. The sign on the fence identifies Centre Street. (Courtesy of Arizona State Library, Archives and Public Records, History and Archives Division, Phoenix, No. 96-3983.jpg.)

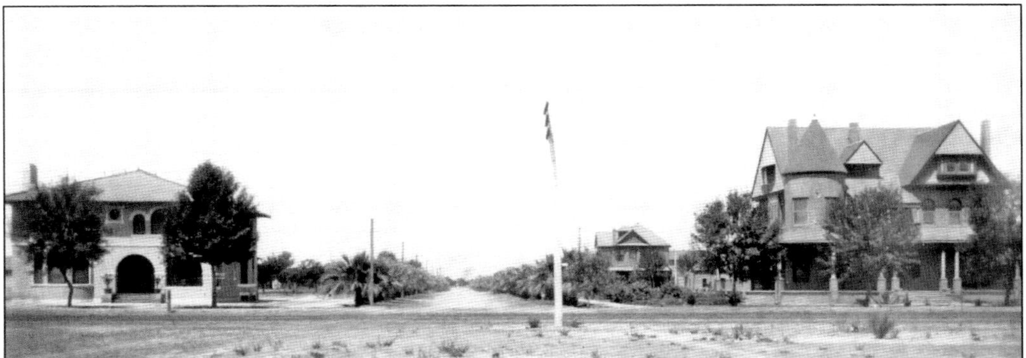

This view shows McKinley Street looking east from Central Avenue around 1905. The floods of 1890 and 1891, along with a desire for large houses and lots, drove business and community leaders to construct their homes north of the original townsite. Central Avenue soon became known as Millionaires' Row. The house on the left would be replaced by the Central Christian Church (page 44) about 10 years later. (Courtesy of McClintock Collection, Arizona Room, Phoenix Public Library.)

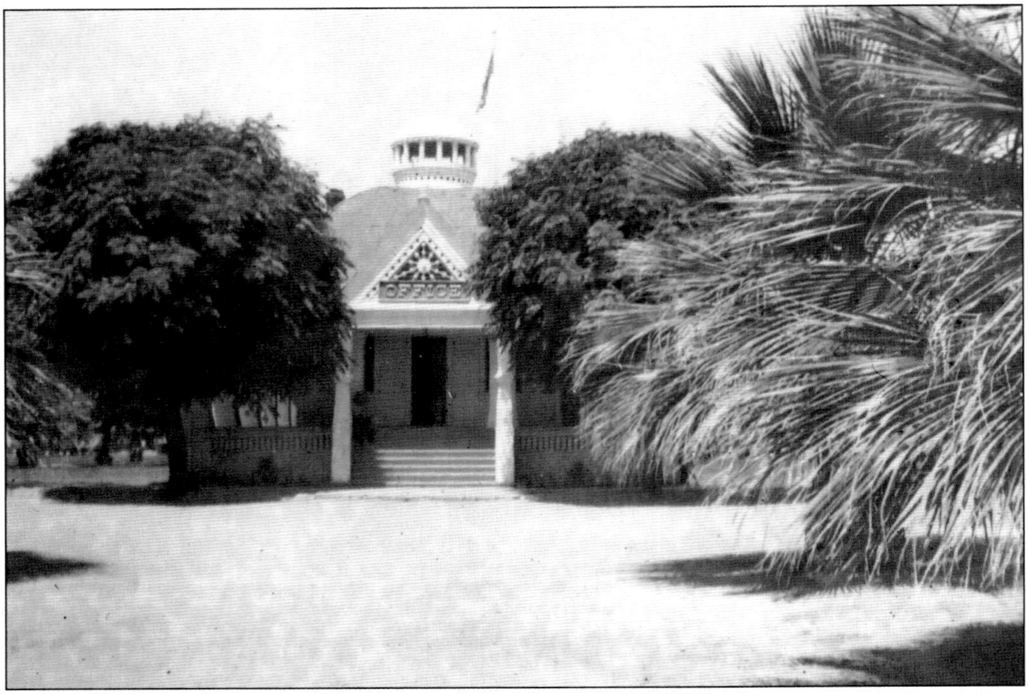

The Phoenix Indian School was established in 1891. A partnership of the Bureau of Indian Affairs and the citizens of Phoenix raised funds to purchase land at the northeast corner of Central Avenue and Indian School Road for the school. This was the first administrative office. By the late 1890s, the school had over 700 students. By 1902, there were 24 buildings on the campus surrounded by 240 acres of farmland. (Author's collection.)

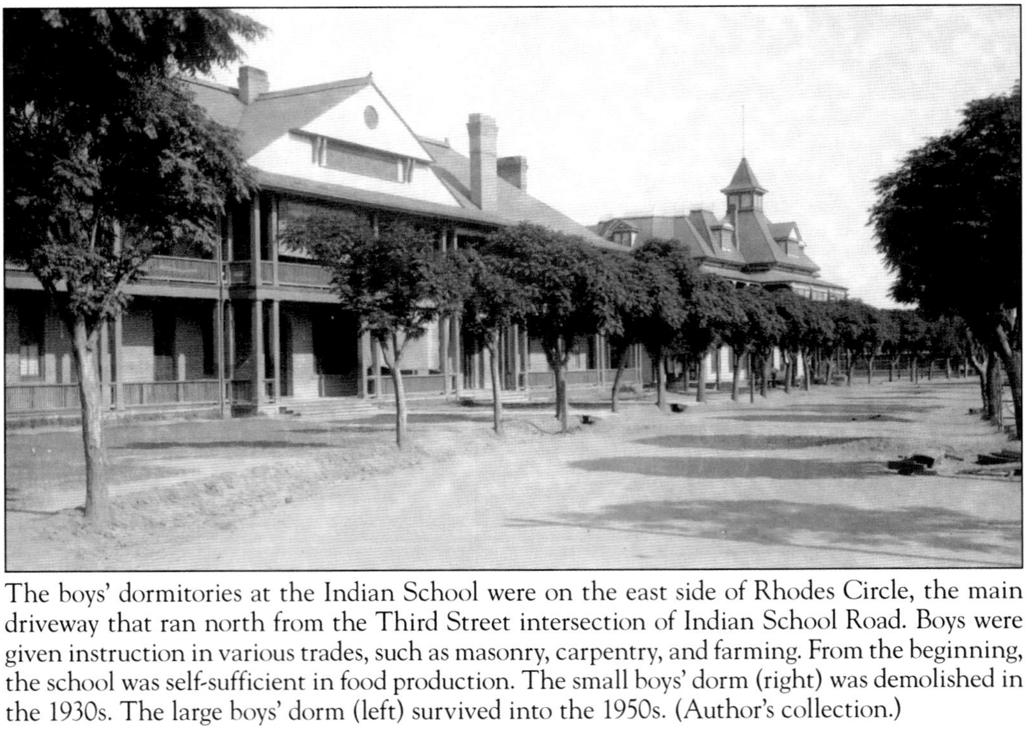

The boys' dormitories at the Indian School were on the east side of Rhodes Circle, the main driveway that ran north from the Third Street intersection of Indian School Road. Boys were given instruction in various trades, such as masonry, carpentry, and farming. From the beginning, the school was self-sufficient in food production. The small boys' dorm (right) was demolished in the 1930s. The large boys' dorm (left) survived into the 1950s. (Author's collection.)

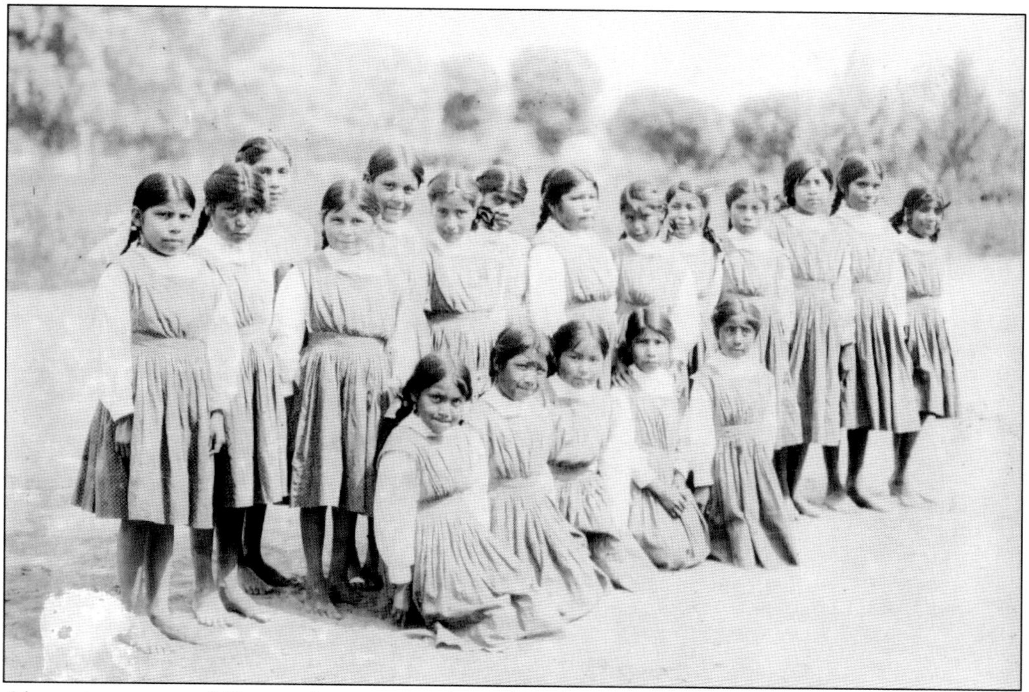

Above is a group of Native American girls at the Phoenix Indian School around 1900. In the school's early years, vocational training and assimilation were emphasized. Girls like these were taught domestic skills, such as sewing and nursing. Below is the girls' dormitory on the west side of Rhodes Circle opposite the boys' dormitories. Designed by noted Phoenix architect James Creighton, it was constructed about 1891 and survived into the 1950s. After nearly 100 years of operation, the school closed its doors in 1990, and the site became the Phoenix Steele Indian School Park. Three buildings from the school campus remain. (Above, author's collection; below, courtesy of Arizona Science Center.)

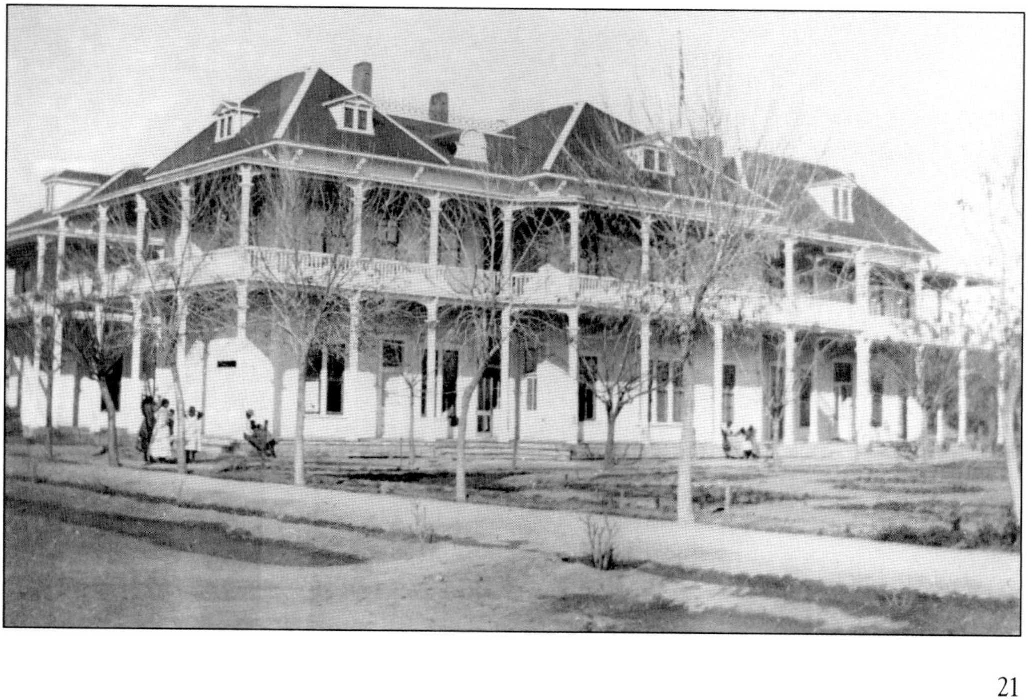

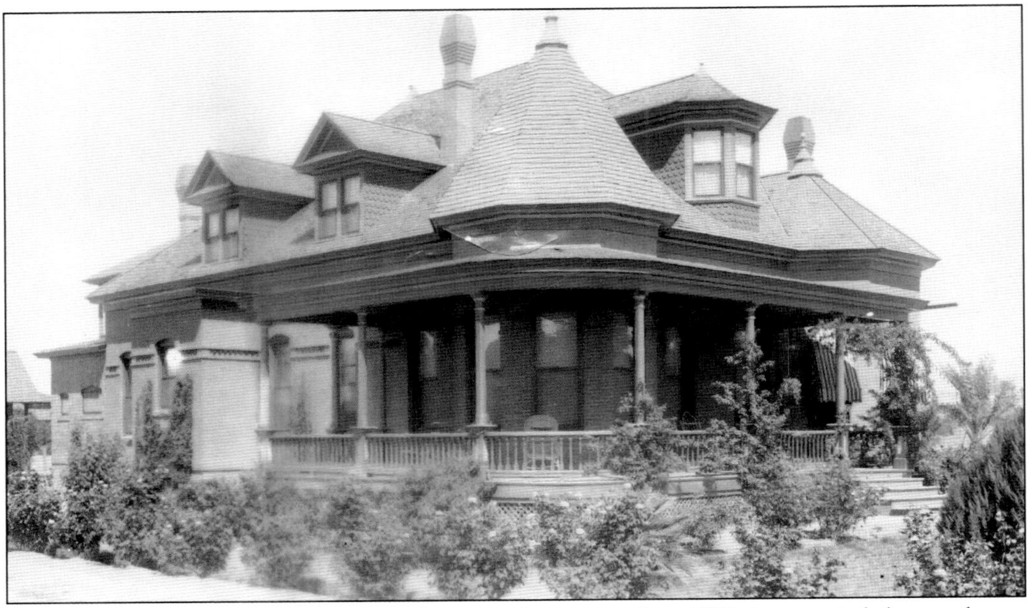

This was the home of Ephraim James Bennitt. Constructed in 1896, it occupied the northwest corner of Central Avenue and Bennitt Lane, now Fillmore Street. A civil engineer by profession, Bennitt was also involved in mining, real estate, and banking, serving as president of the Valley Bank. In 1928, the house was demolished and the Westward Ho Hotel was built on the site. (Courtesy of McClintock Collection, Arizona Room, Phoenix Public Library.)

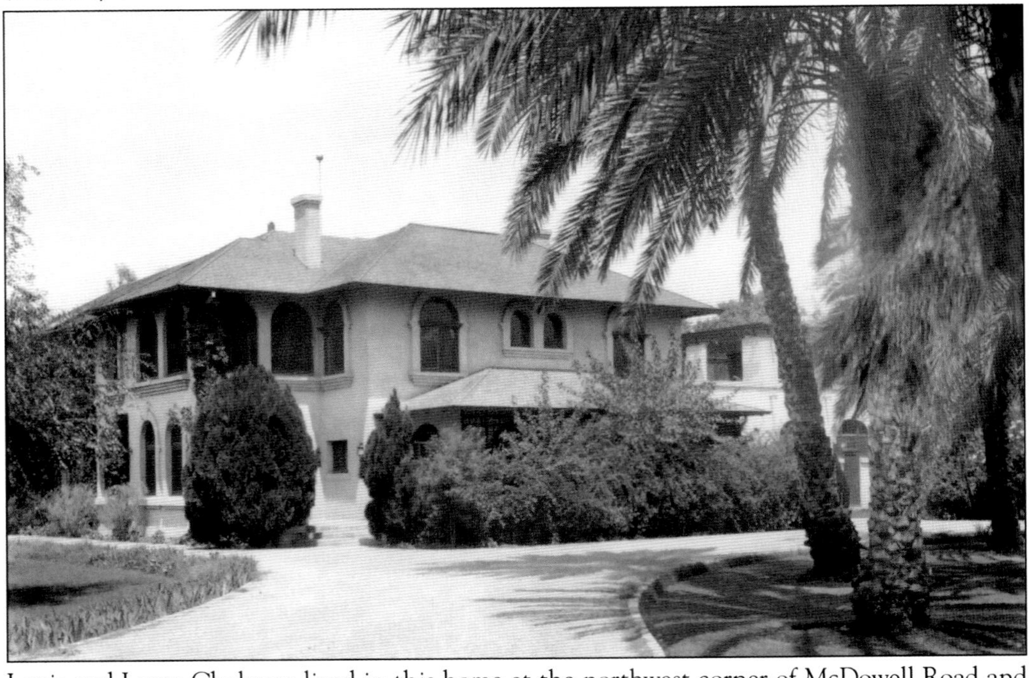

Louis and Laura Chalmers lived in this home at the northwest corner of McDowell Road and Third Street in the country. Louis began his Phoenix law practice in 1885. His firm evolved into Fennemore Craig. After his death in 1934, Laura resided in the house until 1953. The Los Olivos Car Wash now occupies the site. (Courtesy of McCulloch Brothers Photographs, Herb and Dorothy McLaughlin Collection, Arizona State University Libraries.)

Two

Into a New Era
1900–1920

Despite a recession in the early 1890s, Phoenix grew and prospered. The population, over 3,000 in 1890, had nearly doubled to over 5,500 by 1900. The city limits stretched from Nineteenth Avenue on the west to Eleventh Street on the east and from Grant Street on the south beyond Roosevelt Street to the north.

The street railway system encouraged growth in the east and west direction and to the north. The rail spurs that linked Phoenix to both the Southern Pacific and the Atchison, Topeka & Santa Fe Railway took agricultural goods produced in the valley to eastern and western markets. In return, merchandise, construction materials, and people flowed into the area. Soon, the valley became both a tourist destination and a haven for those seeking a cure from lung ailments in the warm, dry air.

Buildings sprung up on vacant lots. Along Washington Street, the primary business thoroughfare, one- and two-story wood structures gave way to new brick edifices, some of them three and four stories tall. Large department stores replaced the smaller general stores. First-class hotels housed winter visitors.

In addition to the east-west growth, commercial development also began along Central Avenue, north from Jefferson Street to Van Buren Street. By 1900, the bustling business core of merchants, shops, offices, hotels, saloons, and restaurants shared its surroundings with homes, churches, and schools. A short walk, horseback ride, or buggy ride would quickly take one from home to the office, shop, school, bank, or church.

In 1900, the first automobiles appeared. While the affluent had already started residing in homes north of Van Buren Street, the automobile accelerated expansion into the suburbs by providing a means for the well-off to live in the country with only a short drive to the city center for business, banking, and shopping.

For the city to grow from an agricultural community into a desert metropolis, several elements were necessary. In addition to its ambitious and industrious citizens, the community also needed reliable local and interstate transportation, access to capital, a dependable supply of water, and a means of mitigating the hot summers.

Despite the challenges, an air of optimism prevailed. Nothing seemed impossible, not even taming a river.

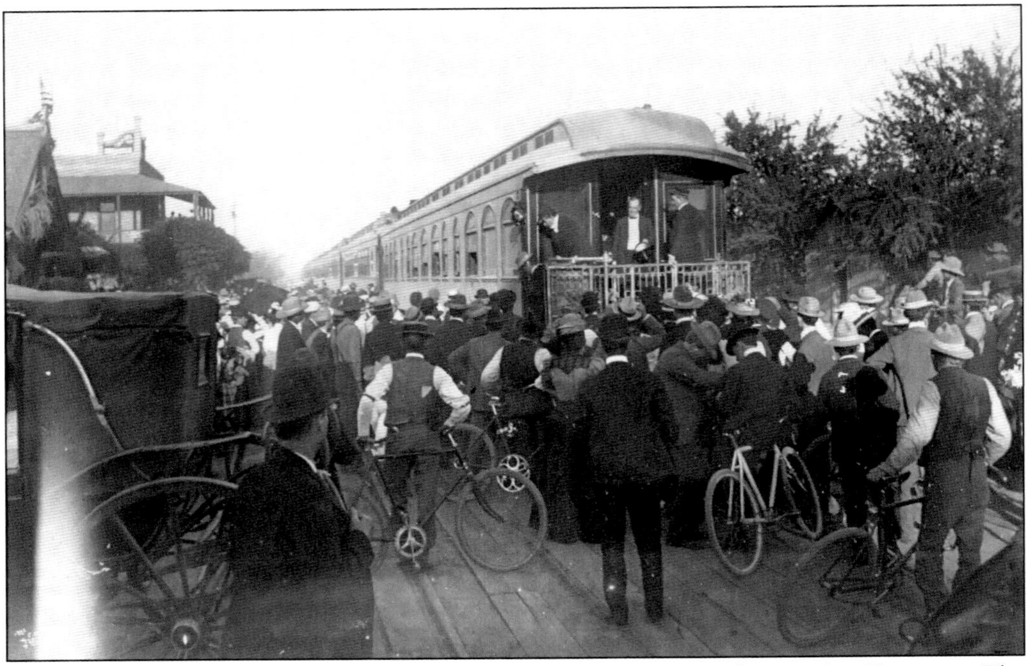

On May 7, 1901, Pres. William McKinley visited Phoenix during a rail trip to San Francisco. The president visited the territorial capital, where he attended a reception and made a speech. Later in the day, he inspected the Phoenix Indian School. In less than four months, President McKinley fell to an assassin's bullet, and Theodore Roosevelt became president. The Roosevelt presidency would have a major impact on Phoenix. McKinley's rival in two presidential elections, William Jennings Bryan (partially obscured), pictured below near a Phoenix Church, also visited Arizona. (Both, courtesy of Arizona Science Center.)

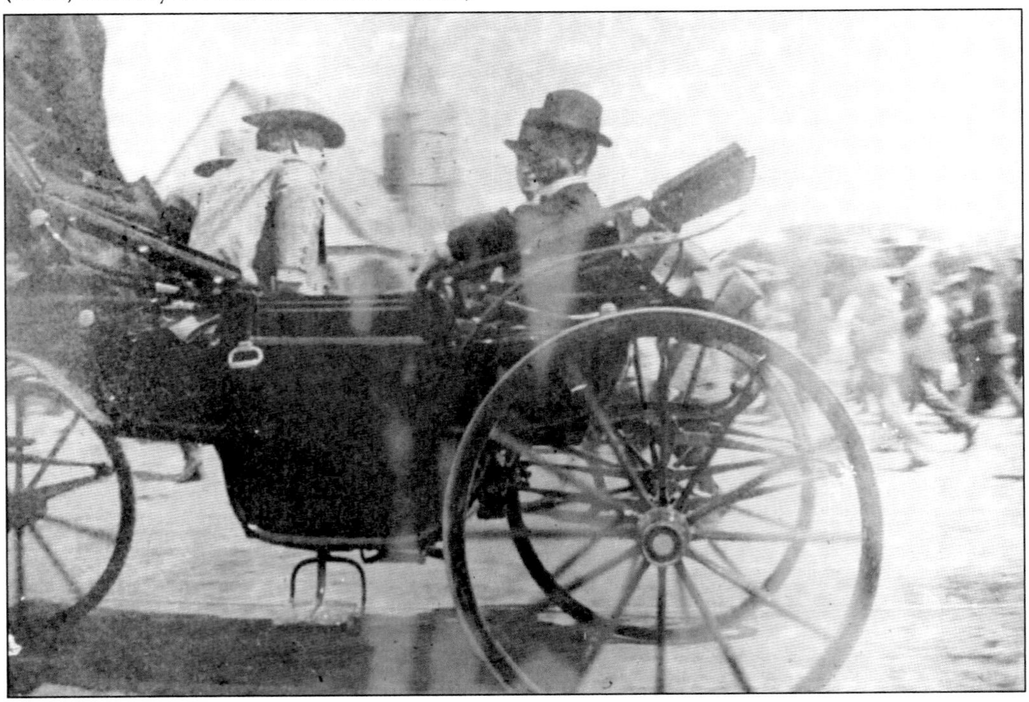

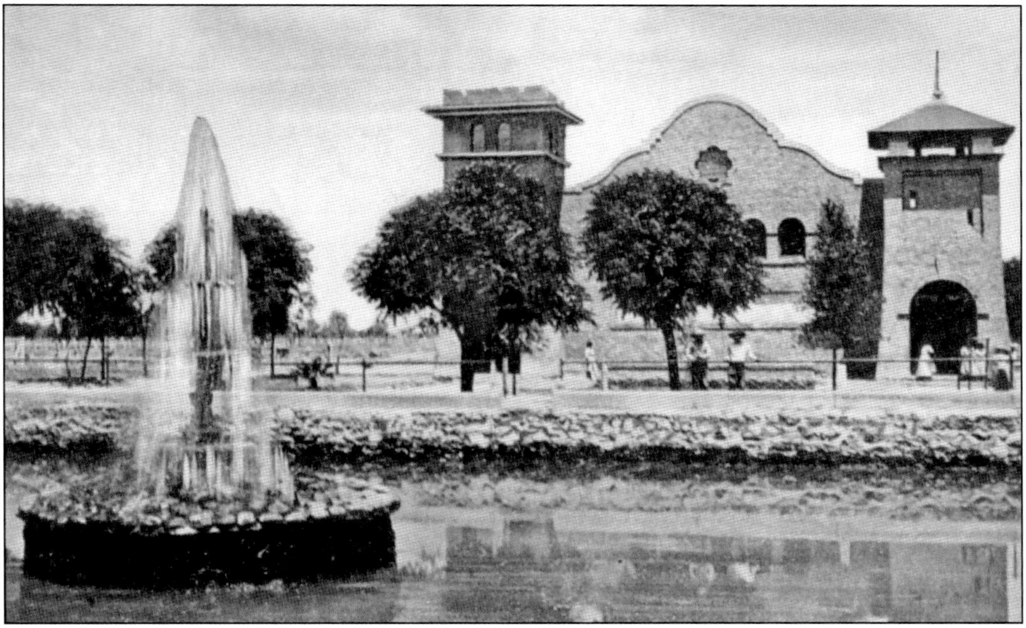

The Phoenix Indian School continued to grow. Students started to receive diplomas, and over 60 would volunteer for military duty during the Great War. This Mission Revival building was first constructed as an auditorium in 1902 but was converted into a dining hall by 1904. It survives to this day as part of the Phoenix Steele Indian School Park. (Author's collection.)

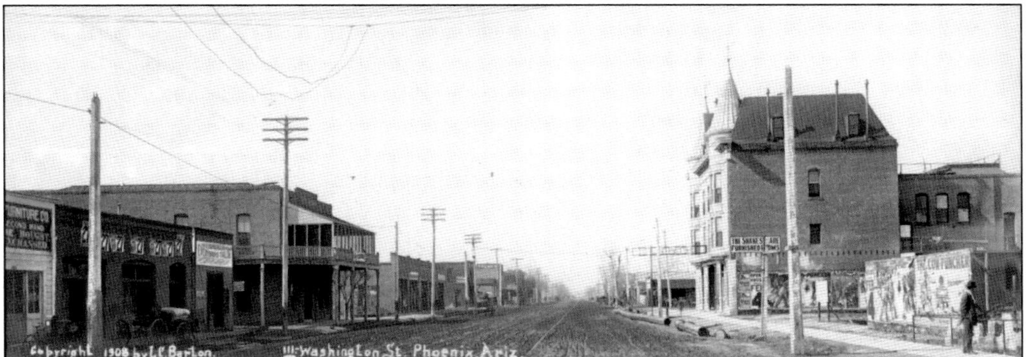

Passage of the National Reclamation Act in 1902 provided for federal loans to construct water projects. In February 1903, a group of valley landowners, which included an up-and-coming young businessman named Dwight Heard, met in the Dorris Opera House (right) on Washington Street west of Third Avenue. They established the Salt River Valley Water Users' Association to provide a reliable water supply for agricultural and urban use, as well as to control floods on the unpredictable Salt River. Over 4,800 individual landowners pledged more than 200,000 acres as collateral to construct a dam east of the city. (Barton photograph; courtesy of Library of Congress.)

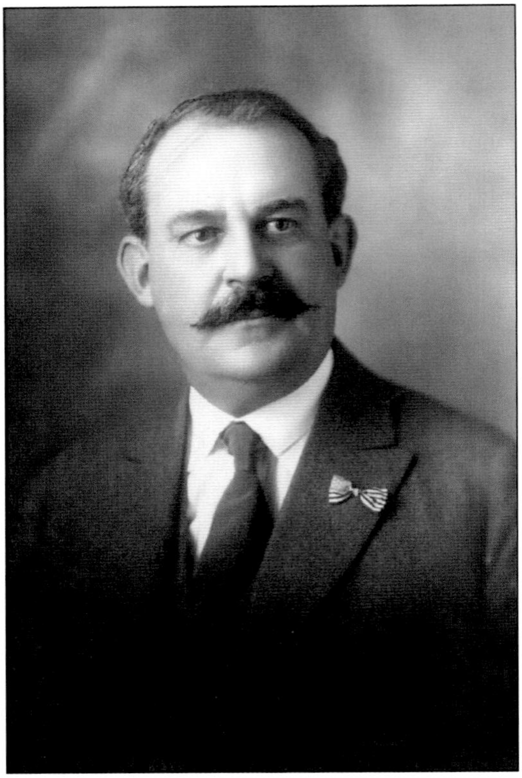

Dwight B. Heard moved from Chicago to Arizona for his health and settled in Phoenix in 1895. He quickly established himself as a leading businessman in the community. His interests included crops, cattle, land development, and journalism. His Bartlett-Heard Land and Cattle Company was one of the largest landholders in the area. Heard was able to access investment capital from the East for local development. In 1912, he also became the owner and publisher of the *Arizona Republican* newspaper. (Photograph by Heath Photography; author's collection.)

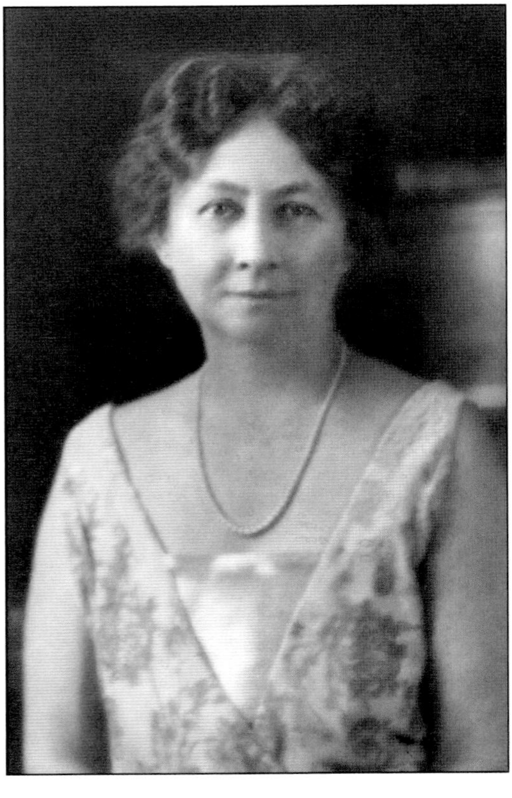

Maie Bartlett married Dwight Heard in 1893. Like her husband, she became active in the community and, over the years, supported many civic and philanthropic projects with boundless energy. Both of the Heards had a significant and lasting impact on the community. They founded the Heard Museum in 1929. (Courtesy of Heard Family Photographs and Ephemera, No. RC8:45.06, Billie Jane Baguley Library and Archives, Heard Museum, Phoenix, Arizona.)

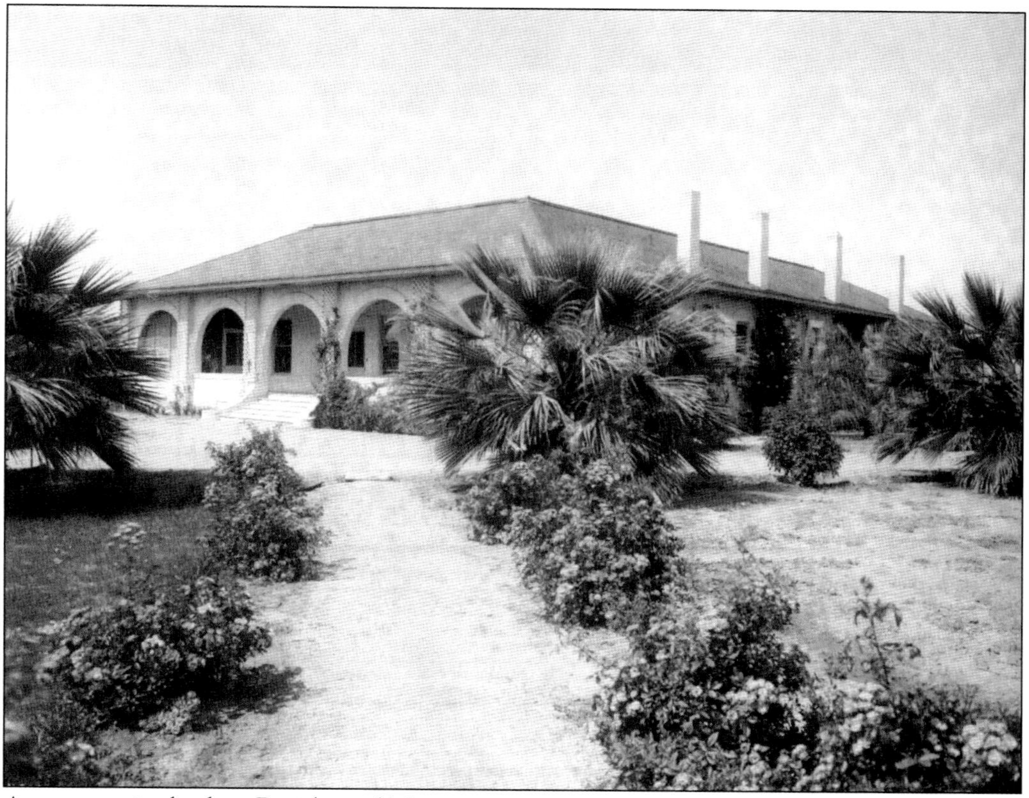

As community leaders, Dwight and Maie Heard were forefront in both the physical and cultural development of the city. The Heard home, named Casa Blanca, or "white house," stood at the northeast corner of Central Avenue and Monte Vista Road. Constructed about 1903, it quickly became a social center, hosting dignitaries who included US presidents. The interior view at right shows some of the numerous artifacts the Heards collected over the years, which later became part of the Heard Museum collection. After Dwight's death in 1929, Maie continued to reside at Casa Blanca until her death in 1951. Then, for a couple of years, it was the home of the Jewish Community Center and Jewish Community Council. The Phoenix Towers cooperative apartments now occupy the site. (Above, courtesy of Heard Family Photographs and Ephemera, No. RC8:80, Billie Jane Baguley Library and Archives, Heard Museum, Phoenix, Arizona; right, courtesy of Frederick W. Bancroft Photographic Album and Correspondence, No. RC9:15, Billie Jane Baguley Library and Archives, Heard Museum, Phoenix, Arizona.)

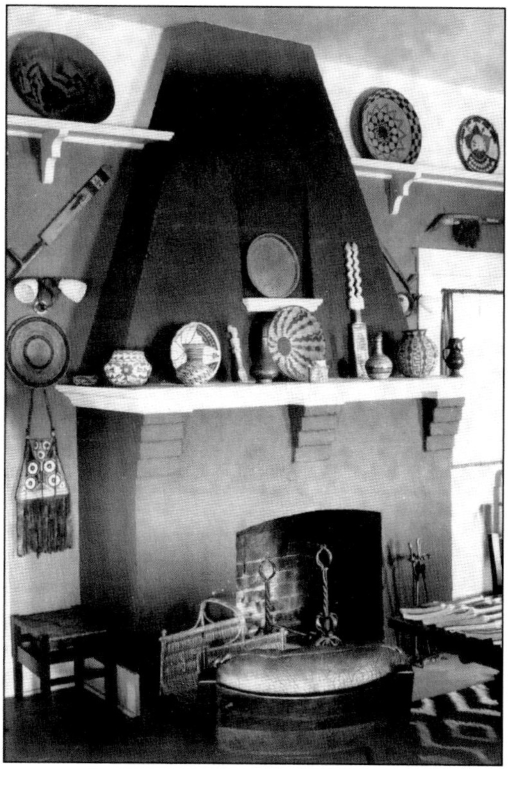

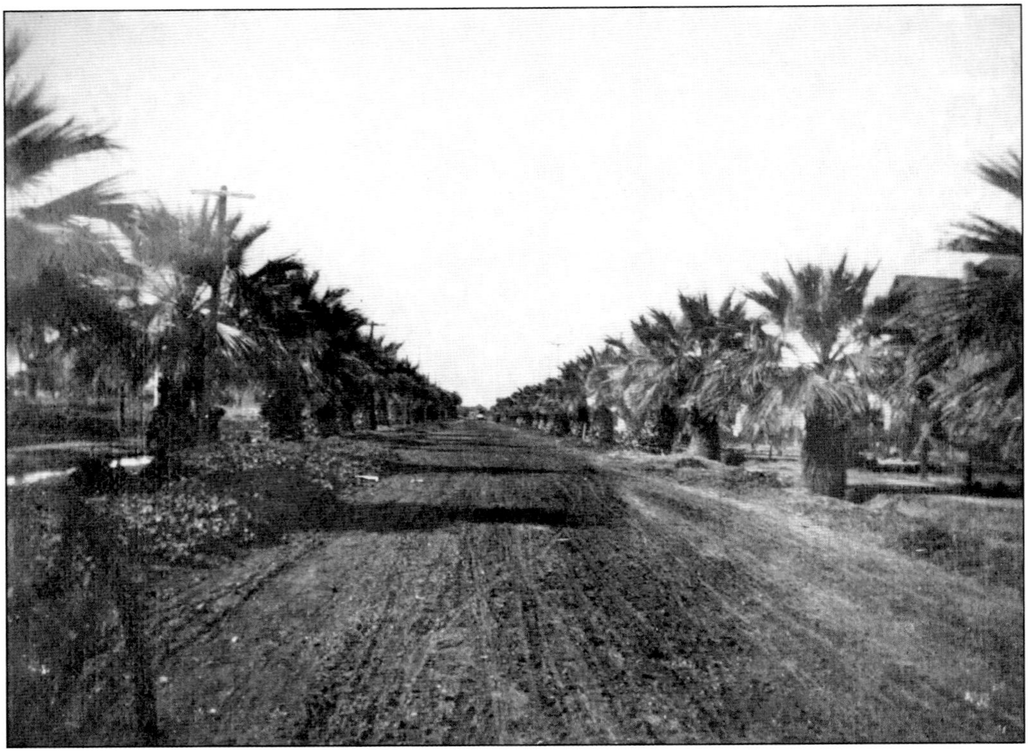

Above is an early-20th-century view of Central Avenue. Palm trees that eventually lined much of Central Avenue in Midtown are shown here. Also note the irrigation ditch on the left of the street. Below is Palm Avenue around 1908. Not to be confused with Palm Lane, this street ran east from Central Avenue, north of Thomas Road. Even though this was out in the country, two streetlights are visible. Unpaved streets were the norm in Phoenix at this time. The first paved streets were downtown, and that was not until 1912. Wider use of the automobile generated more street paving over the years. Palm Avenue is now Earll Drive. (Above, courtesy of Arizona Science Center; below, Barton photograph, courtesy of Library of Congress.)

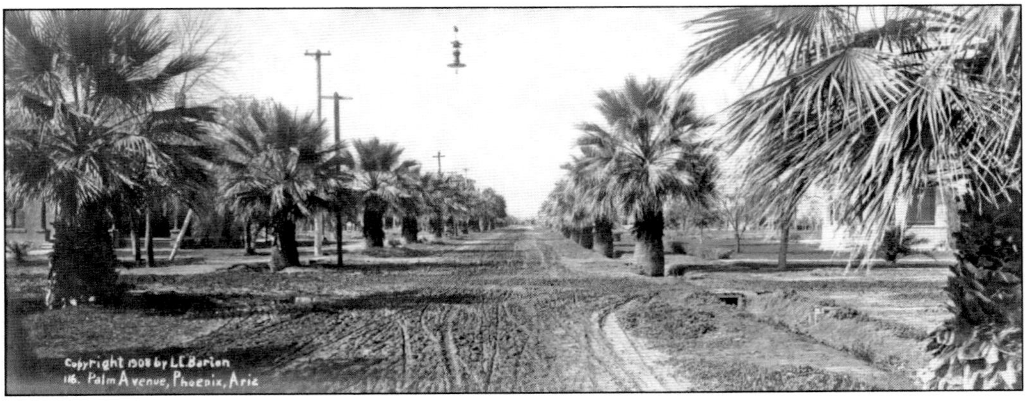

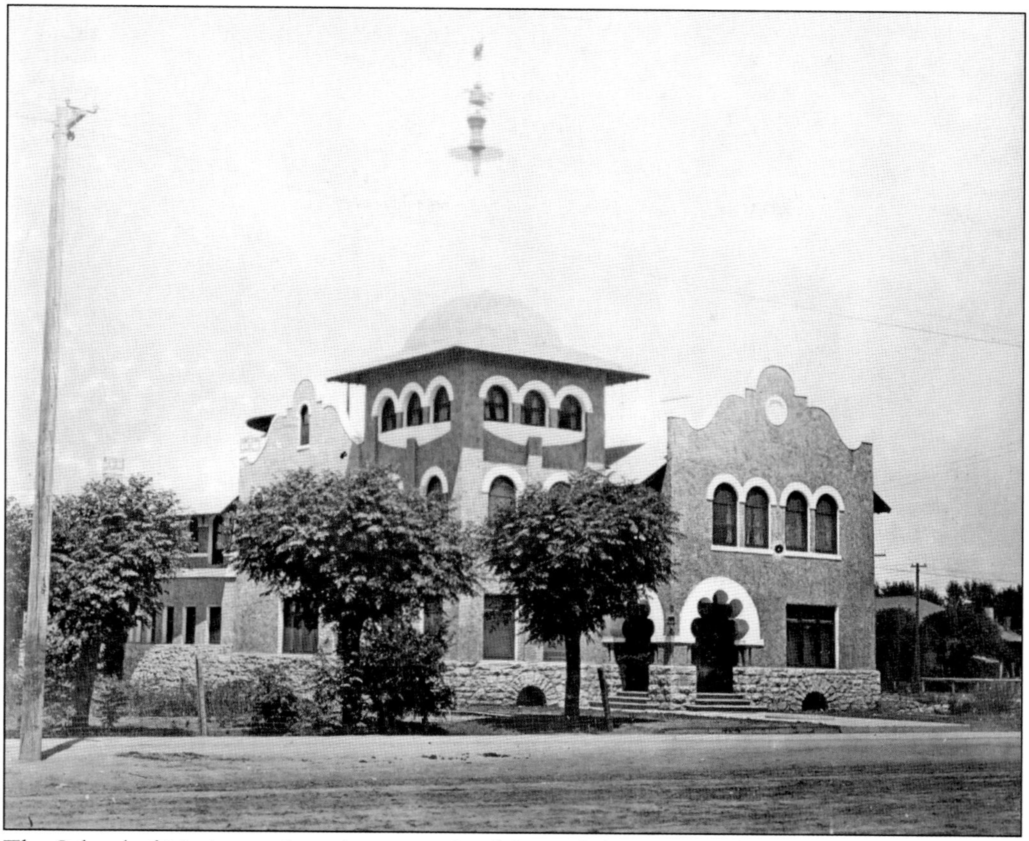

The School of Music stood on the west side of Central Avenue, two blocks north of Van Buren Street. It was one of the first significant commercial buildings on Central Avenue north of downtown. Abilena Creighton Christy founded the school in 1904 and moved it into this structure in 1907. The building survived into the 1950s. (Author's collection.)

On the west side of Central Avenue and south of McDowell Road stood the home of Lloyd B. Christy, a director and cashier of the Valley Bank. He also served as mayor of Phoenix from 1909 to 1914. Christy was very involved with the YMCA and was instrumental in the construction of its new downtown building (page 37). (Courtesy of McClintock Collection, Arizona Room, Phoenix Public Library.)

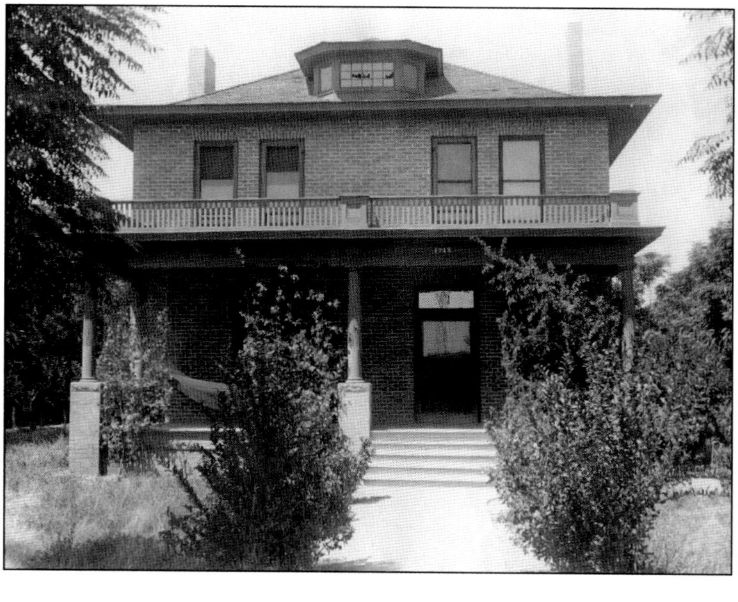

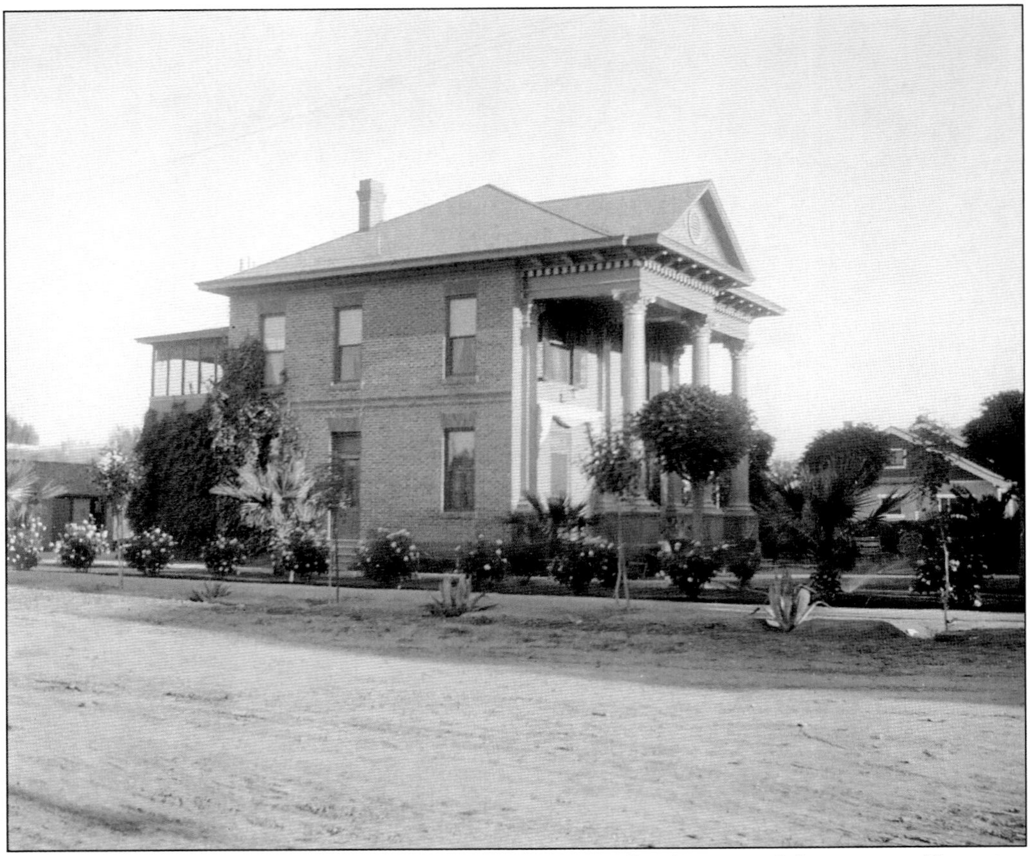

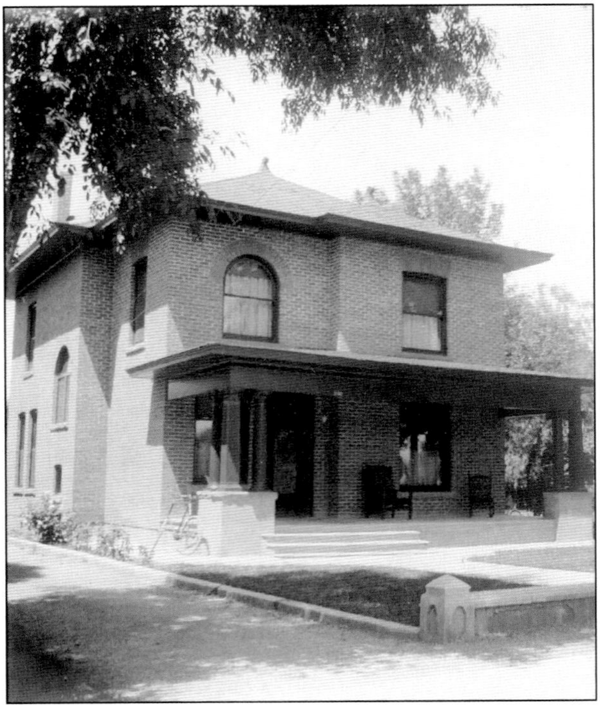

By the turn of the century, Phoenix had started to grow beyond the boundaries of its original townsite. Many community and business leaders began constructing large homes along Central Avenue, north of Van Buren. The Simon Oberfelder house, shown above around 1910, was on the northwest corner of McKinley Street and Central Avenue. Oberfelder was cashier for the National Bank of Arizona. The H.B. Wilkinson house, left, stood on the southwest corner of Central Avenue and Fillmore Street. Wilkinson was the law partner of Louis Chalmers. (Both, courtesy of Frederick W. Bancroft Photographic Album and Correspondence; above, No. RC9:114; below, No. RC9:113, Billie Jane Baguley Library and Archives, Heard Museum, Phoenix, Arizona.)

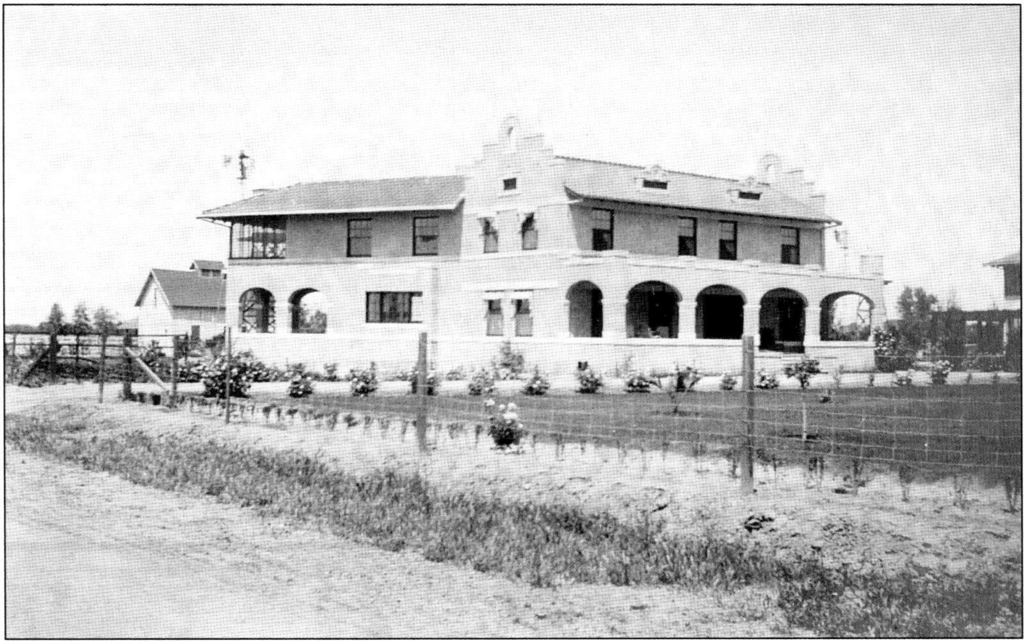

These are two more large houses that stood on Central Avenue. Above is the Tweed home at the northwest corner of Central Avenue and McDowell Road. To its north was the Hartranft house, pictured below. Gordon Tweed was a rancher; William Hartranft manufactured cement. Hartranft was instrumental in the city's early planning and zoning efforts as well as the inspired creator of the Phoenix parks system. (Both, courtesy of Frederick W. Bancroft Photographic Album and Correspondence; above, No. RC9:119; below, No. RC9:112, Billie Jane Baguley Library and Archives, Heard Museum, Phoenix, Arizona.)

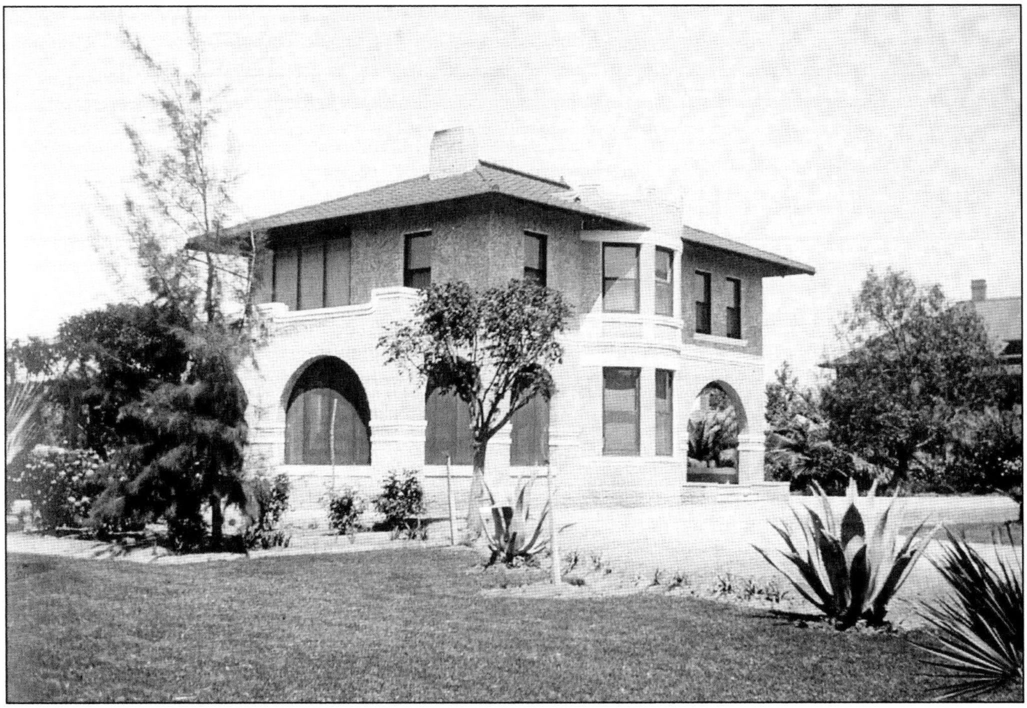

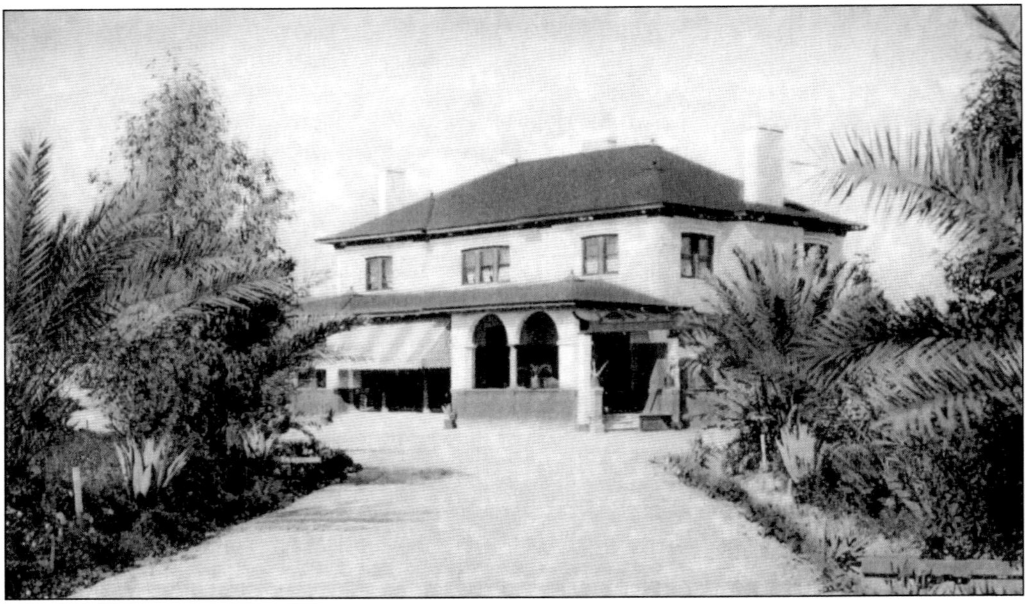

Arizona became a haven for people suffering from lung illnesses, such as tuberculosis. Called "lungers," many flocked to Phoenix and its warm, dry climate in hope of recovery. Palm Lodge (above), a sanatorium on the northeast corner of Central Avenue and Thomas Road, was operated by Dr. Henry Stone early in the century. It later served as a resort that attracted winter visitors before becoming a private home. The Phoenix Indian School had its own sanatorium for Native Americans (below). During the first decade, there was a major tuberculosis outbreak at the school. (Above, author's collection; below, courtesy of Arizona State Library, Archives and Public Records, History and Archives Division, Phoenix, No. 01-8212.)

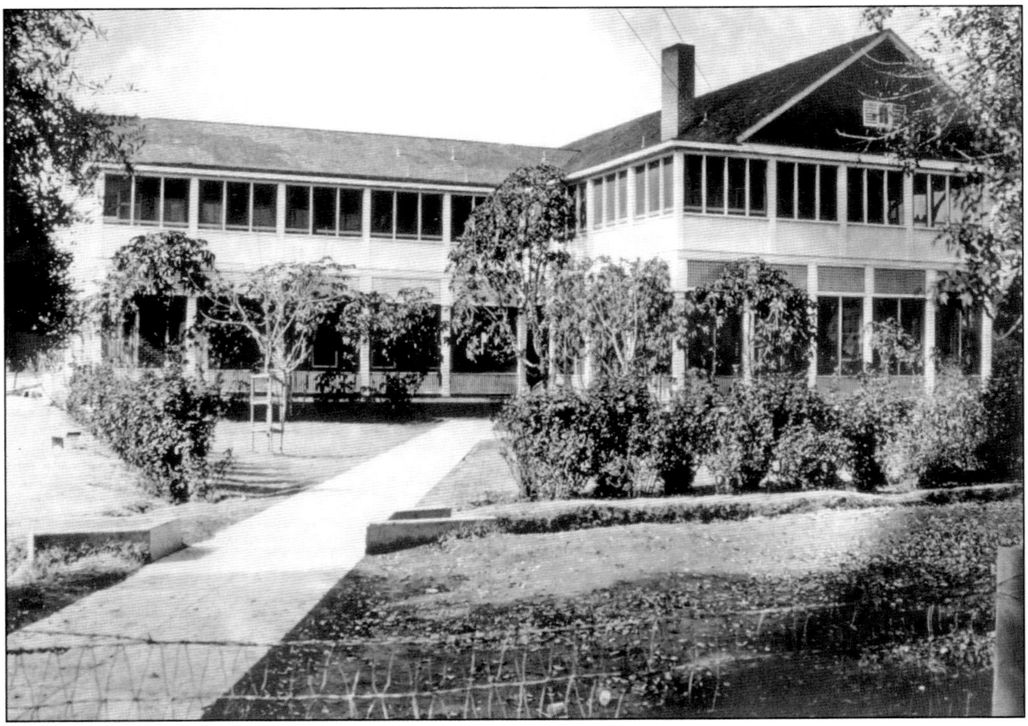

Dwight Heard, along with family and other partners, created the Los Olivos subdivision on 160 acres at the northeast intersection of McDowell Road and Central Avenue in 1907. The subdivision originally had 32 large multi-acre lots to attract those willing to construct estate homes just north of the city. The Otto Plath house, shown here, was constructed on East Palm Lane in 1910 and fit the vision of Los Olivos. Slow sales, however, drove more subdividing over the years that created a larger number of smaller lots. This advertisement from 1912 outlines the amenities of Los Olivos, which included city water, electricity, and the Indian School street rail line—amenities of the city, along with "the comforts of the country." Development occurred steadily over the next several decades. Today, this area is home to both the Alvarado and Los Olivos historic districts. (Right, courtesy of Library of Congress, *Arizona Republican*, March 24, 1912, Vol. XXII, Number 303, Section 2, page 1; below, photograph by the author.)

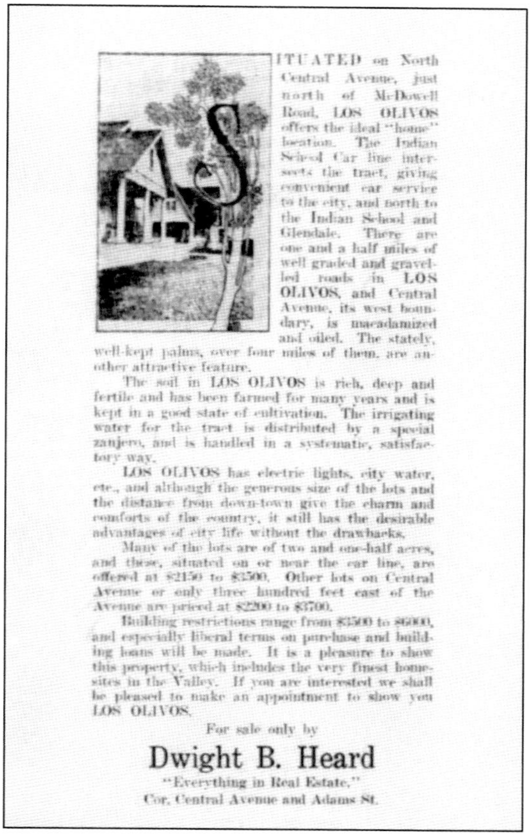

SITUATED on North Central Avenue, just north of McDowell Road, **LOS OLIVOS** offers the ideal "home" location. The Indian School Car line intersects the tract, giving convenient car service to the city, and north to the Indian School and Glendale. There are one and a half miles of well graded and gravelled roads in **LOS OLIVOS**, and Central Avenue, its west boundary, is macadamized and oiled. The stately, well-kept palms, over four miles of them, are another attractive feature.

The soil in **LOS OLIVOS** is rich, deep and fertile and has been farmed for many years and is kept in a good state of cultivation. The irrigating water for the tract is distributed by a special zanjero, and is handled in a systematic, satisfactory way.

LOS OLIVOS has electric lights, city water, etc., and although the generous size of the lots and the distance from down-town give the charm and comforts of the country, it still has the desirable advantages of city life without the drawbacks.

Many of the lots are of two and one-half acres, and these, situated on or near the car line, are offered at $2150 to $3500. Other lots on Central Avenue or only three hundred feet east of the Avenue are priced at $2200 to $3700.

Building restrictions range from $3500 to $6000, and especially liberal terms on purchase and building loans will be made. It is a pleasure to show this property, which includes the very finest homesites in the Valley. If you are interested we shall be pleased to make an appointment to show you **LOS OLIVOS**.

For sale only by

Dwight B. Heard

"Everything in Real Estate."

Cor. Central Avenue and Adams St.

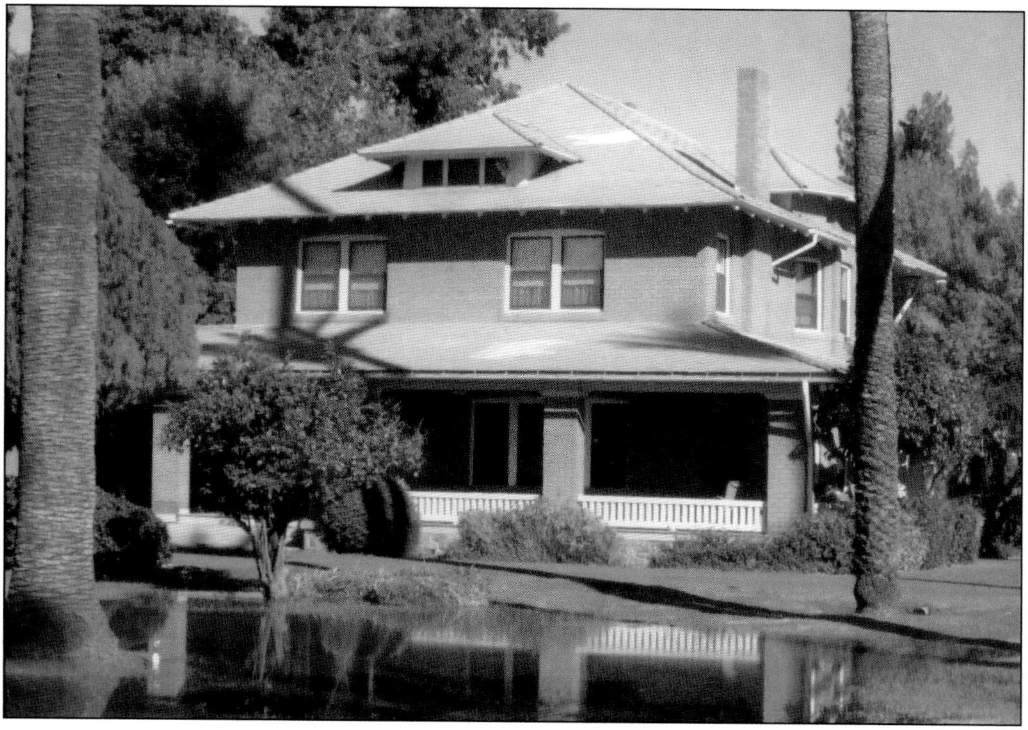

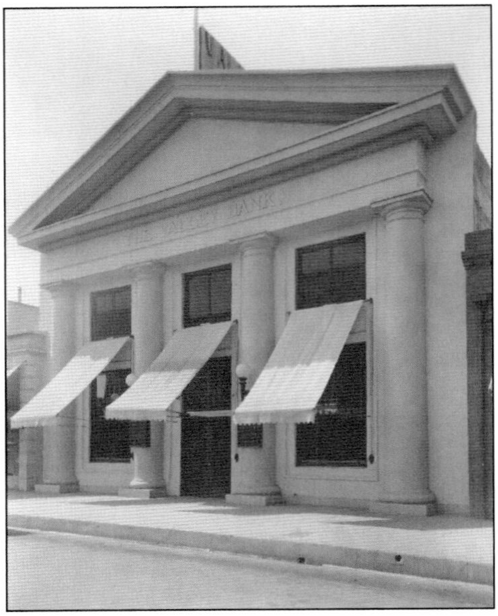

The Valley Bank was one of the financial institutions in turn-of-the-century Phoenix. Founded in 1884, the bank moved to Adams Street, west of Central Avenue, in 1909. Capital for development was essential for Phoenix growth. The Valley Bank failed in November 1914 but was reconstituted a month later. It eventually evolved into the Valley National Bank. (Courtesy of McClintock Collection, Arizona Room, Phoenix Public Library.)

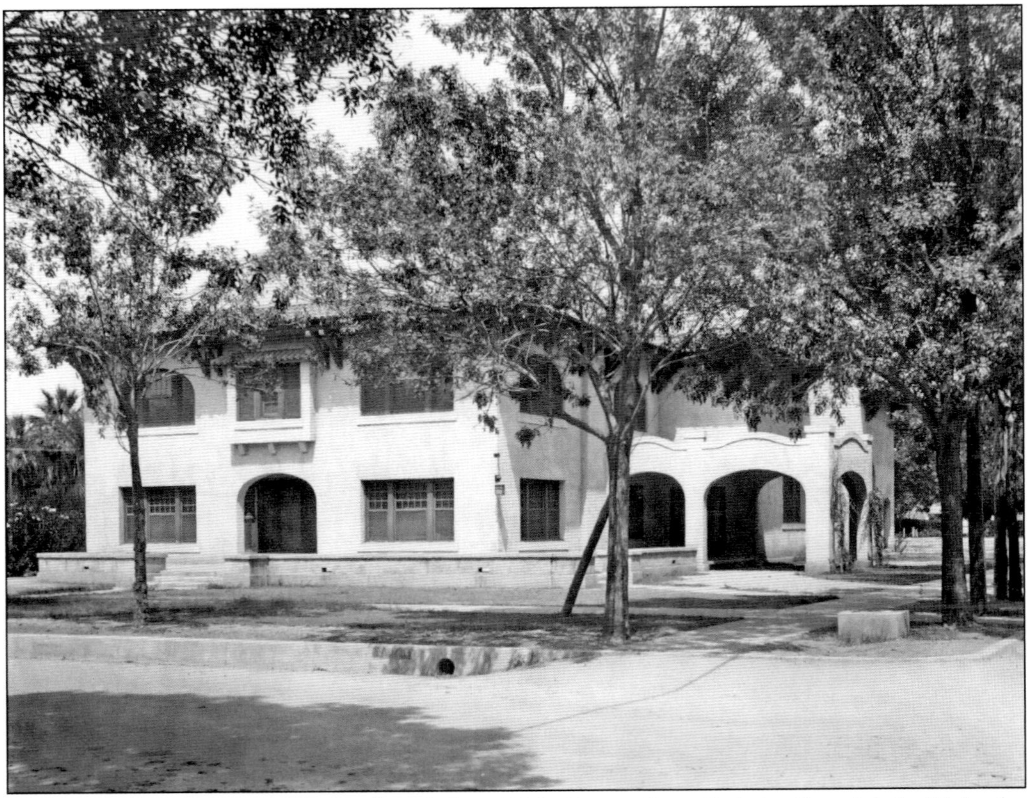

The Phoenix Women's Club was founded in 1900. Originally called the Fortnightly Club, the women's organization constructed this building at the northeast corner of First Avenue and Fillmore Street in 1911. The club promoted many civic activities, which included establishment of the first public library and formation of the Phoenix Fine Arts Association (later Phoenix Art Museum). Part of the Westward Ho Hotel now occupies the site. (Courtesy of McClintock Collection, Arizona Room, Phoenix Public Library.)

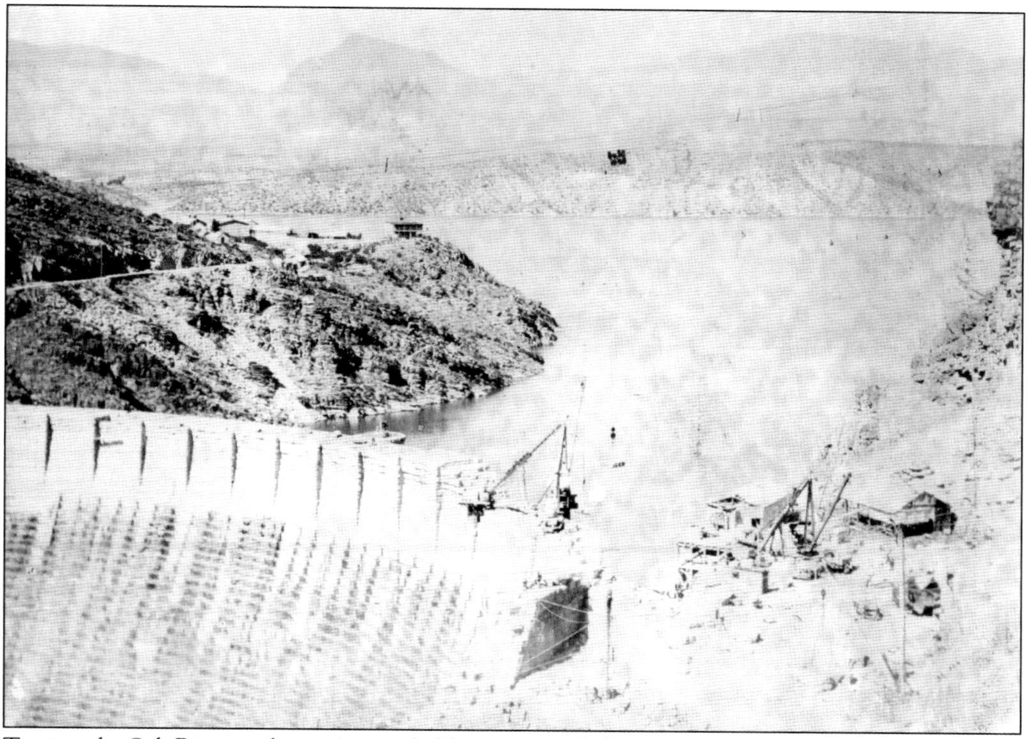

Taming the Salt River and securing a reliable water supply became a community priority in the late 19th century. In 1889, surveyors located a dam site in the Tonto Valley, 60 miles east of Phoenix. After formation of a water users' association and securing of funds, construction began in 1904. Italian masons were brought in to carve the stone that gave the dam its unique appearance, as shown here during construction. When completed, it had cost over $10 million and stood almost 300 feet high. On March 19, 1911, former president Theodore Roosevelt visited Phoenix to dedicate the dam that bore his name. After driving north on Central Avenue and stopping at the Phoenix Indian School, Roosevelt and his motorcade arrived at the dam, where he gave the dedication speech. (Above, author's collection; below, courtesy of McClintock Collection, Arizona Room, Phoenix Public Library.)

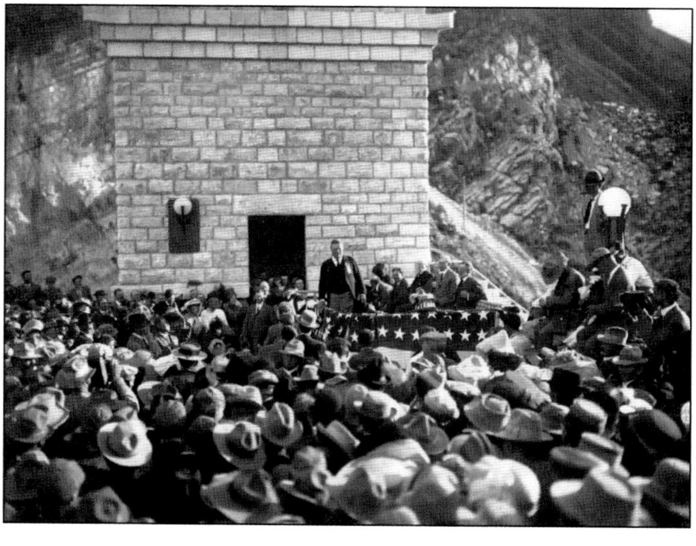

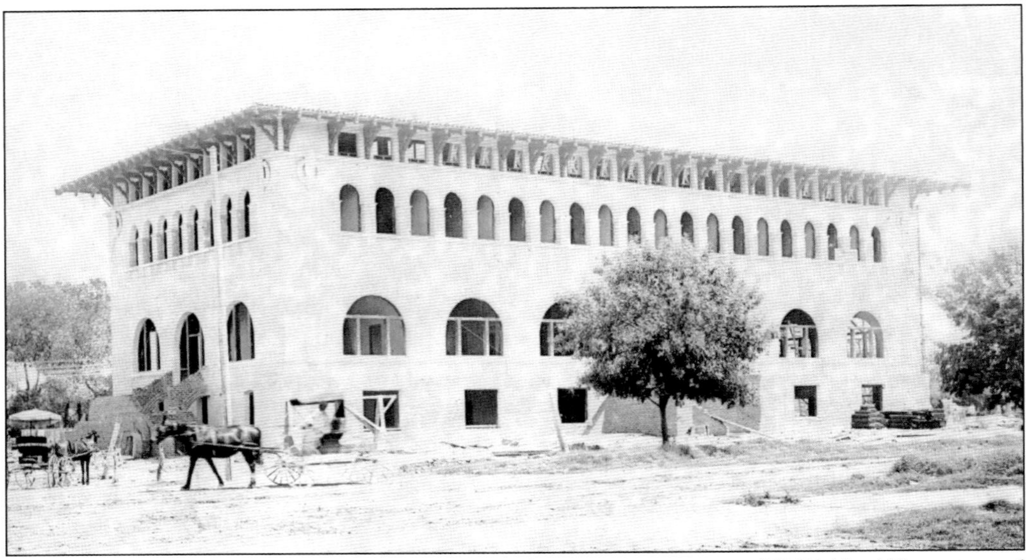

In 1892, local leaders formed the Young Men's Christian Association (YMCA) of Phoenix and the Valley of the Sun, a place for the improvement of the spiritual, mental, physical, and social conditions of boys and young men. The new organization grew steadily, and by 1907, work had begun on their new building, shown here under construction around 1910, at the northeast corner of Monroe Street and Second Avenue. (Author's collection.)

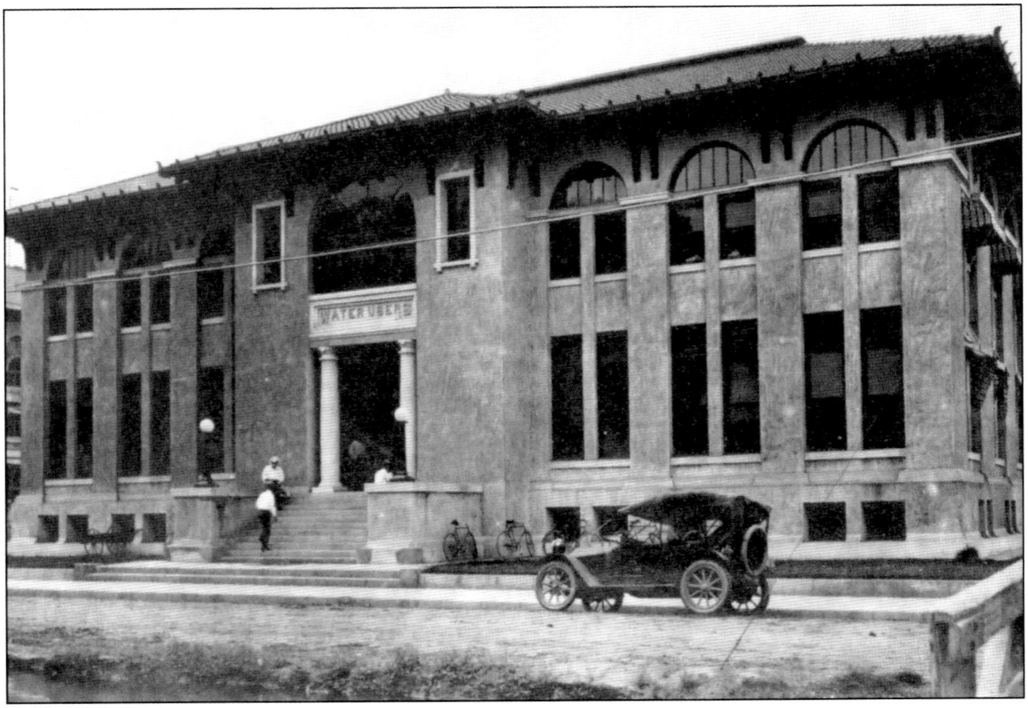

The Salt River Valley Water Users' Association constructed its headquarters on Van Buren Street between First and Second Avenues in 1911. It is shown here shortly after completion. The Town Ditch that flowed just north of Van Buren Street can be seen in the foreground. The association eventually became Salt River Project, which still provides water and power to the valley. (Courtesy of Salt River Project.)

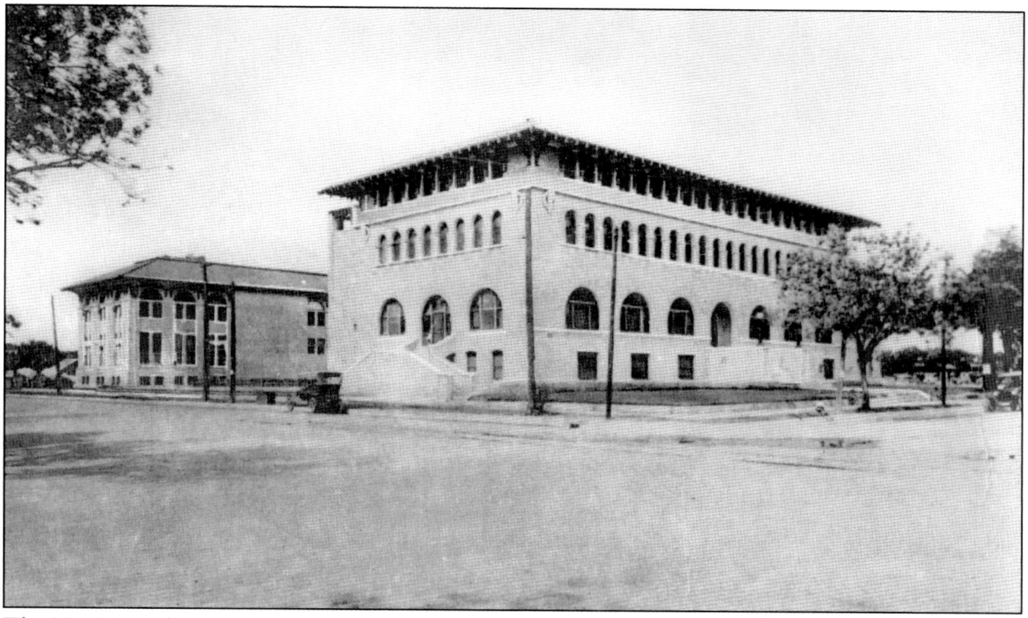

The YMCA and Water Users buildings, both completed in 1911, shared the same block. They formed the civic center of that time, capping the north end of downtown and providing an important hub of community activity. Both of these buildings lasted until 1961. (Author's collection.)

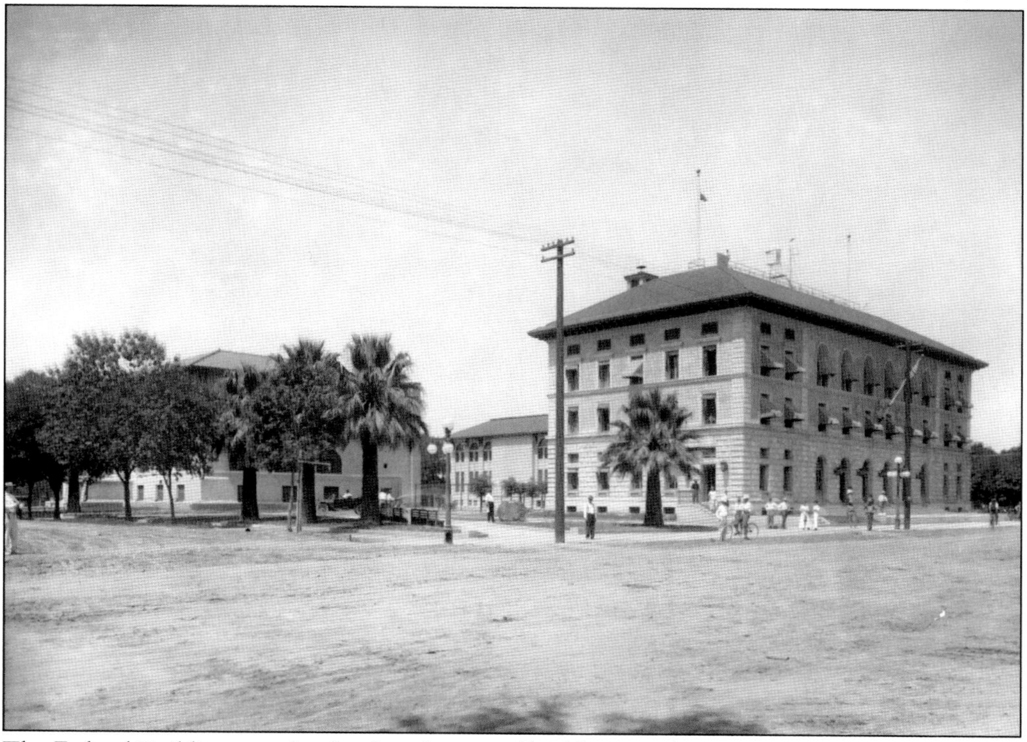

The Federal Building was the third in the trio of buildings at the civic center. It was located on First Avenue between Monroe and Van Buren Streets. Completed in 1913, it housed the post office as well as courts and other federal operations. It was demolished in the late 1950s for a new federal court building. (Courtesy of McClintock Collection, Arizona Room, Phoenix Public Library.)

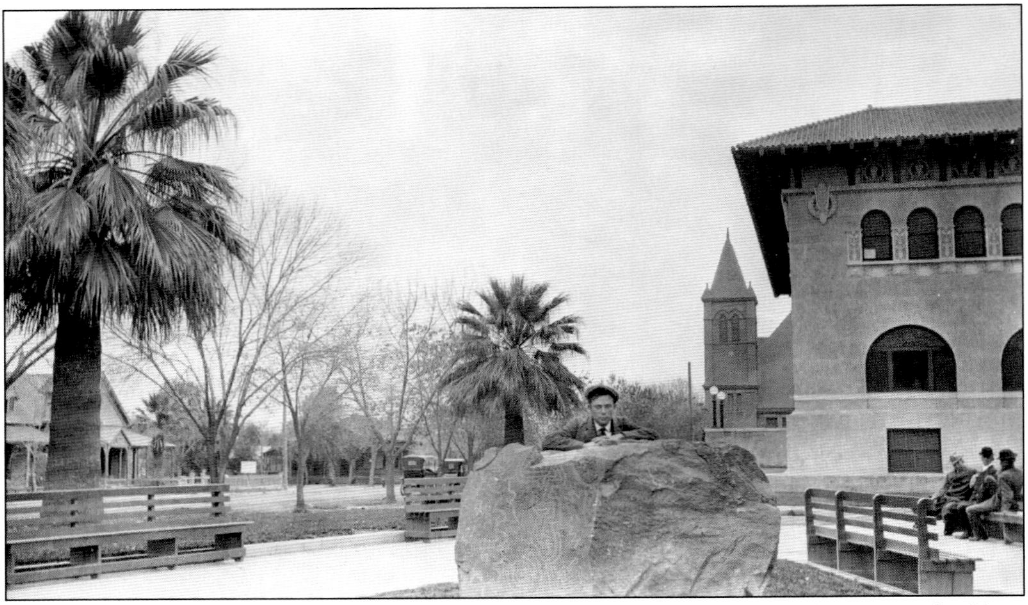

Here are closer views of the civic center plaza. Above is the east side of the YMCA building around 1914. Monroe Street runs east and west on the left. One can see the residential character of the area. Note the houses at the intersection of Monroe Street and Second Avenue along with the picket fences and vintage cars. The Methodist Church is visible behind the YMCA. Below is the same view with the south end of the Federal Building on the right. This pleasant plaza had places for strollers and patrons to sit and relax. The large stone on which the young man rests his arms had petroglyphs that can be seen in the photograph. (Above, author's collection; below, courtesy of McCulloch Brothers Photographs, Herb and Dorothy McLaughlin Collection, Arizona State University Libraries.)

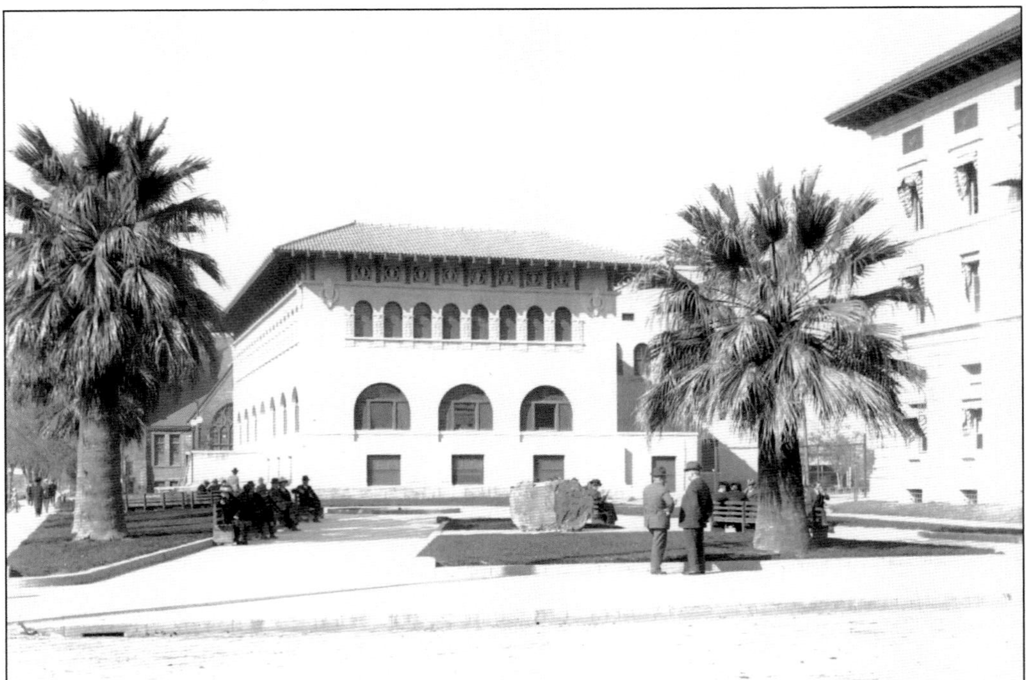

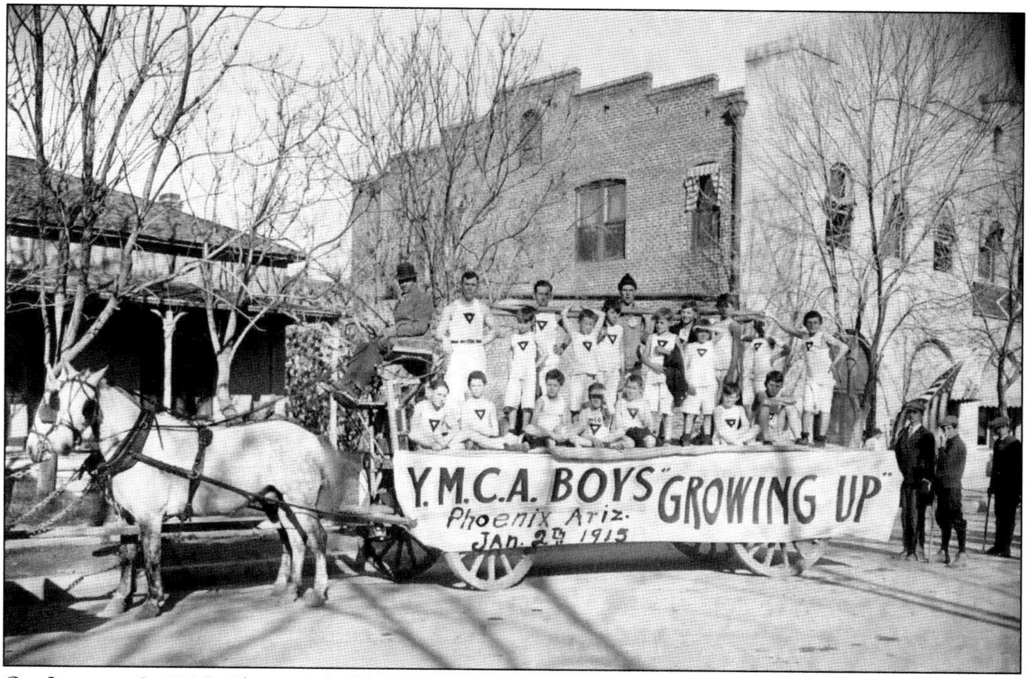

On January 2, 1915, Phoenix held a Prosperity Festival featuring a parade and other events to celebrate the past success of the community and generate optimism for the year ahead. Evening events featured a gala dinner at the Adams Hotel with Vice Pres. Thomas Marshall and Gov. George Hunt in attendance. Boys from the YMCA participated in the parade with this float. (Author's collection.)

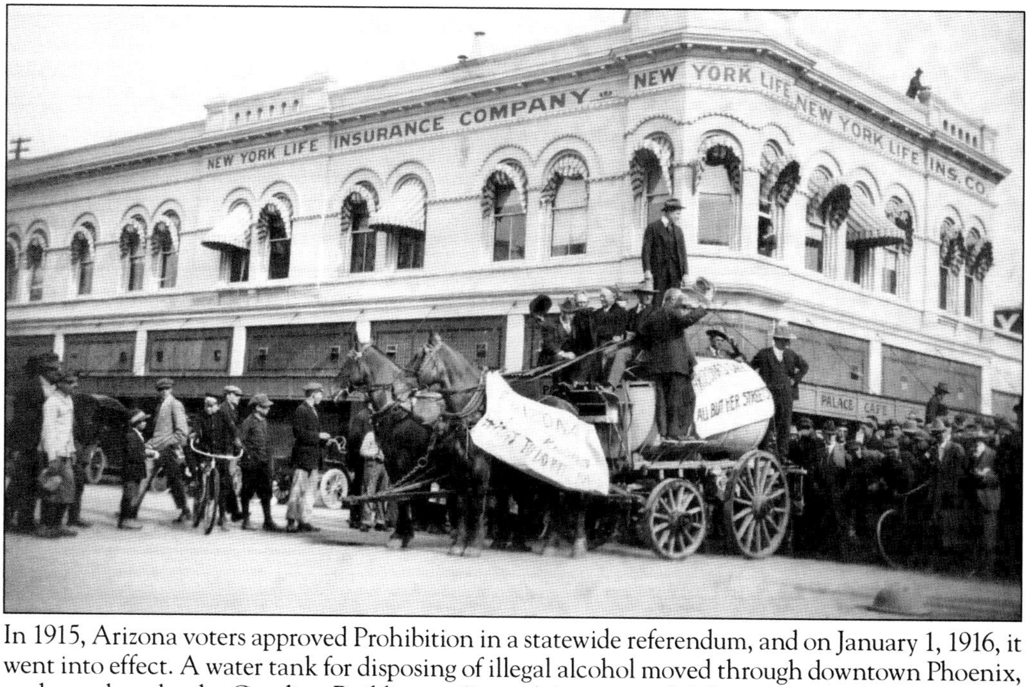

In 1915, Arizona voters approved Prohibition in a statewide referendum, and on January 1, 1916, it went into effect. A water tank for disposing of illegal alcohol moved through downtown Phoenix, as shown here by the Gooding Building at Central Avenue and Adams Street. The banner says, "Arizona knows what to do with booze." (Courtesy of Arizona Science Center.)

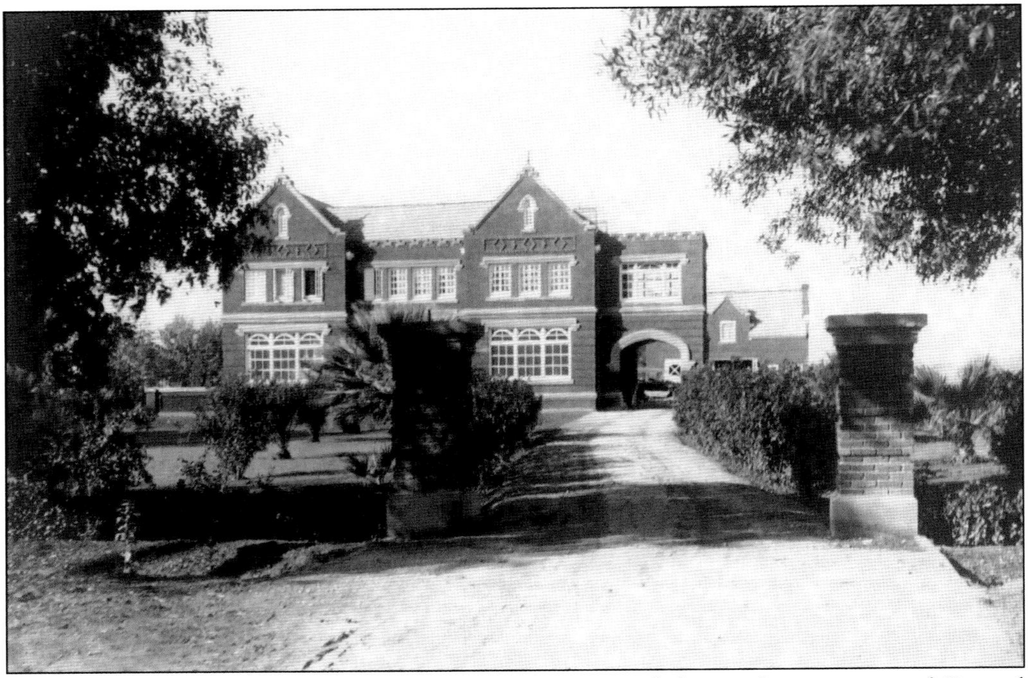

Constructed in 1914, the home of Dr. R.W. Craig occupied the northwest corner of Central Avenue and Encanto Boulevard. One of the large houses on Millionaires' Row, it was designed by architects Fitzhugh & Fitzhugh and constructed at a cost of $25,000. Though absorbed by an office building over the years, parts of the house could be seen into the 1980s. (Courtesy of Arizona Science Center.)

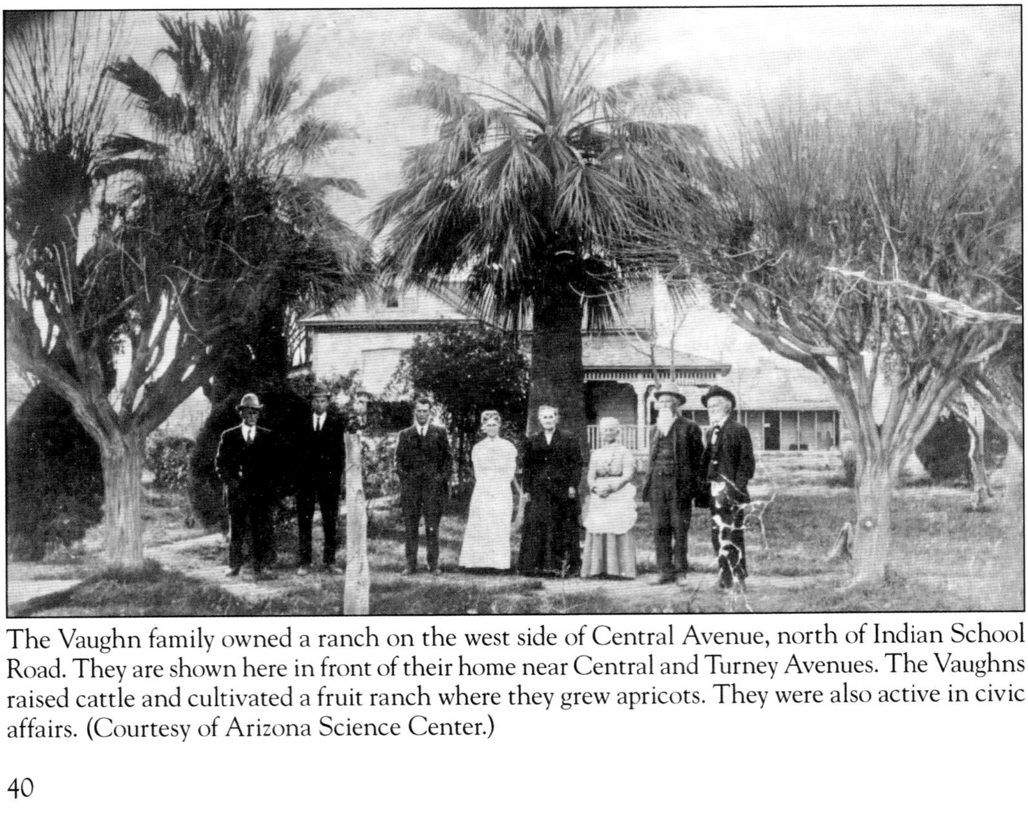

The Vaughn family owned a ranch on the west side of Central Avenue, north of Indian School Road. They are shown here in front of their home near Central and Turney Avenues. The Vaughns raised cattle and cultivated a fruit ranch where they grew apricots. They were also active in civic affairs. (Courtesy of Arizona Science Center.)

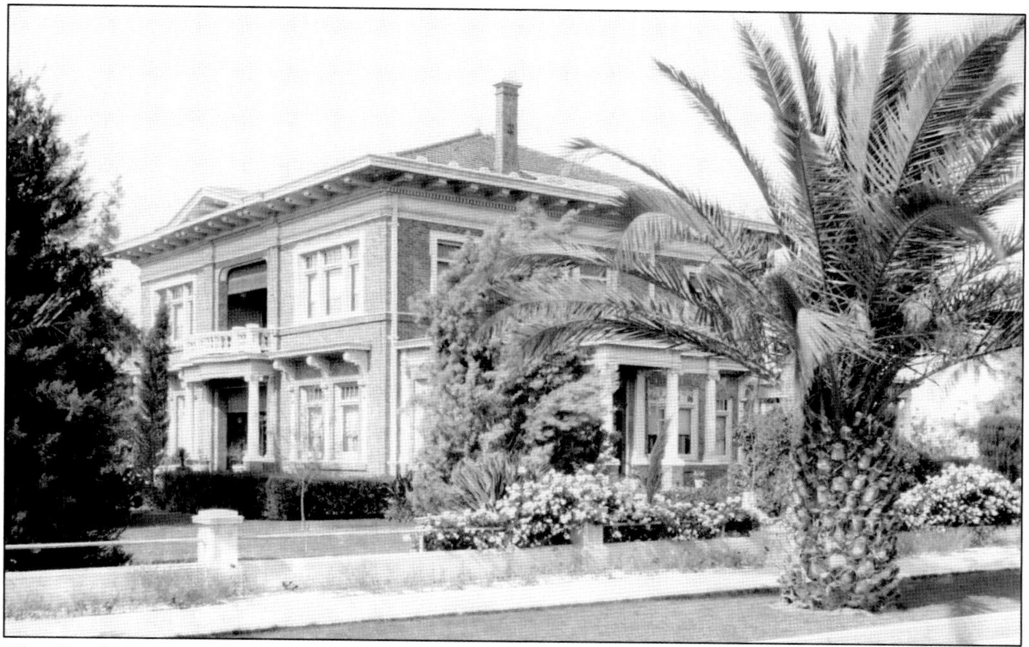

The Eisele-Diamond House stood at the northeast corner of Central Avenue and Coronado Road. Built for Edward Eisele, the proprietor of Phoenix Bakery, it was later purchased by Isaac and Nellie Diamond, who ran the Boston Store downtown. The house was demolished in 1961 for an office building. The Phoenix Art Museum and Phoenix Theatre campus now occupy the site. (Courtesy of McCulloch Brothers Photographs, Herb and Dorothy McLaughlin Collection, Arizona State University Libraries.)

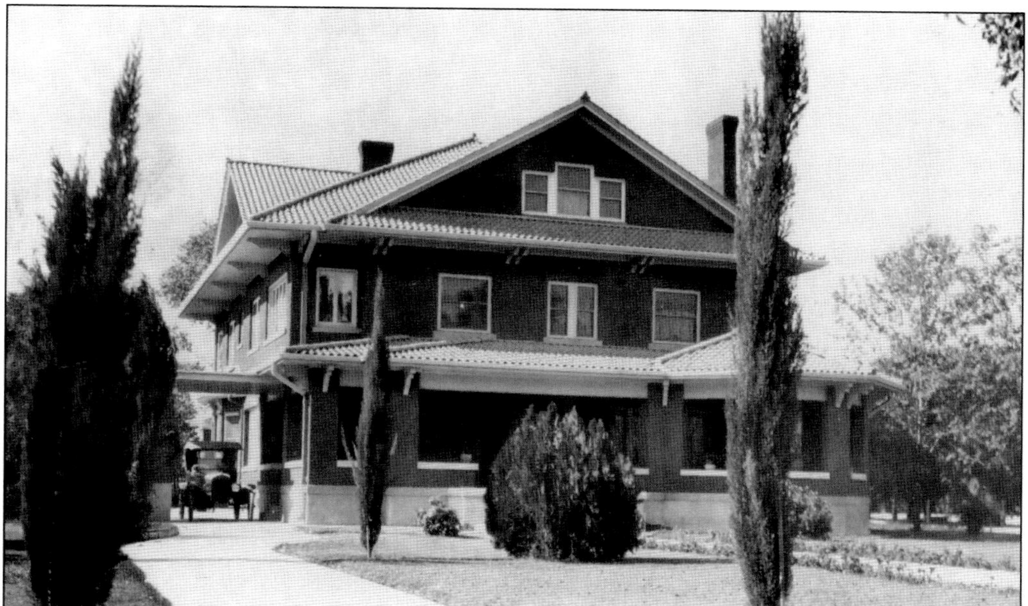

Dr. William C. Ellis constructed his home on the southwest corner of Central Avenue and Culver Street. A prominent local physician, Dr. Ellis was instrumental in setting up Deaconess Hospital. Nearly lost to freeway construction, the house still stands as the last intact example of the Central Avenue mansions that once occupied Millionaires' Row. (Courtesy of the Shackelford family.)

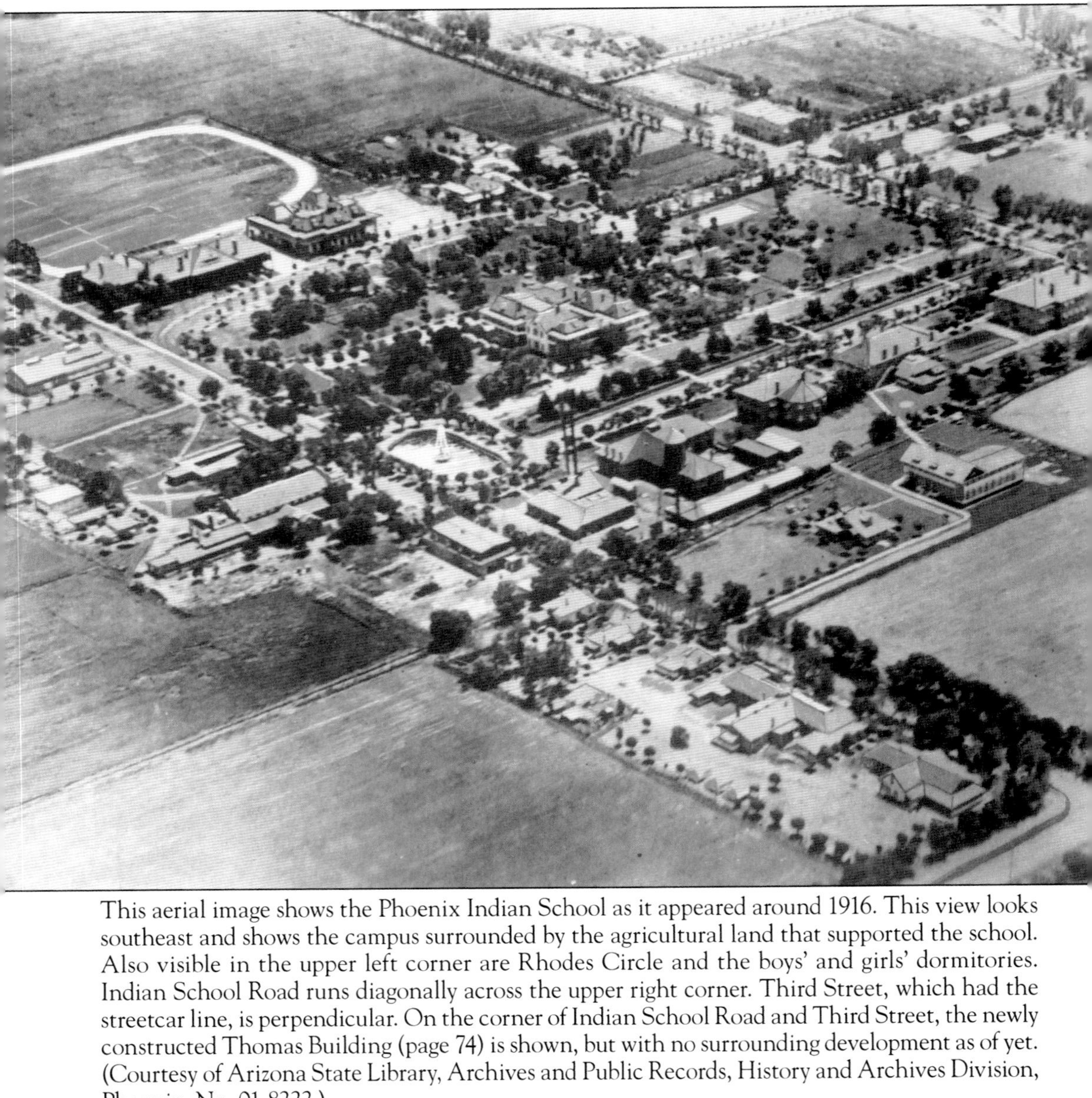

This aerial image shows the Phoenix Indian School as it appeared around 1916. This view looks southeast and shows the campus surrounded by the agricultural land that supported the school. Also visible in the upper left corner are Rhodes Circle and the boys' and girls' dormitories. Indian School Road runs diagonally across the upper right corner. Third Street, which had the streetcar line, is perpendicular. On the corner of Indian School Road and Third Street, the newly constructed Thomas Building (page 74) is shown, but with no surrounding development as of yet. (Courtesy of Arizona State Library, Archives and Public Records, History and Archives Division, Phoenix, No. 01-8222.)

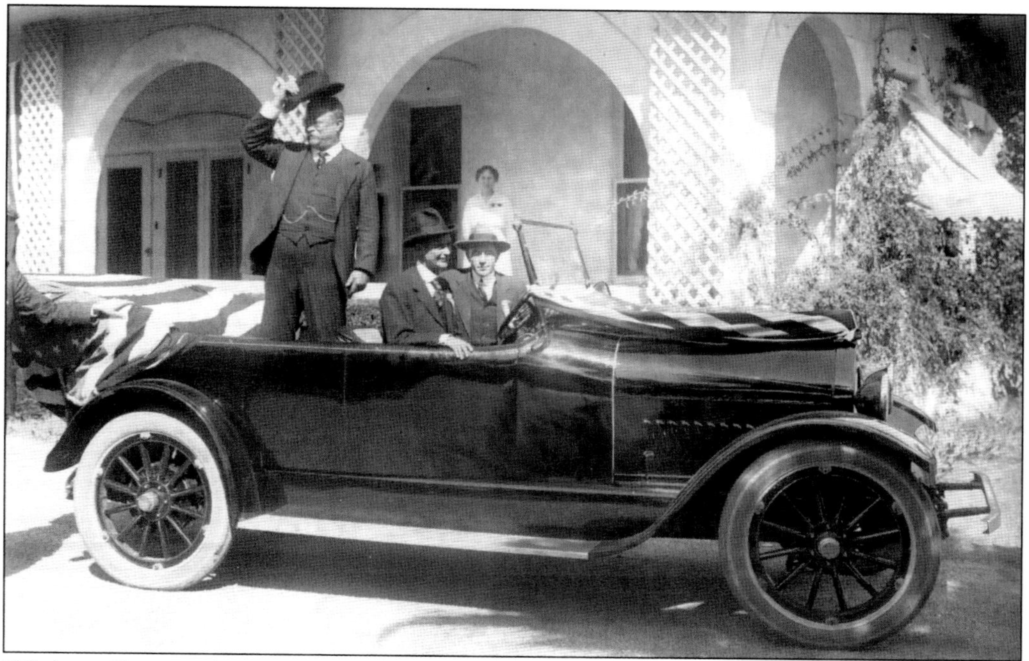

While in Phoenix for a speech on October 21 during the 1916 presidential election campaign, former president Theodore Roosevelt stopped at Casa Blanca to visit the Heards. He is shown here in his automobile, with Maie Heard looking on from the porch. He spoke for two hours on foreign affairs and relations with Mexico at the Polk Street Grounds, northeast of the Van Buren Street and Central Avenue intersection. (Courtesy of Arizona Science Center.)

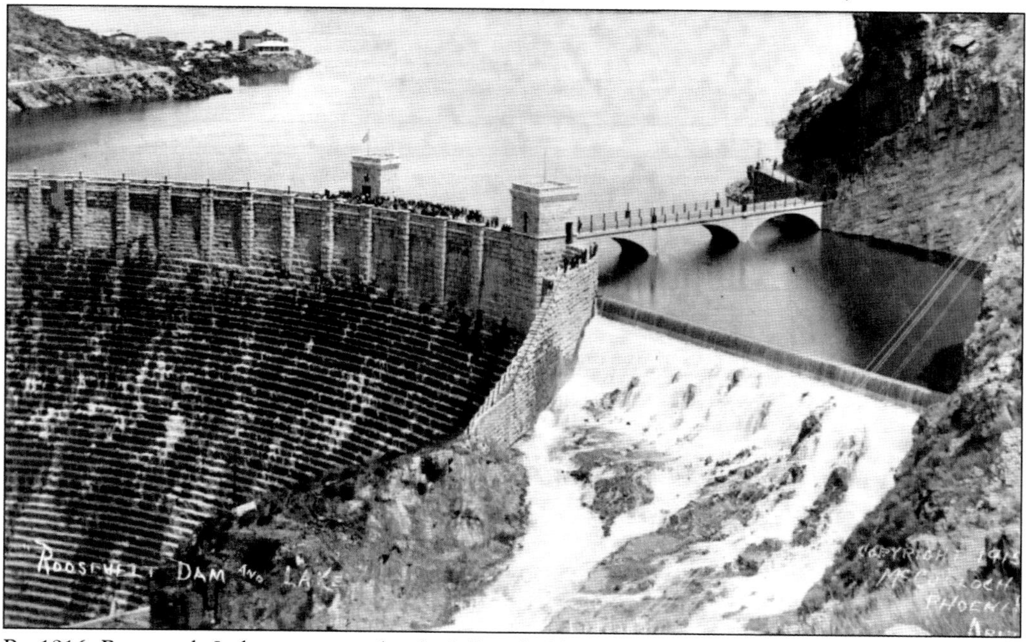

By 1916, Roosevelt Lake was completely full. It held a multiyear supply of water and produced electric power for the valley's farms and cities. While the water levels would rise and fall over the decades, the reliable supply of water and power, along with flood control, helped drive Phoenix development in the years ahead. (Barton photograph, courtesy of Library of Congress.)

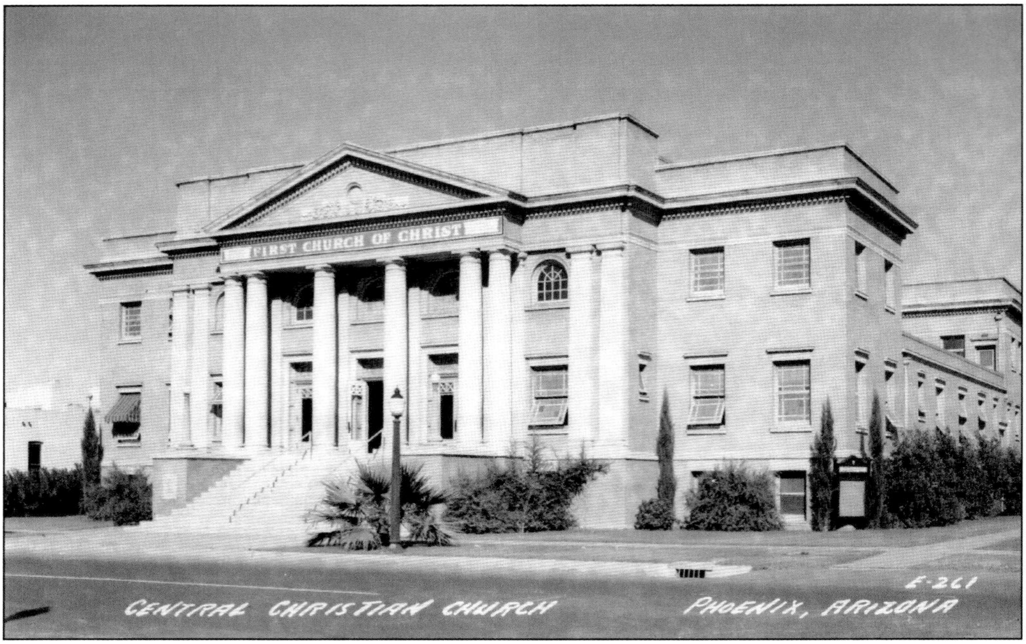

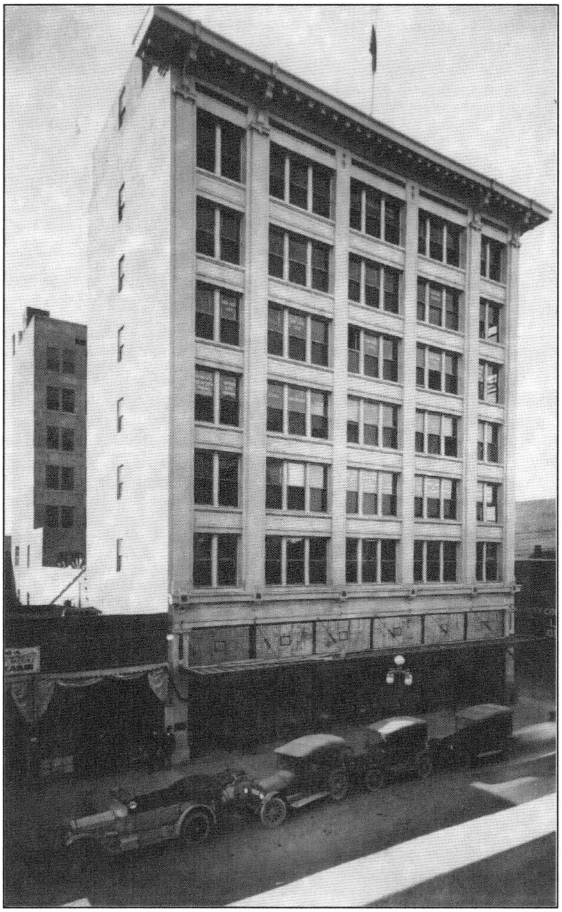

The Christian Church congregation constructed this building at the northeast corner of McKinley Street and Central Avenue. Designed by architect Robert Orr of Los Angeles, it had seating capacity for over 1,100 and cost about $75,000. A dedication on March 31, 1918, drew over 1,500 people. The church lasted into the 1980s. (Author's collection.)

In 1919, work began on the Heard Building on the west side of Central Avenue between Adams and Monroe Streets. Designed by Llewellyn Adelbert Parker and built by Dwight Heard, it housed his offices as well as those of the *Arizona Republican* newspaper. Completed in 1920, at seven stories it was Phoenix's first high-rise. It held that title until 1924 when the Luhrs Building was completed. (Courtesy of McClintock Collection, Arizona Room, Phoenix Public Library.)

Three

The Jazz Age, Depression, and War 1920–1945

By 1920, the population stood at just over 29,000, a fivefold increase from 1900. North Central Avenue was firmly established as Millionaires' Row, a place for the city's wealthy, business, and community leaders. Large homes, often surrounded by beautiful gardens or multiple acres of agricultural land, lined the avenue. As the century progressed, things started to change.

More commercial establishments appeared in the Corridor, both to support the growing population and escape from an increasingly crowded downtown core. Encouraged by the street railway system, more paved streets, and affordable automobiles, the Corridor saw the establishment of new subdivisions that became homes for the middle class. The streets were lined with trees and different styles of homes that ranged from the traditional bungalow to period revival. Two streetcar lines, several blocks on either side of Central Avenue, took people into the downtown to work and shop, then brought them home again when their business was complete.

A downturn in the 1920s brought on by a collapse in cotton prices after the end of the Great War drove some retrenchment and diversity in the local agricultural economy. The area quickly recovered, and the 1920s became a time of steady growth in the Corridor and Midtown areas. The Great Depression slowed this growth but did not entirely stop the construction of new homes and businesses. The next war would bring more opportunity for growth and change.

By 1920, Phoenix had established important elements to ensure steady growth: a reliable water supply, along with flood control, for both agricultural and urban use; a transportation system that linked Phoenix to national and international markets; a local transportation system that connected the northern suburbs with the downtown core; and financial institutions willing to supply the capital that fueled growth.

The region still suffered from brutally hot summers that sent much of its population to cooler climes for relief and kept tourists away during the hot months, but the mid-century decades saw increasing availability of refrigeration air-conditioning that provided relief from the heat and further encouraged growth.

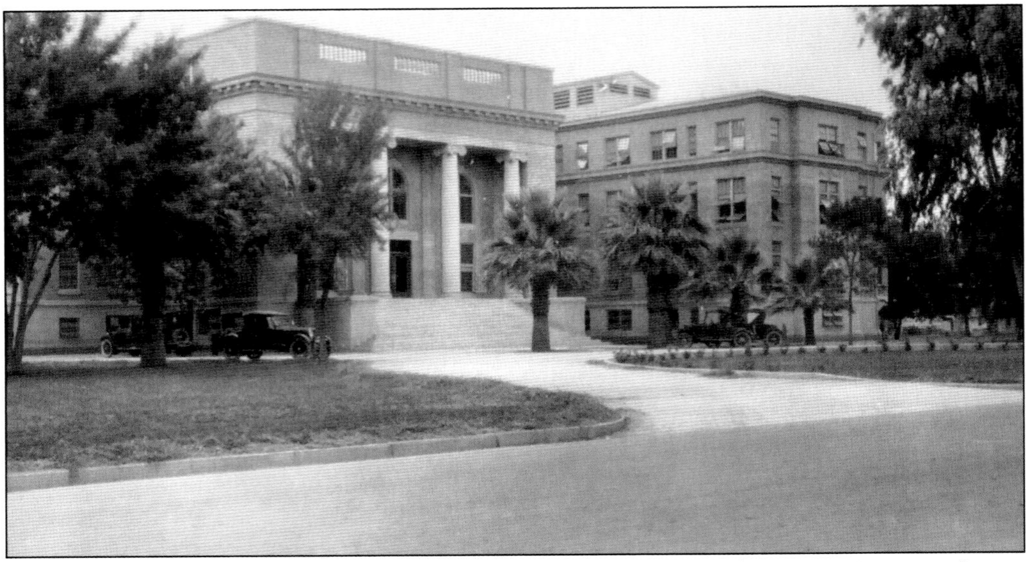

Established in 1911, Arizona Deaconess Hospital was initially located downtown. It acquired a site at the southeast corner of McDowell Road and Tenth Street in 1917. Construction began on the new facility in early 1918 but was soon halted due to the high cost of materials during wartime. Work occurred intermittently until completion in 1923. This early view shows the administration and west wings. It was renamed Good Samaritan Hospital in 1928. (Author's collection.)

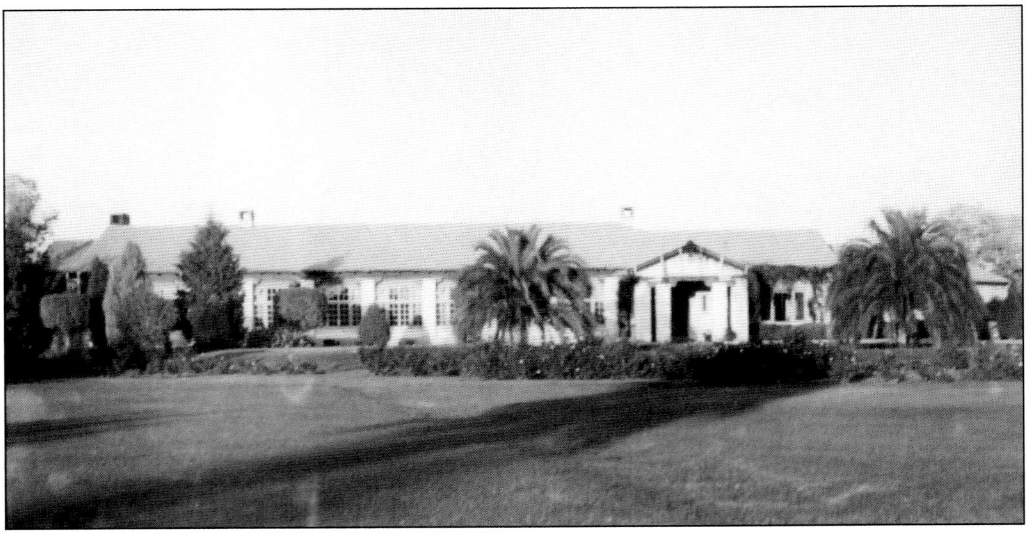

In October 1921, the Phoenix Country Club opened at its new location on the northeast corner of Seventh Street and Thomas Road with a three-day celebration. Located on 160 acres, it boasted an 18-hole golf course as well as 50 acres that were set aside for building lots, which became prime home locations. Phoenix architects Lescher, Kibby & Mahoney designed the clubhouse shown here. (Author's collection.)

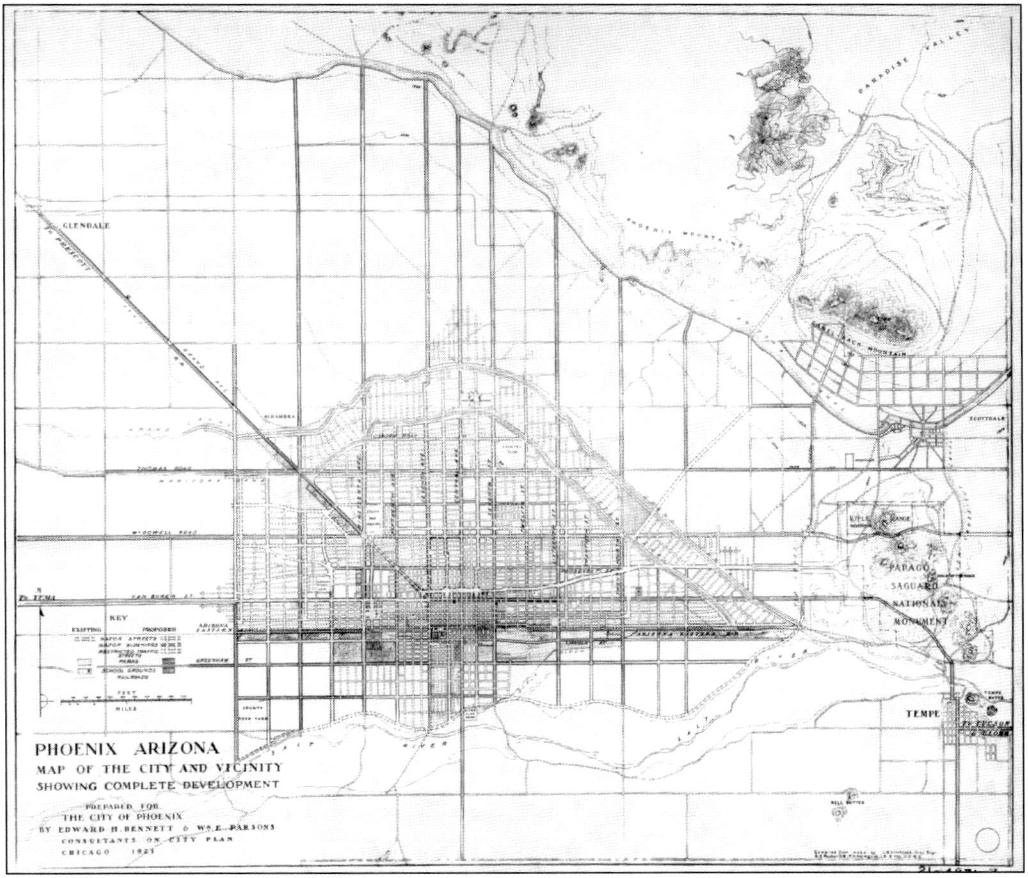

At the urging of the Chamber of Commerce, the city commission (now council) engaged Edward H. Bennett with the firm of Bennett & Parsons of Chicago to develop the city's first urban plan in 1920. Completed the following year, it provided for a street system, civic center, parks, an aviation field, and planning and zoning legislation. Though never fully implemented, the Bennett Plan marked the city's first effort to manage long-range growth and develop zones for different uses. (Courtesy of Edward H. Bennett Collection, Ryerson and Burnham Archives, The Art Institute of Chicago, Digital File No. 197301_150925-001.)

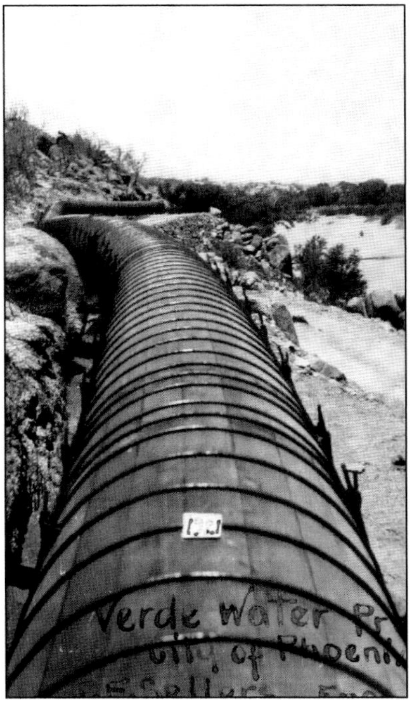

In 1916, Phoenix commissioned a study on obtaining an additional supply of water from the Verde River, and in 1919 construction began on a 36-inch-diameter redwood pipe that delivered water from the river to a reservoir at Fifty-Second Street and Thomas Road. Much of the line ran above grade and was a target for cowboys, who would shoot holes in it for a drink or bath. By 1930, concrete pipe had replaced the redwood. (Author's collection.)

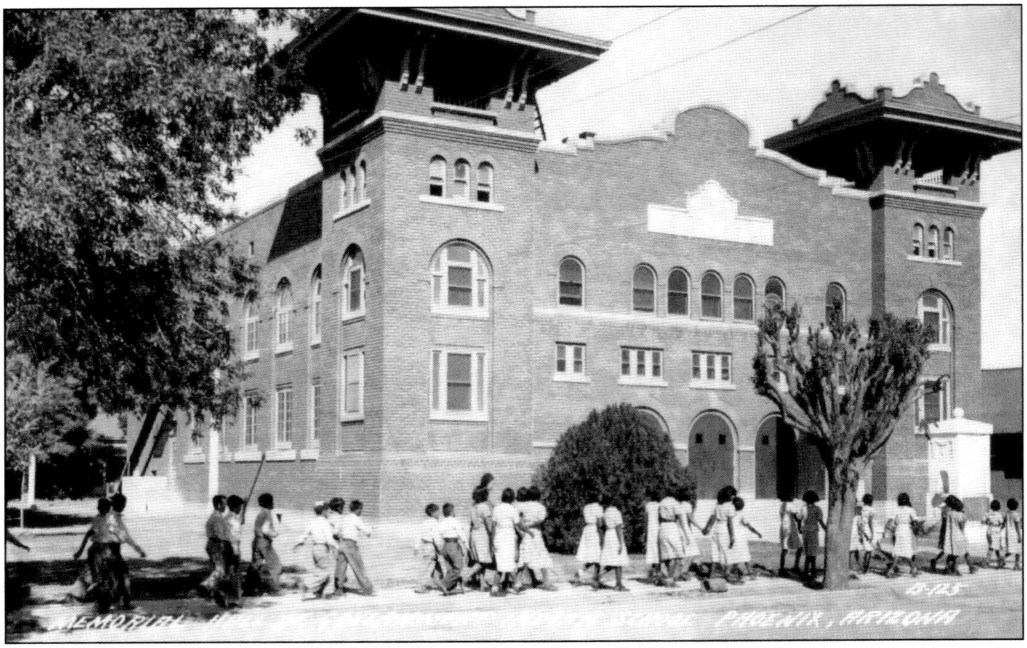

Growth continued at the Phoenix Indian School during the early 20th century. Above is the Memorial Building, constructed in 1922 and dedicated to the Phoenix Indian School students who served in the Great War. The Memorial Building still stands at the Phoenix Steele Indian School Park. Below is a new administration building. (Both, author's collection.)

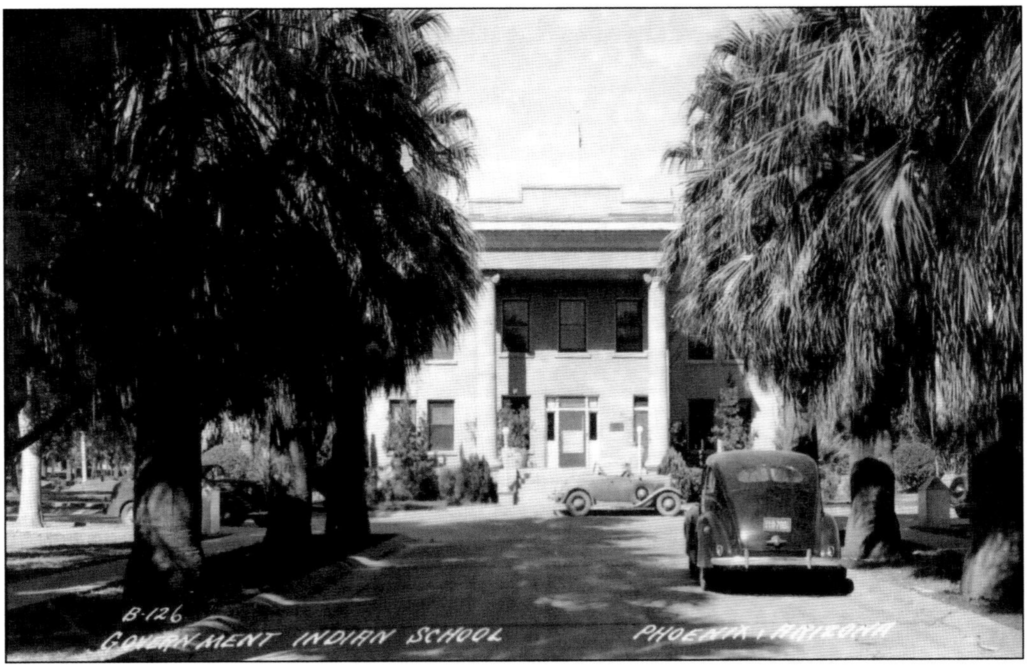

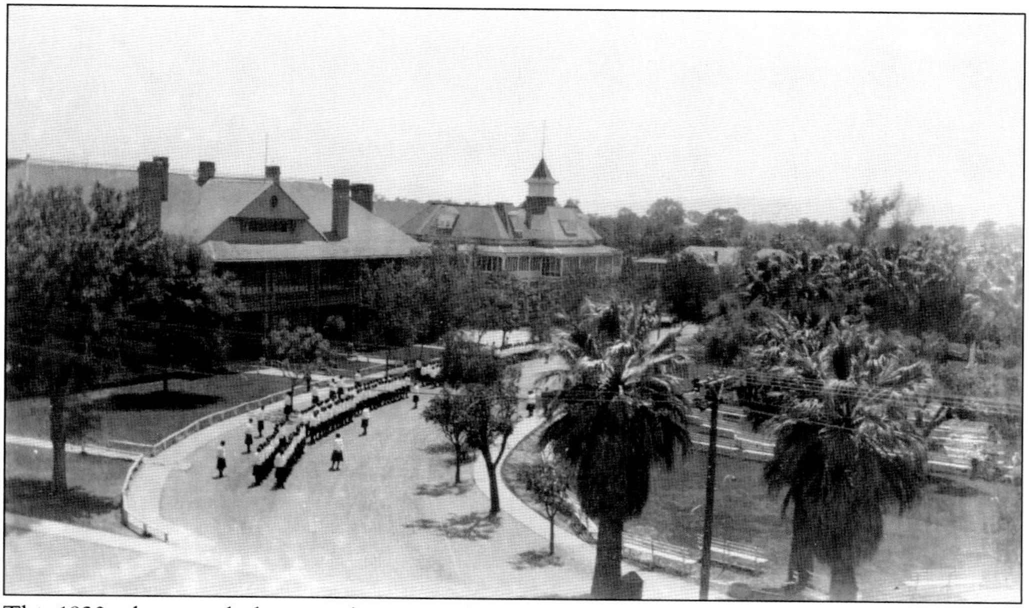

This 1920s photograph shows students attending an assembly at the Phoenix Indian School. While the campus was constantly changing, some of the original buildings still stood, as seen here with both of the first boys' dormitories (page 20). (Courtesy of Phoenix Indian School Collection, No. RC284(1)2.1, Billie Jane Baguley Library and Archives, Heard Museum, Phoenix, Arizona.)

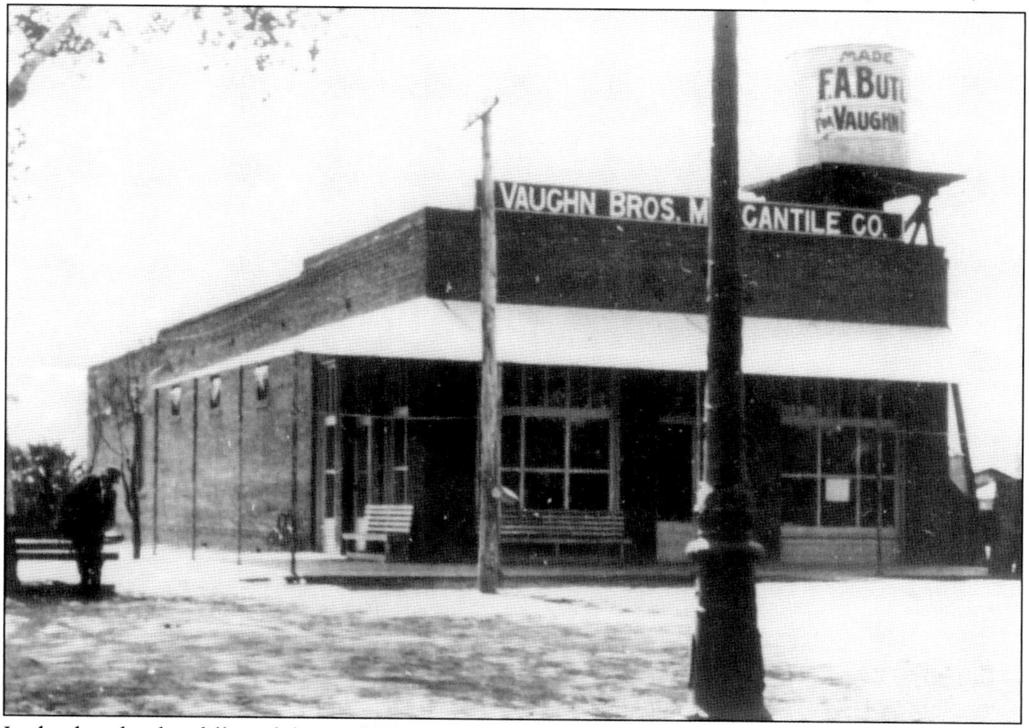

In the decades that followed the establishment of the school, a small commercial center developed on its south side along Indian School Road. The Vaughn brothers (page 40) were merchants. They established Vaughn Brothers Mercantile Company at the southwest corner of Indian School Road and Third Street. It later became Vaughn Brothers Real Estate. (Courtesy of Arizona Science Center.)

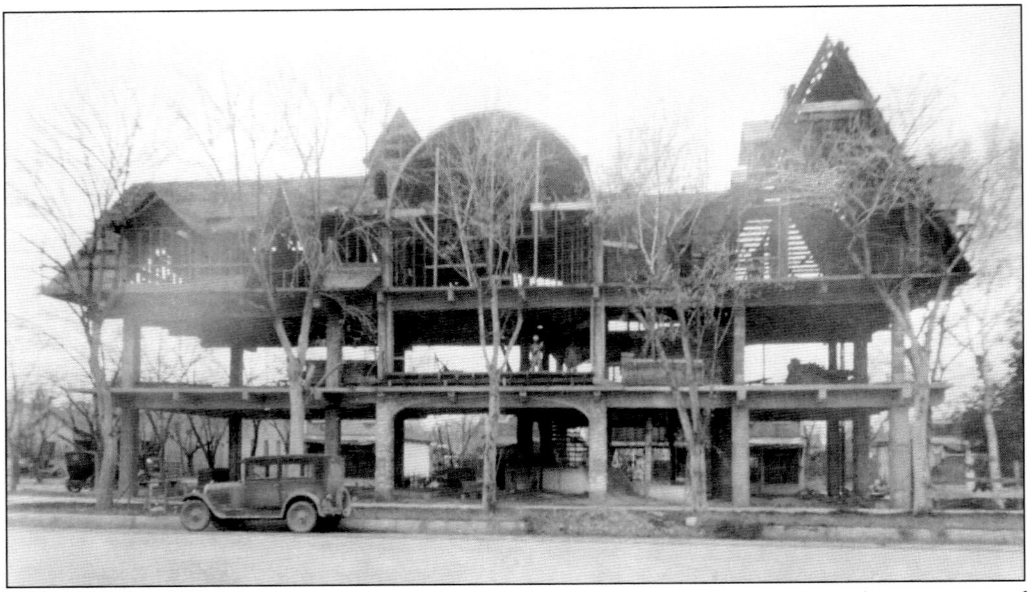

Hattie Mosher, a local businesswoman, started building this house on the southeast corner of Central Avenue and Taylor Street in the early 1920s. Throughout the 1920s and 1930s, Mosher, once a civic leader, had long legal battles that included stints in jail and the eventual loss of her property. She died in poverty in 1945. Never completed, the structure stood empty for many years until it was converted into an office building. The downtown campus of Arizona State University now occupies the site. (Courtesy of McCulloch Brothers Photographs, Herb and Dorothy McLaughlin Collection, Arizona State University Libraries.)

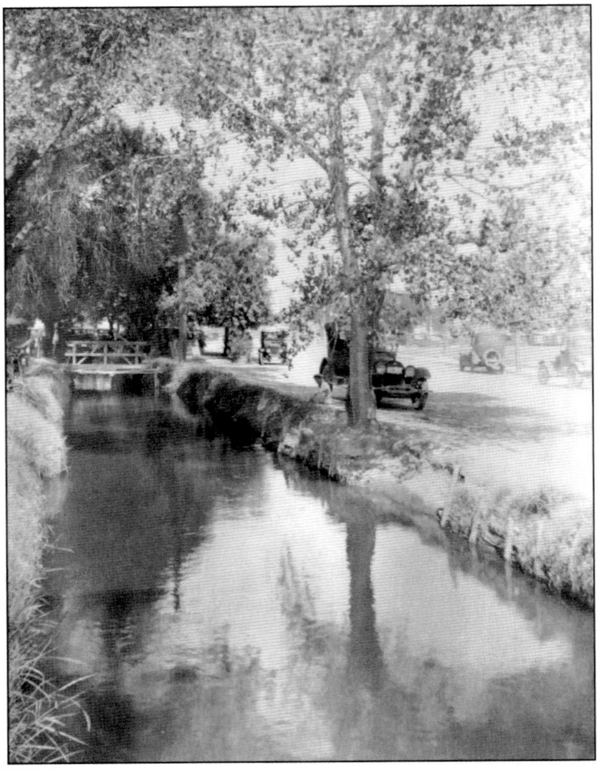

Well into the 1920s, the Town Ditch (page 10) still flowed along Van Buren Street, north of downtown. The canal was later rerouted. (Courtesy Herb and Dorothy McLaughlin Collection, Arizona State University Libraries.)

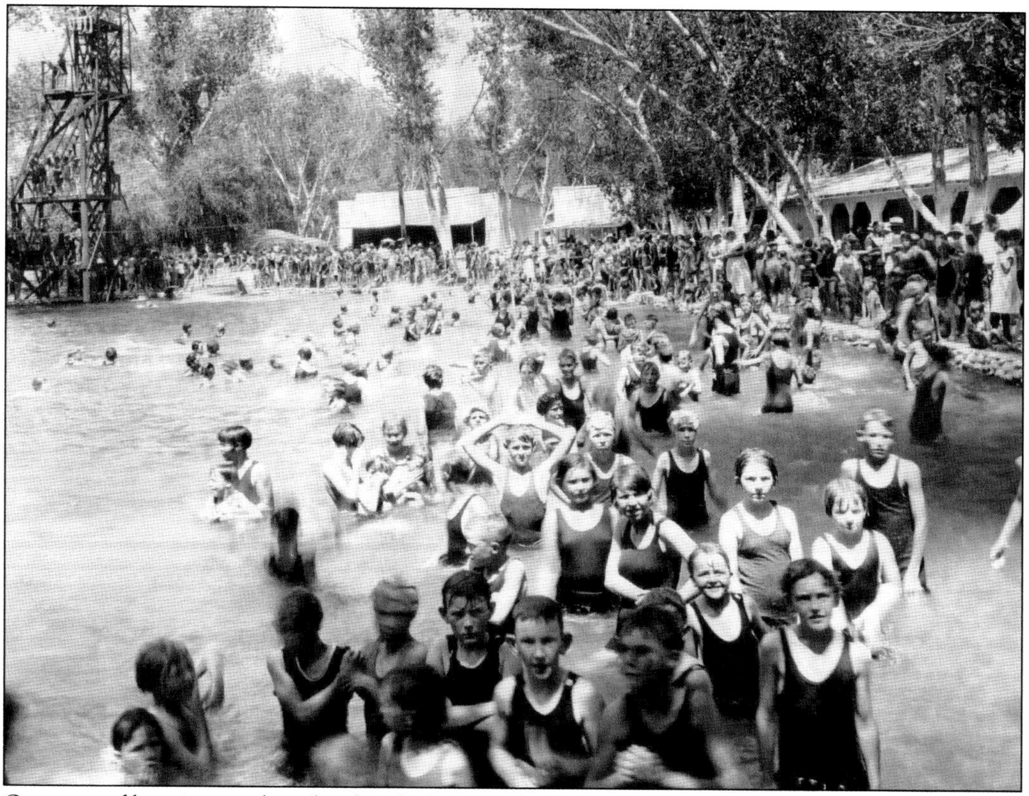

One way of keeping cool in the days before nearly everyone had refrigeration air-conditioning was swimming. There were public pools for people to enjoy on a hot day. In the early 1920s, the *Arizona Republican* newspaper hosted an annual picnic for children and their families at Riverside Park at South Central Avenue and the Salt River. The event attracted thousands for swimming, games, and food. (NEA photograph; author's collection.)

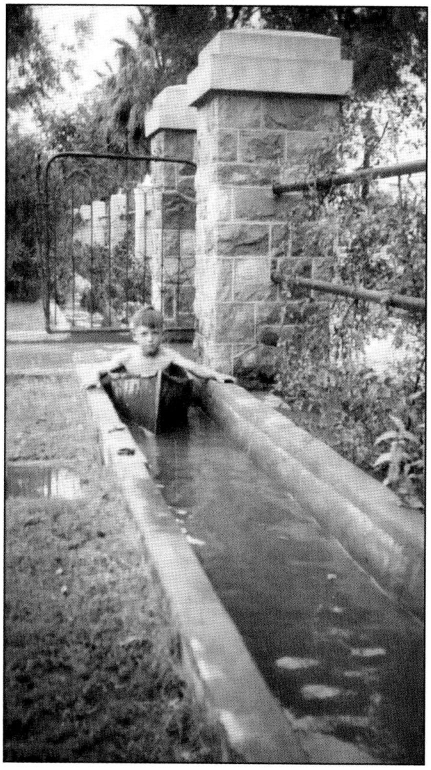

Another way of keeping cool was swimming or playing in the irrigation ditches. This photograph shows Ellis Shackelford in a boat in the irrigation ditch that ran along Central Avenue. (Courtesy of the Shackelford family.)

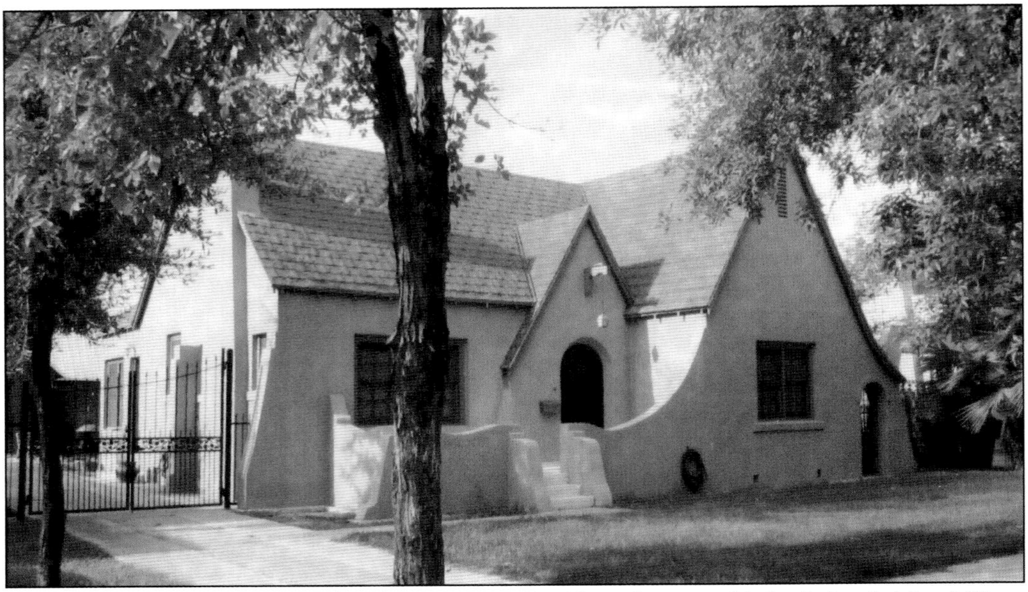

In 1920, Phoenix residential developers Home Builders, Inc., established the Ashland Place subdivision on East Hoover Avenue and Vernon Street between Central Avenue and Third Street. The development was very successful. Convenient to the streetcar line that ran along Third Street, most of Ashland had been built out by the end of the decade. The homes were intended for the middle class and encompassed a variety of architectural styles. Home Builders also developed in the Chelsea North subdivision at the northwest corner of McDowell Road and Central Avenue. (Photograph by the author.)

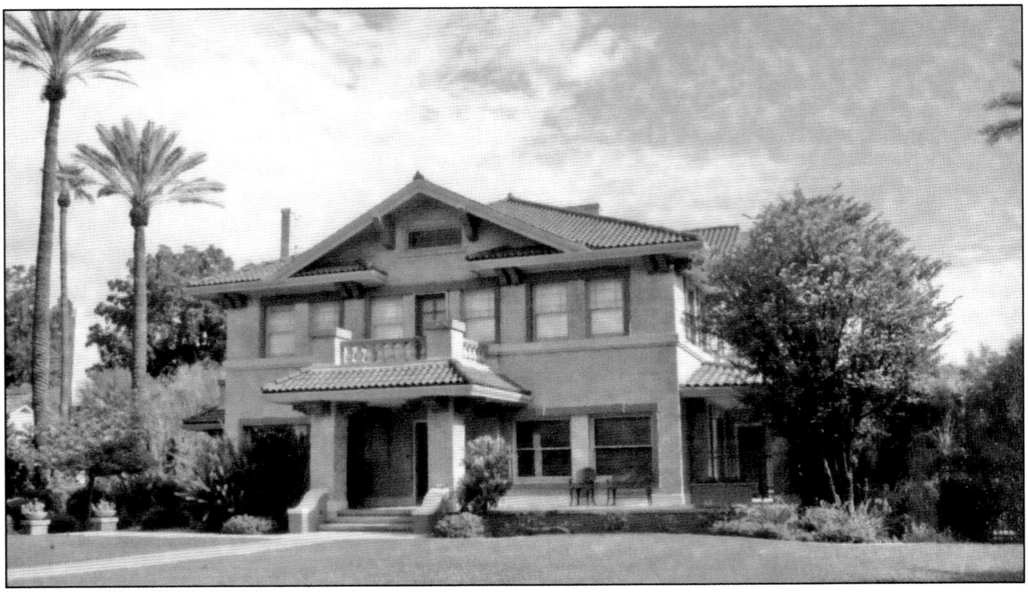

During the 1920s, the pace of development quickened as the benefits of a reliable water supply, improved interstate transportation, capital investment, more diversified economy, and in-migration were realized. The Salim Ackel House was constructed in the Los Olivos neighborhood in 1920. Development in Dwight Heard's subdivision had been slow but steady, and most of the district was established by 1932. The Ackel House is now in the Alvarado Historic District. (Photograph by the author.)

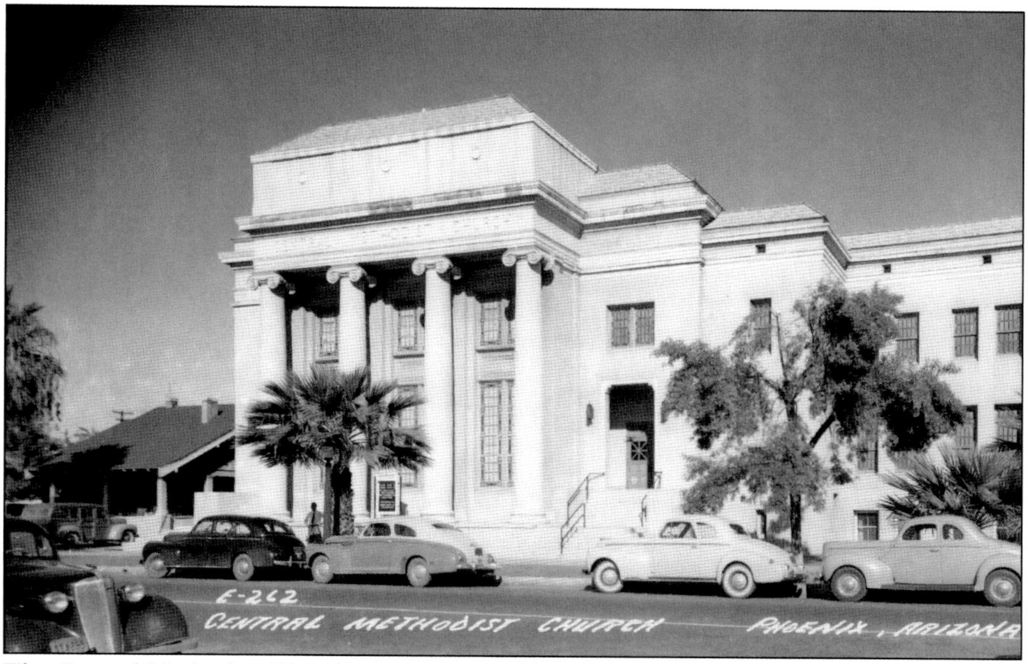

The Central Methodist Church was constructed at the northeast corner of Pierce Street and Central Avenue in 1926 when the congregation had outgrown its home at Central Avenue and Monroe Street (page 38). The congregation eventually outgrew this building and moved farther up Central Avenue in 1951. (Author's collection.)

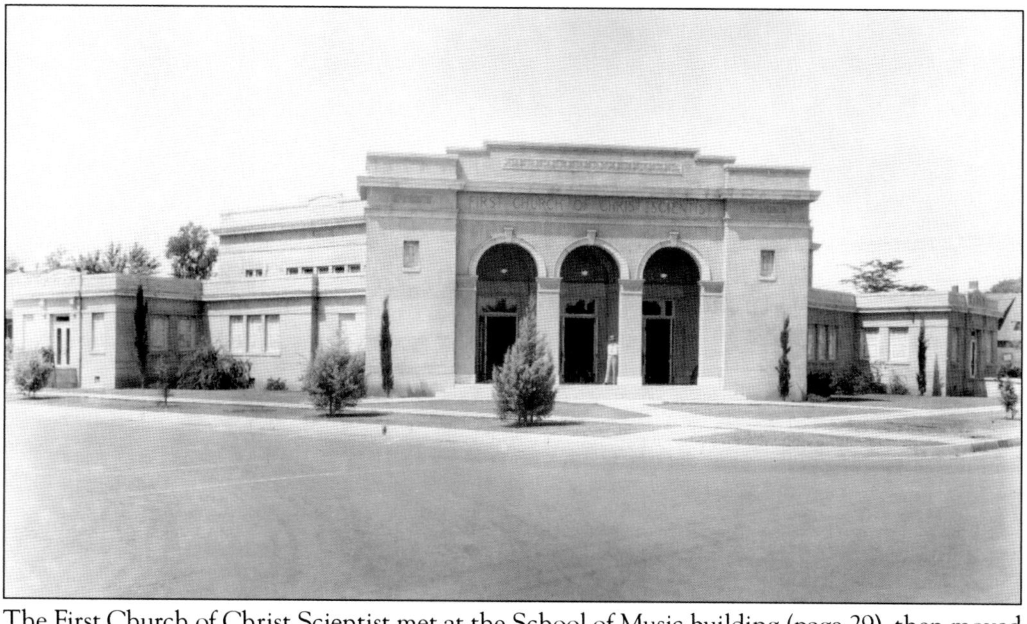

The First Church of Christ Scientist met at the School of Music building (page 29), then moved to this new facility at the southwest corner of First and Roosevelt Streets in 1925. Designed by Fitzhugh & Byron, its entrance was placed at an angle to attract attention from both streets. It is now the location of the Roosevelt Community Church. (Courtesy of Arizona Science Center.)

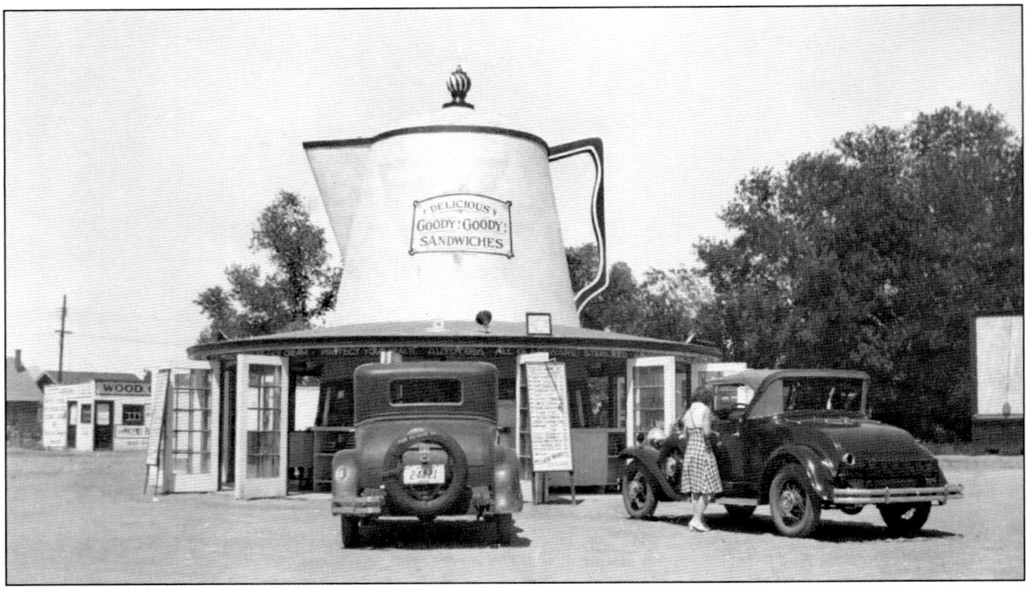

The Coffee Pot occupied the northeast corner of Seventh Street and McDowell Road. Started during the Great Depression in the early 1930s, the café sold coffee and sandwiches. The wall of French doors could be opened to take advantage of nice weather. The sign indicates hamburgers cost 15¢. The building survived into the early 1950s. (Courtesy of Herb and Dorothy McLaughlin Collection, Arizona State University Libraries.)

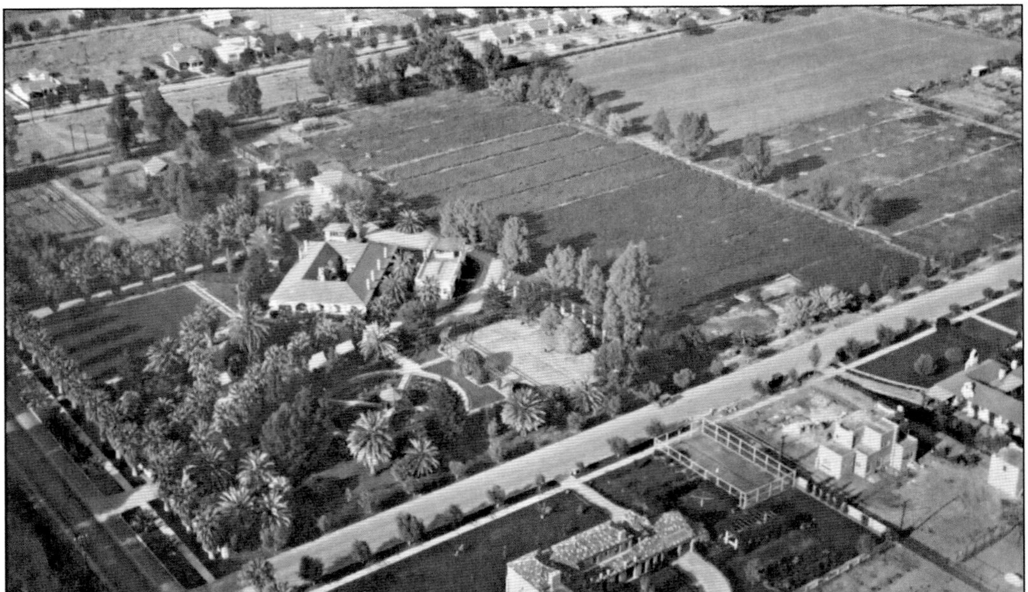

This aerial view looks northeast from Central Avenue and Monte Vista Road and shows the Heard estate Casa Blanca (page 27), along with its neighborhood, in the 1920s. In the upper left corner of the photograph are the first homes constructed along Hoover Avenue in Ashland Place. The south branch of the Maricopa Canal, below the houses on Hoover, brought irrigation water into the surrounding area. The house in the lower right corner later became the University Club. (Courtesy of Large Format Photography Collection, No. PCD263:RC233_OV331, Billie Jane Baguley Library and Archives, Heard Museum, Phoenix, Arizona.)

This photograph shows the Security Building at the southwest corner of Central Avenue and Van Buren Street just before completion in 1928. Designed in the Renaissance Revival style, it replaced the Phoenix High School (page 14) and was the home of the Security Improvement Company, a Dwight Heard business. Another floor for a penthouse residence was added in 1958. Maricopa County now owns the building. (Photograph by Ben Cooley, author's collection.)

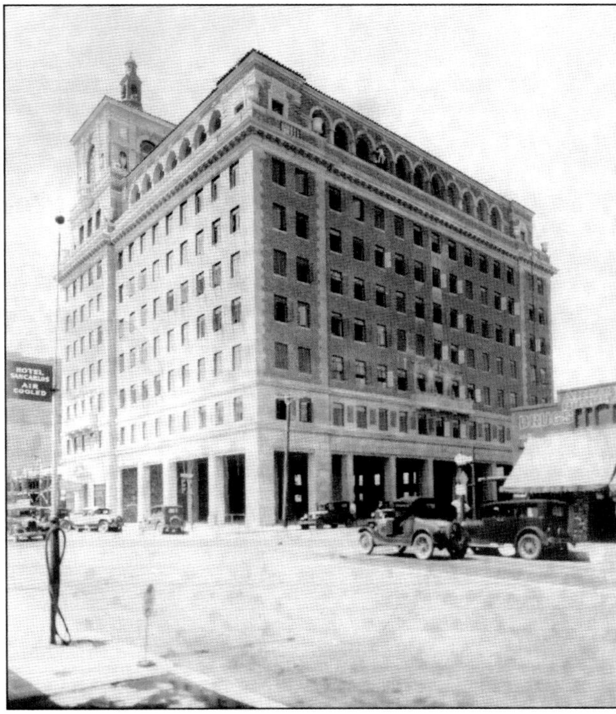

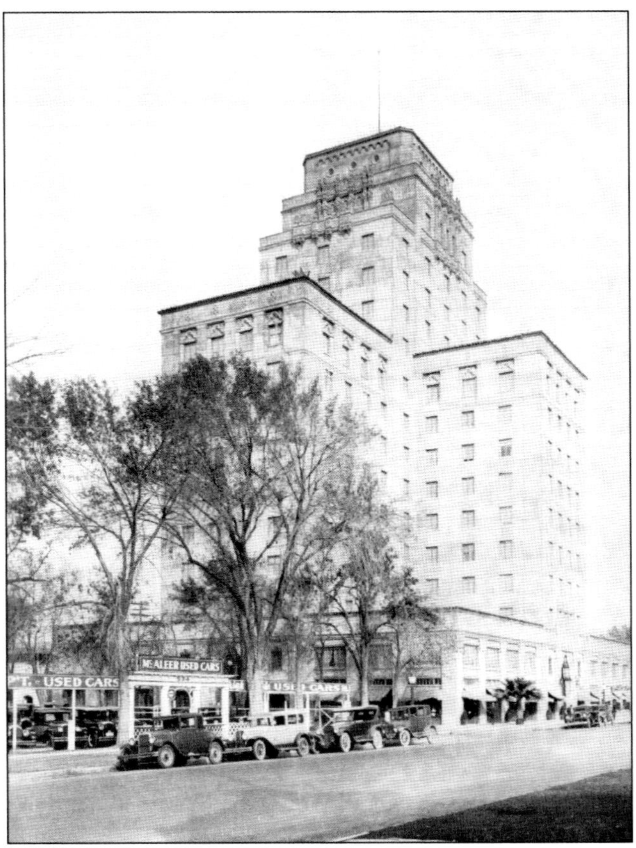

Opened in 1928, the Westward Ho Hotel was located on the northwest corner of Fillmore Street and Central Avenue where the Bennitt house (page 22) once stood. It attracted the rich and famous. The facility expanded in the 1940s and 1950s over the site of the Women's Club (page 34). At 16 stories, it reigned as the tallest building in Phoenix for over 30 years. (Author's collection.)

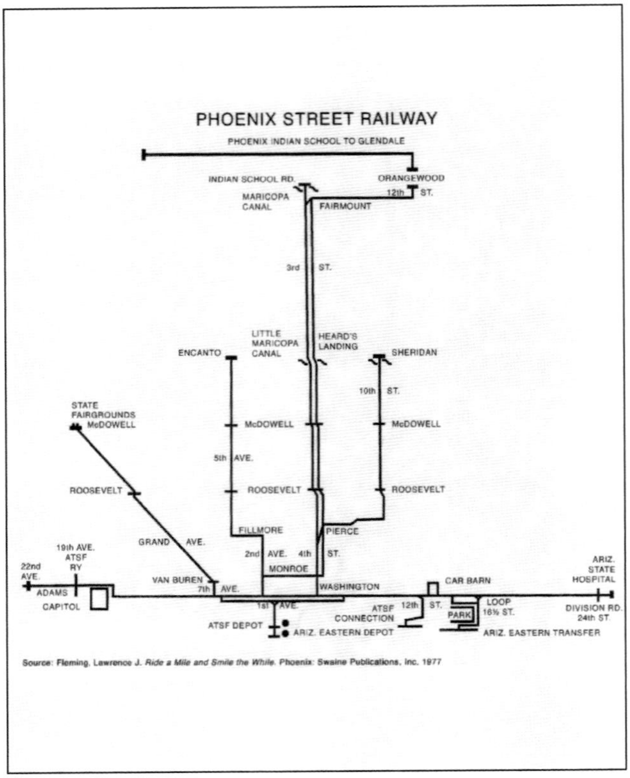

This diagram shows the Phoenix Street Railway in the early 1920s. It had 32 miles of track and a suburban line that extended to downtown Glendale. During this time, the privately owned system suffered declining ridership and deteriorating equipment. After much debate, the City of Phoenix purchased it in 1925 and began rehabilitation. It procured 18 new passenger cars and terminated the money-losing Glendale Line in 1929. While things improved for the system, the Great Depression and competition from automobiles and buses had nearly forced discontinuation of the service by 1940. The war postponed the inevitable, and it continued operating into the 1940s. A catastrophic fire at the car barn in late 1947 destroyed all but six of the cars, and in early 1948 streetcar service ended. (Courtesy of Creative Brand Consulting.)

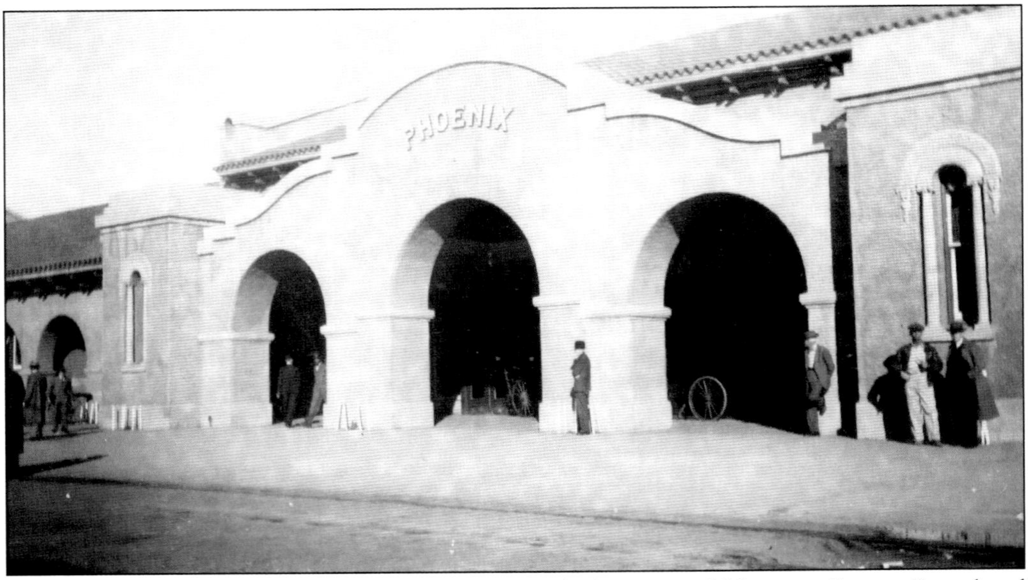

In 1921, work began on the Union Station at Fourth Avenue and Harrison Street. Completed in 1923, this Mission Revival structure was the main gateway for travelers into Phoenix. During the heyday of rail travel in the 1930s, 1940s, and 1950s, as many as 18 passenger trains passed through daily. Passenger rail service declined with the rise of air travel, and the last passenger train left the station in 1996. (Author's collection.)

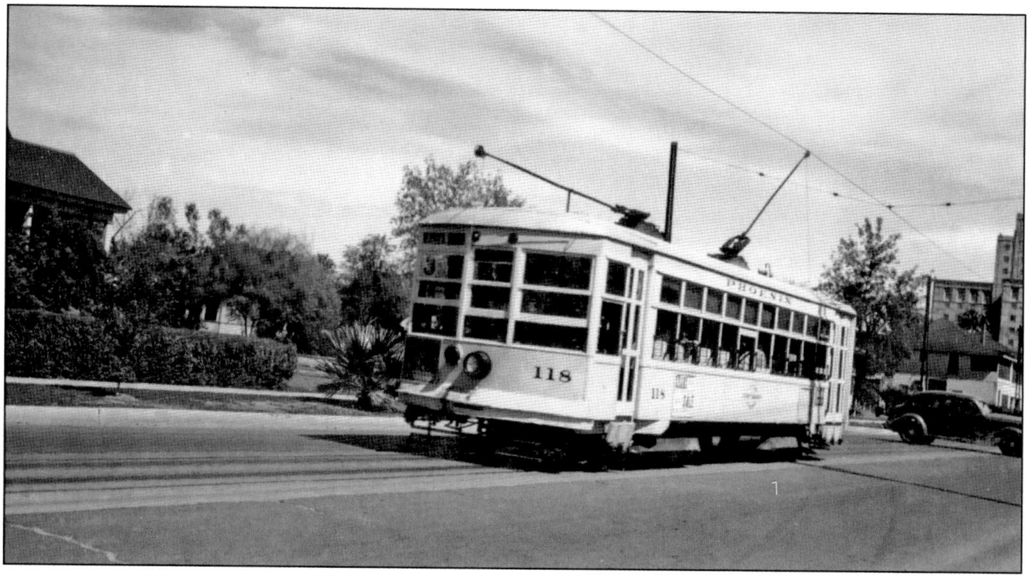

Midtown Phoenix had two streetcar lines: the Indian School Line, which ran along Third Street to the Phoenix Indian School, and the Second Avenue Line, which ran along Second and Fifth Avenues to Encanto Boulevard. A third, called the Brill Line, ran along Tenth Street to Sheridan. Developers located new subdivisions along the lines to make their homes attractive to buyers who needed access to downtown. This encouraged suburban growth north of downtown. Above is one of the cars on the Second Avenue Line as it heads west along Fillmore Street. The Westward Ho can be seen in the background. Below is an Indian School Line car in front of St. Joseph's Hospital at Fourth and Polk Streets. Both photographs are from the 1930s. (Both, author's collection.)

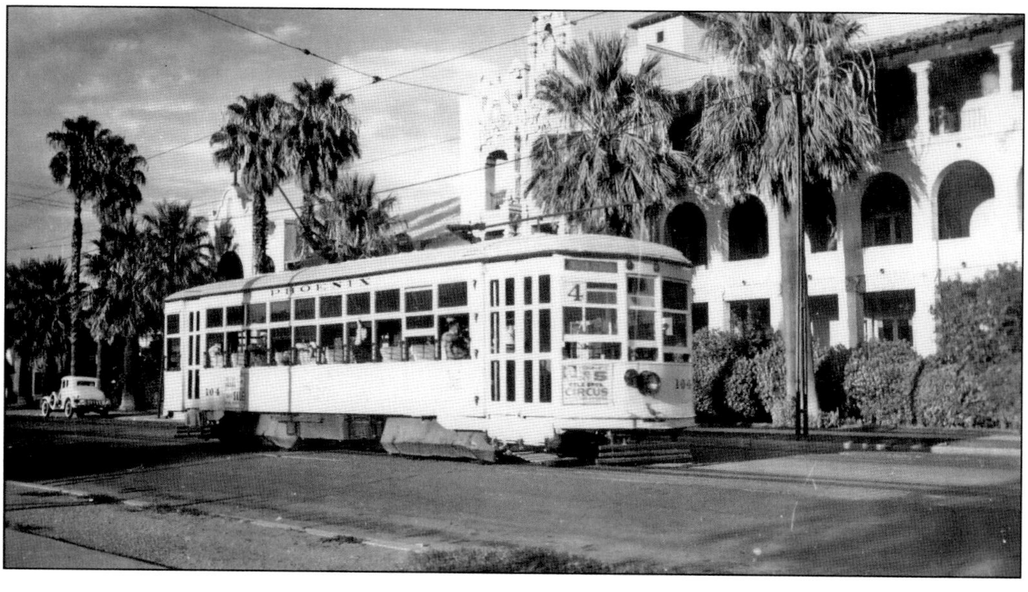

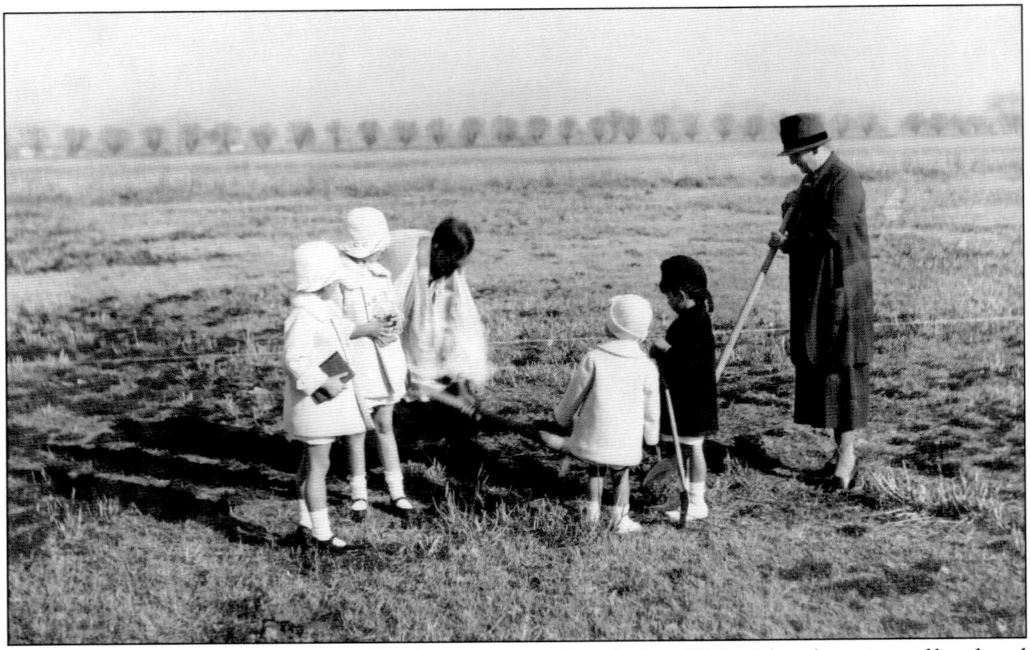

The Brophy College Preparatory school for boys was founded in 1928 with a donation of land and funds from Ellen Brophy in honor of her late husband, William Brophy. Set on 25 acres on the east side of Central Avenue, north of the Grand Canal, it was initially surrounded by farmland, a few homes, and the Phoenix Indian School on the south. It closed in 1935 due to the Great Depression but reopened in 1952. Above is the school's ground-breaking ceremony in 1928. Below is the newly constructed school with a view east to Camelback Mountain. (Both, courtesy of Herb and Dorothy McLaughlin Collection, Arizona State University Libraries.)

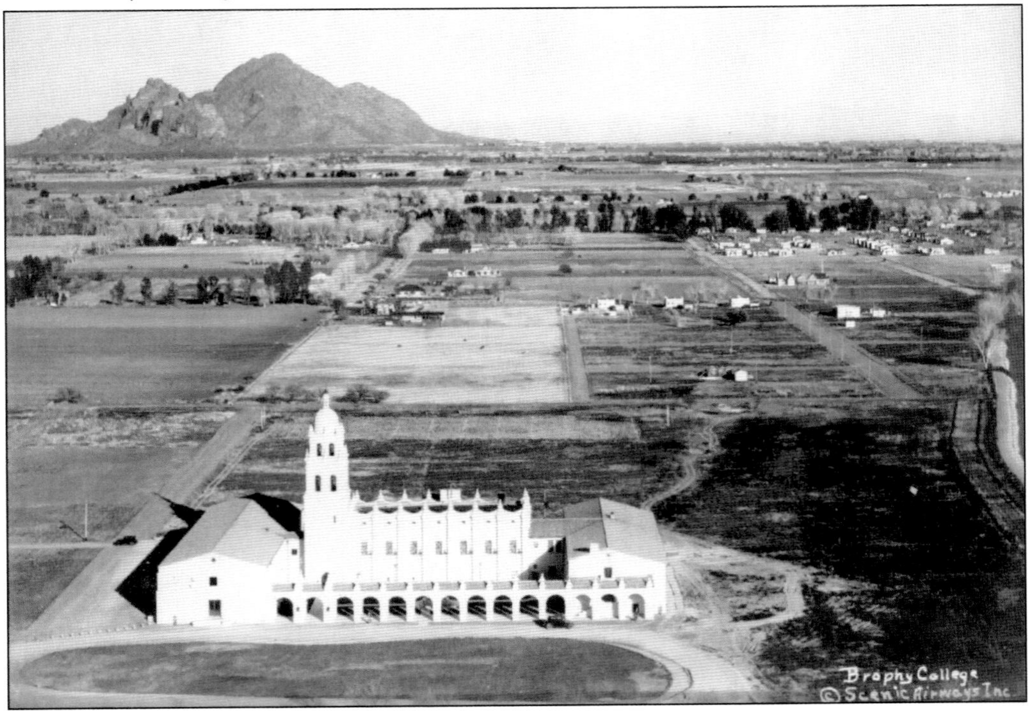

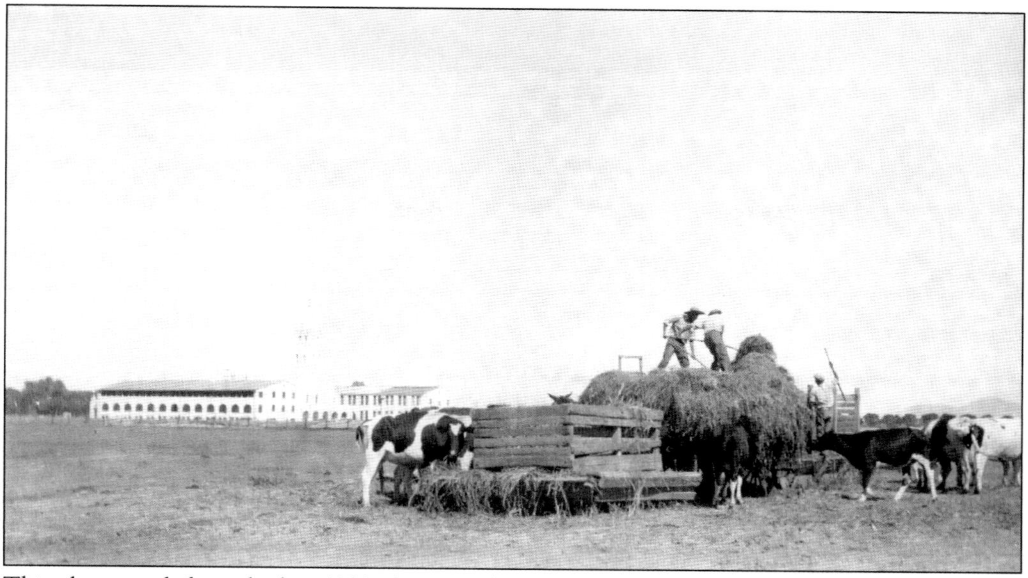

This photograph from the late 1920s shows students at the Phoenix Indian School as they feed hay to cows in the agricultural fields north of the school. By the 1930s, the curriculum had come to emphasize vocational education and agricultural studies. The newly constructed Brophy College Preparatory is seen in the background. (Courtesy of Phoenix Indian School Collection, No. RC284(1)2.4, Billie Jane Baguley Library and Archives, Heard Museum, Phoenix, Arizona.)

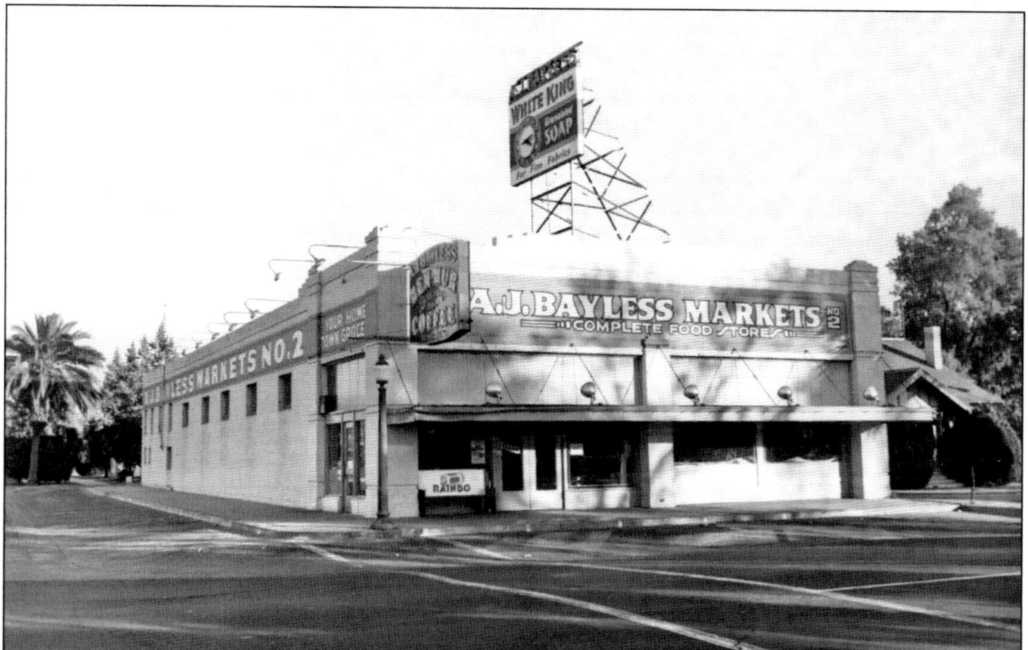

Del Webb Construction built this grocery store for A.J. Bayless at the northwest corner of Moreland Street and Central Avenue in 1931. This was store number two in the Bayless chain that grew to be the largest in Arizona. The Bayless family sold the chain in 1984. This store was demolished in 1971 for the Papago Freeway construction. (Courtesy of Del Webb Corporation Photographs, Arizona Collection, Arizona State University Libraries.)

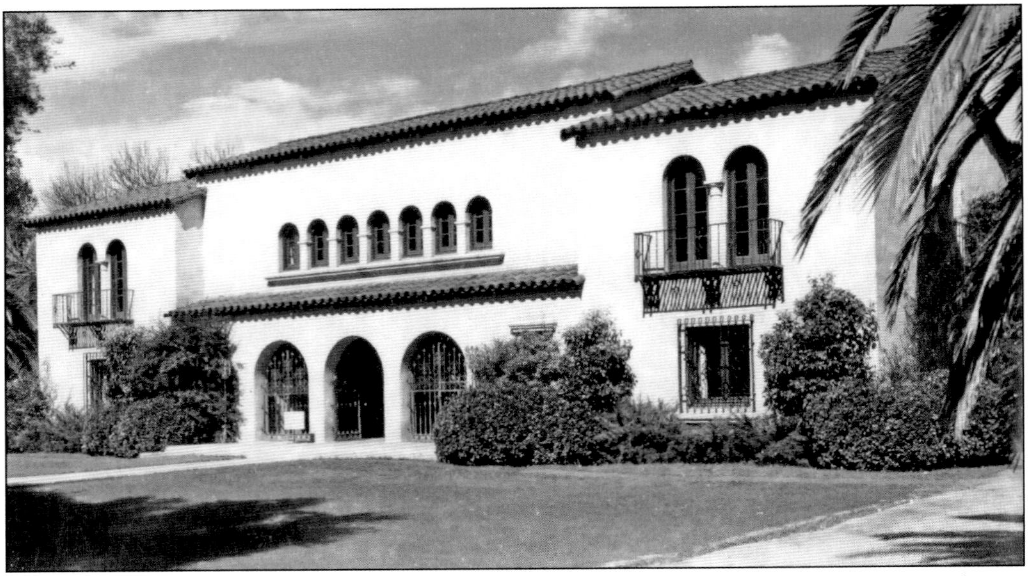

Dwight and Maie Heard (page 26) founded the Heard Museum in 1929. They constructed it on Monte Vista Road, east of their home on Central Avenue, and entrusted to it much of their private collection of Native American art. Dwight died a few months before the museum opened, but Maie remained active in the organization for the rest of her life. The museum is world renowned for its collection and its efforts to promote and educate the public on Native American art and history. (Author's collection.)

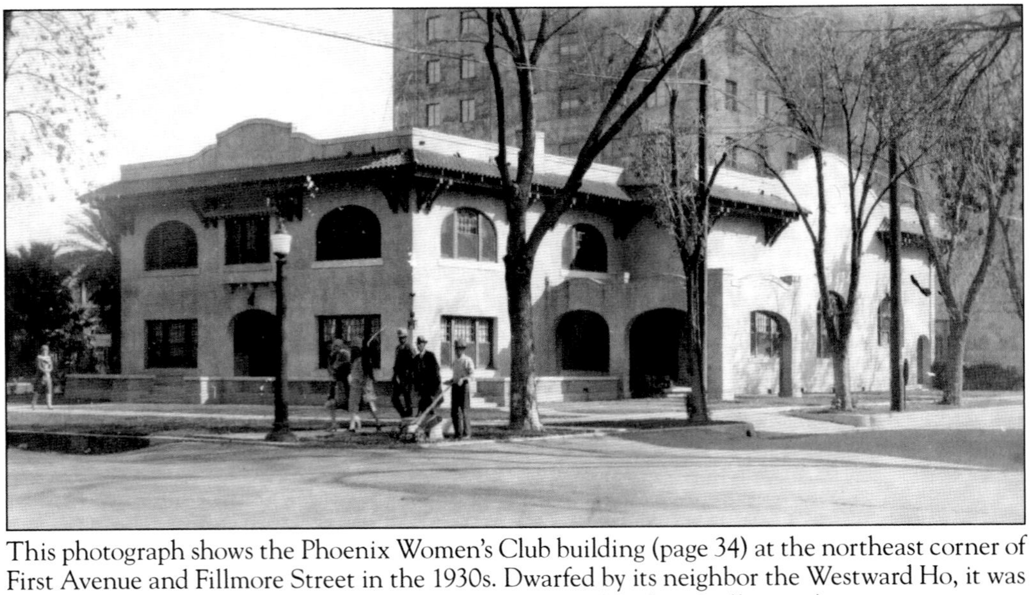

This photograph shows the Phoenix Women's Club building (page 34) at the northeast corner of First Avenue and Fillmore Street in the 1930s. Dwarfed by its neighbor the Westward Ho, it was demolished in the 1950s for an expansion to the hotel. (Author's collection.)

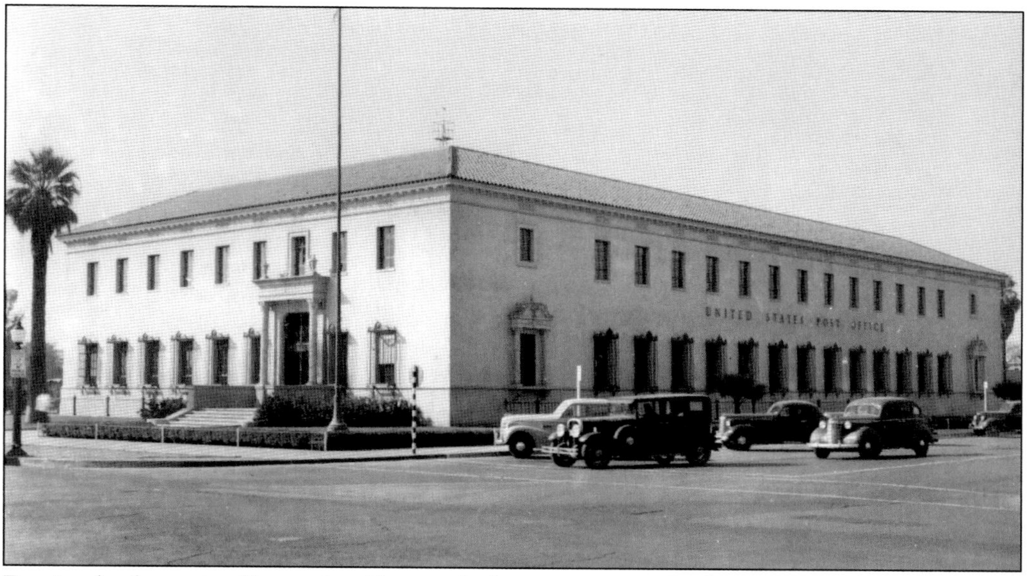

Despite the deepening Depression, Phoenix had outgrown its main downtown post office (page 37) by the early 1930s. Located just south of the Westward Ho Hotel, the new post office was part of the federal building program to combat the Depression. It opened in 1936. Still a functioning post office, it is now part of the downtown campus of Arizona State University. (Author's collection.)

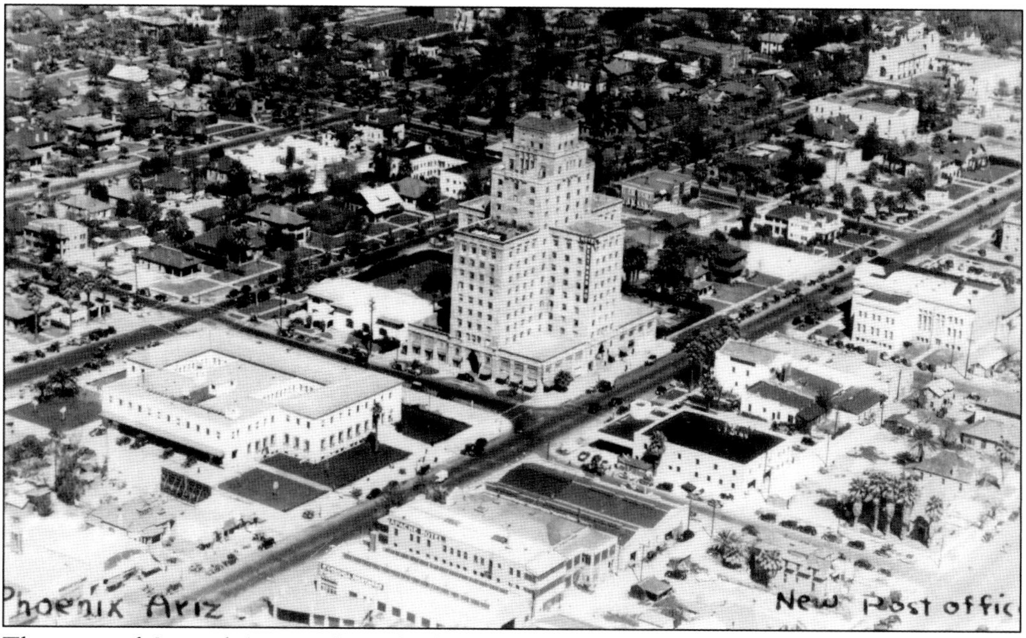

This view of Central Avenue from the late 1930s shows the commercial buildings that began replacing the houses that once lined the street. Central Avenue runs diagonally through the center of the photograph. The Westward Ho Hotel and the new post office are above the street. The second house right of the hotel belonged to the Baron Goldwater family. Left of the hotel is the Phoenix Women's Club. In the foreground below Central Avenue is the Apache Hotel (page 65) before its 1939 makeover. The Central Methodist Church and a corner of the Central Christian Church can also be seen along this frontage. Trinity Episcopal Cathedral is in the upper right corner at Roosevelt Street and First Avenue. (Author's collection.)

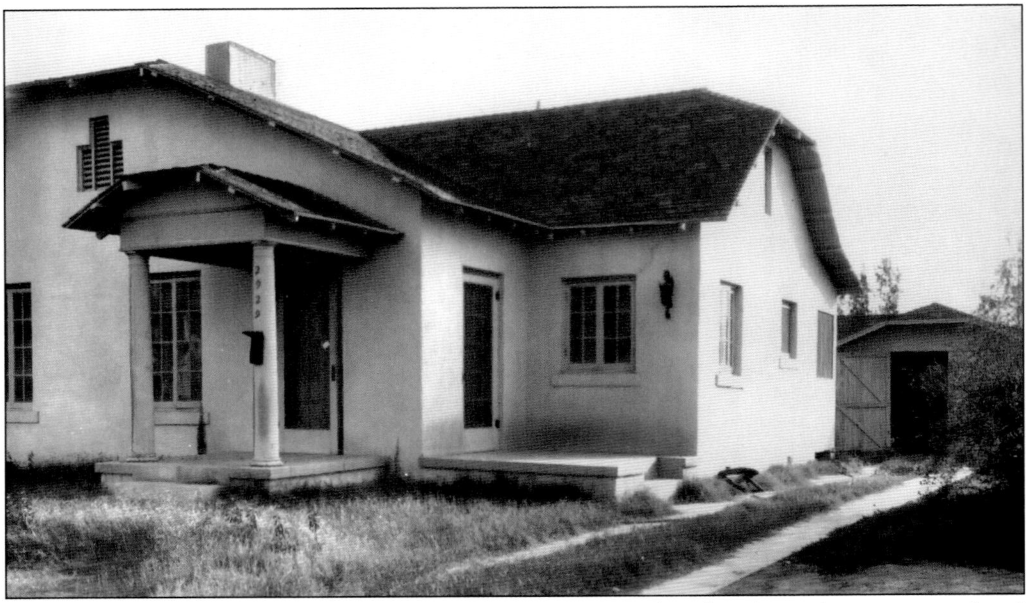

On the night of October 16, 1931, roommates Anne LeRoi and Hedvig Samuelson were murdered in this house on the southeast corner of Second Street and Catalina Drive. The women's bodies were placed into trunks and shipped by rail to Los Angeles, where they were discovered. Winnie Ruth Judd, pictured below in the courtroom with her legal team, stood trial for the murders. She was convicted and sentenced to death, but her sentence was later suspended at a post-sentencing sanity hearing where she was judged insane. She was then sent to the Arizona State Hospital. The "trunk murderess," as she became known, escaped a number of times. The last time, in 1962, she eluded capture for nearly seven years. Discovered, she returned to prison but was paroled in 1971 and died in 1998. This case, especially assertions that Judd had accomplices in committing the murders and attempted cover-up, fascinated people for decades. (Above, Acme photograph, author's collection; below, courtesy of Herb and Dorothy McLaughlin Collection, Arizona State University Libraries.)

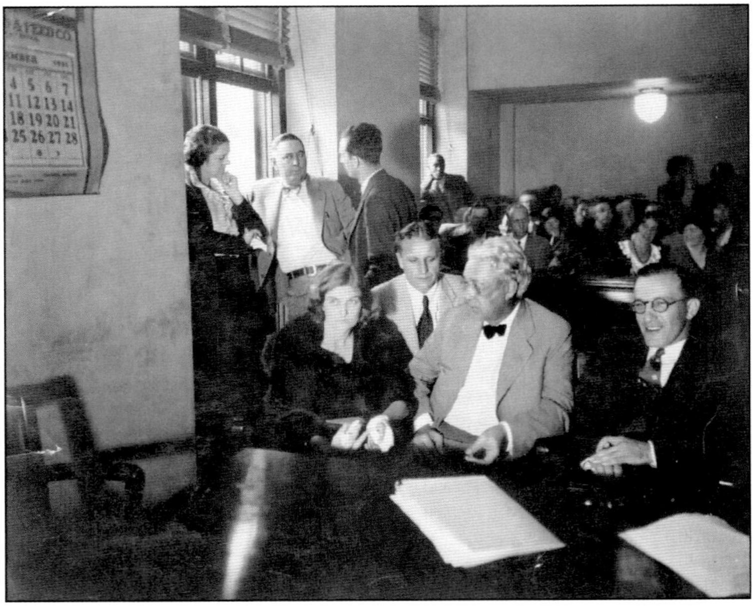

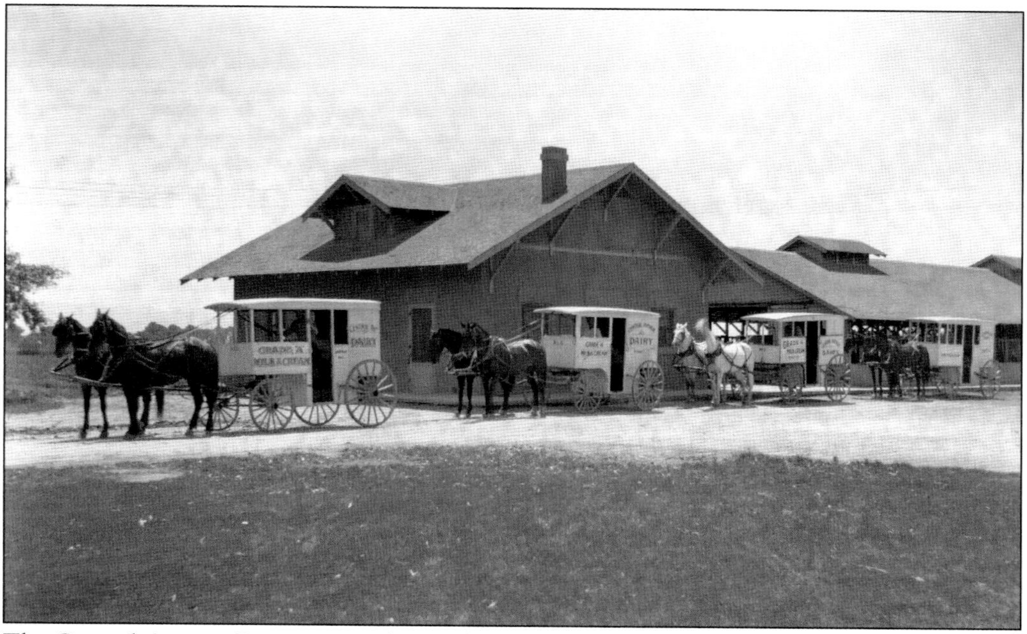

The Central Avenue Dairy operated at its location on the west side of Central Avenue at Earll Drive for many years. The dairy lasted into the 1950s, when it was taken over by developers for residential development and a shopping center. (Courtesy of McCulloch Brothers Photographs, Herb and Dorothy McLaughlin Collection, Arizona State University Libraries.)

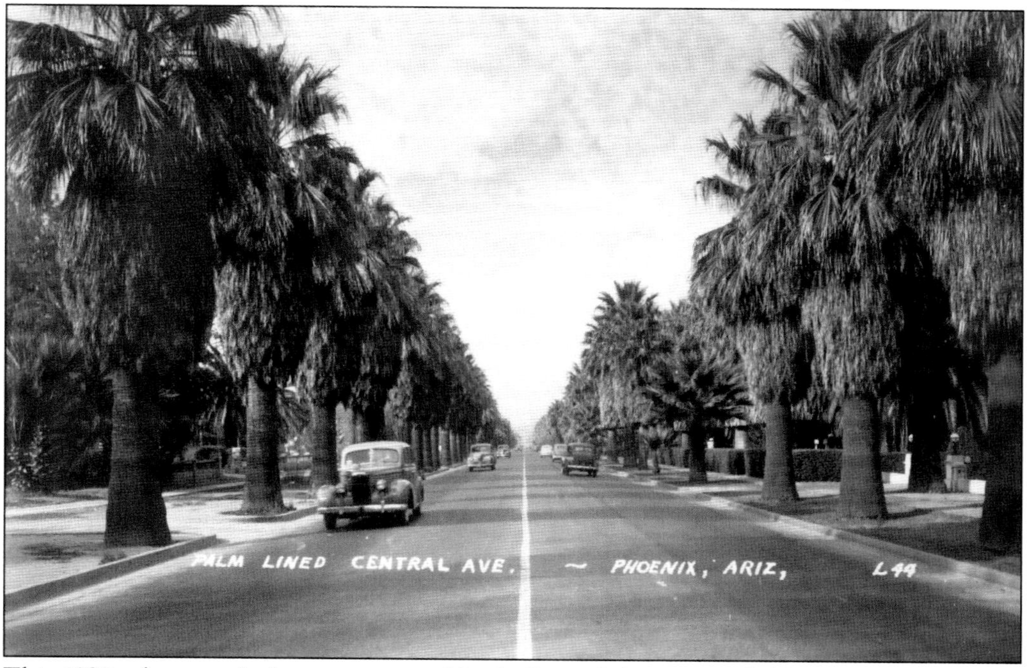

This 1930s photograph shows a view up North Central Avenue, probably north of McDowell Road. Contrast this view with those on pages 12 and 28. The road has been paved, and the palm trees have grown. The landscape is so lush that it is difficult to make out the houses behind the hedges and trees. (Courtesy of Arizona State Library, Archives and Public Records, History and Archives Division, Phoenix, No. 97-0967.)

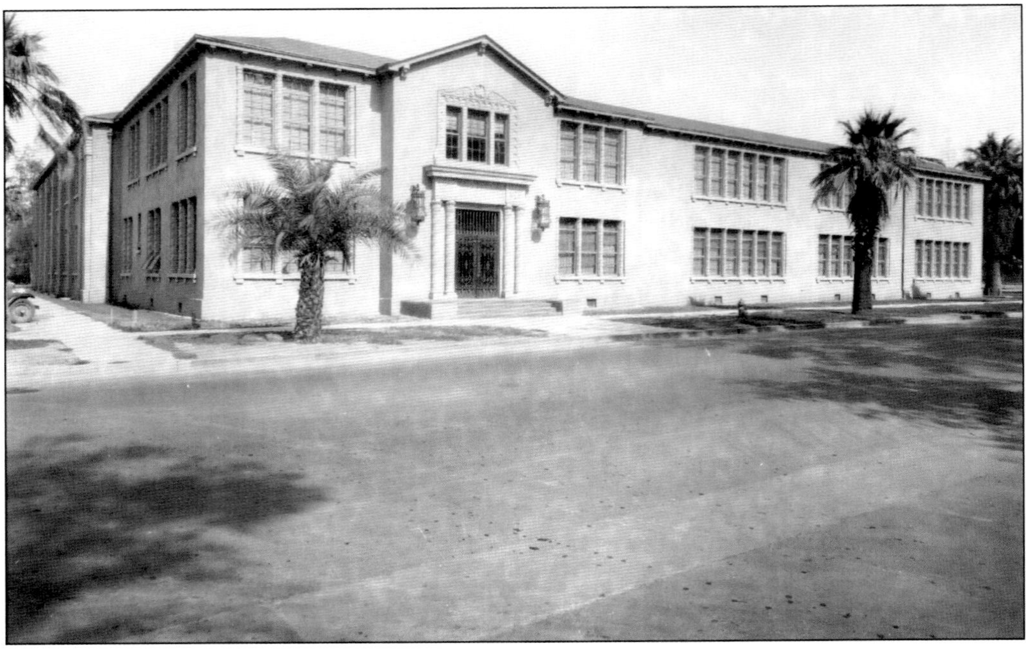

Phoenix Junior College, now Phoenix College, was founded in 1920 and started classes in a small building on the Phoenix Union High School campus at Seventh and Van Buren Streets. It later moved to the above building at Seventh and Fillmore Streets that was constructed around 1928. During the Great Depression, money from New Deal programs flowed into Arizona. The Works Progress Administration (WPA) built a new campus for the college at Thomas Road and Eleventh Avenue where it moved in 1939. The facility consisted of a library and auditorium as well as classroom and administration buildings. The Science Building is shown here shortly after construction. Phoenix College is still located at its Thomas Road campus, but it has grown considerably over the years. (Above, courtesy of Arizona Science Center; below, author's collection.)

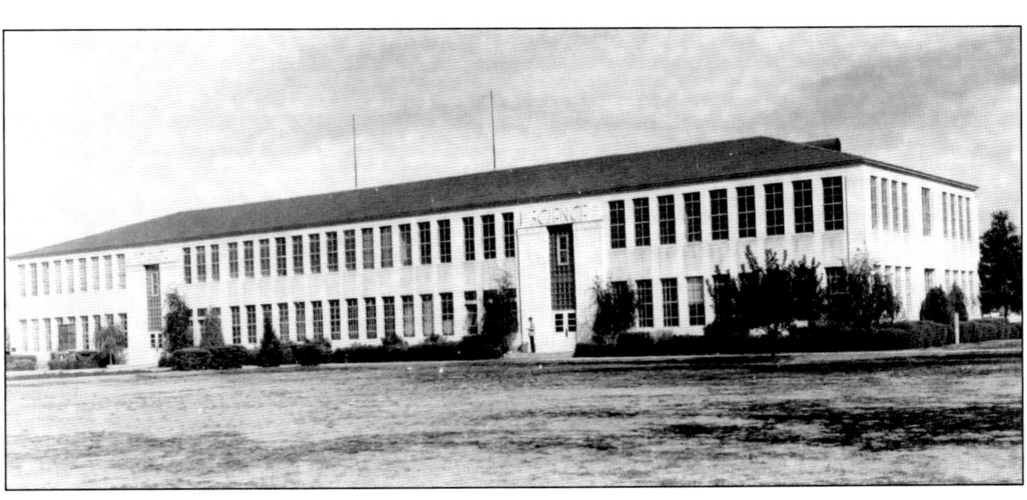

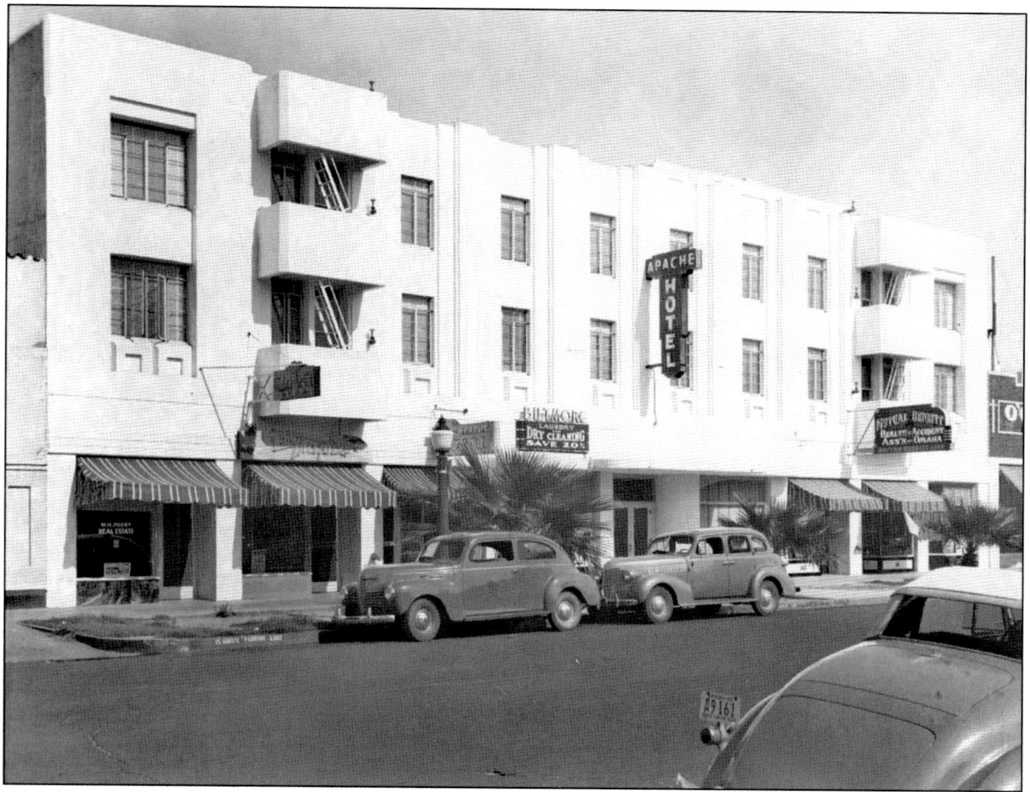

The Apache Hotel occupied the east side of Central Avenue between Taylor and Fillmore Streets. It was the Annex Hotel, then became the Apache in 1922. This 1940s view shows the hotel after the front addition was added by architect Orville Bell in 1939. The building was demolished in the 1980s, and the Arizona State University Cronkite School of Journalism now occupies the site. (Courtesy of McCulloch Brothers Photographs, Herb and Dorothy McLaughlin Collection, Arizona State University Libraries.)

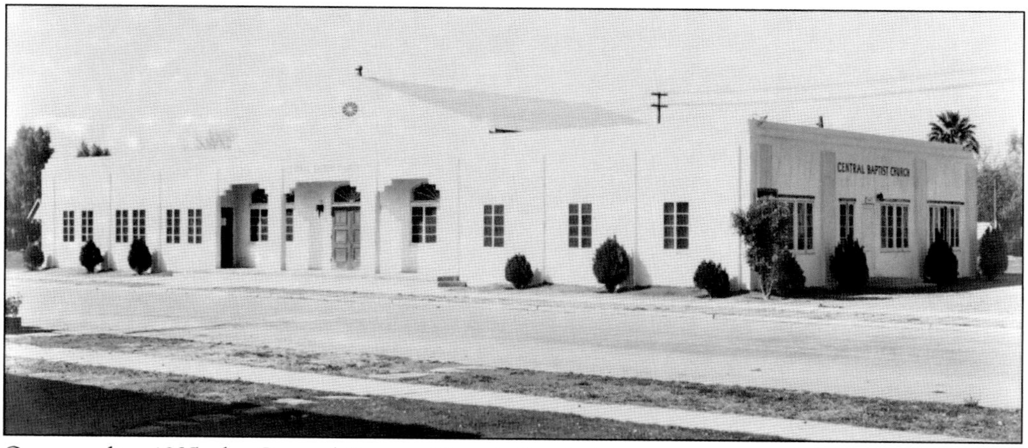

Organized in 1935, the Central Baptist Church first held its meetings in the Phoenix Women's Club before constructing this assembly building on the northwest corner of Wilshire Drive and Central Avenue in 1939. The church expanded over the years but was torn down in the early 1980s for redevelopment. (Courtesy of McCulloch Brothers Photographs, Herb and Dorothy McLaughlin Collection, Arizona State University Libraries.)

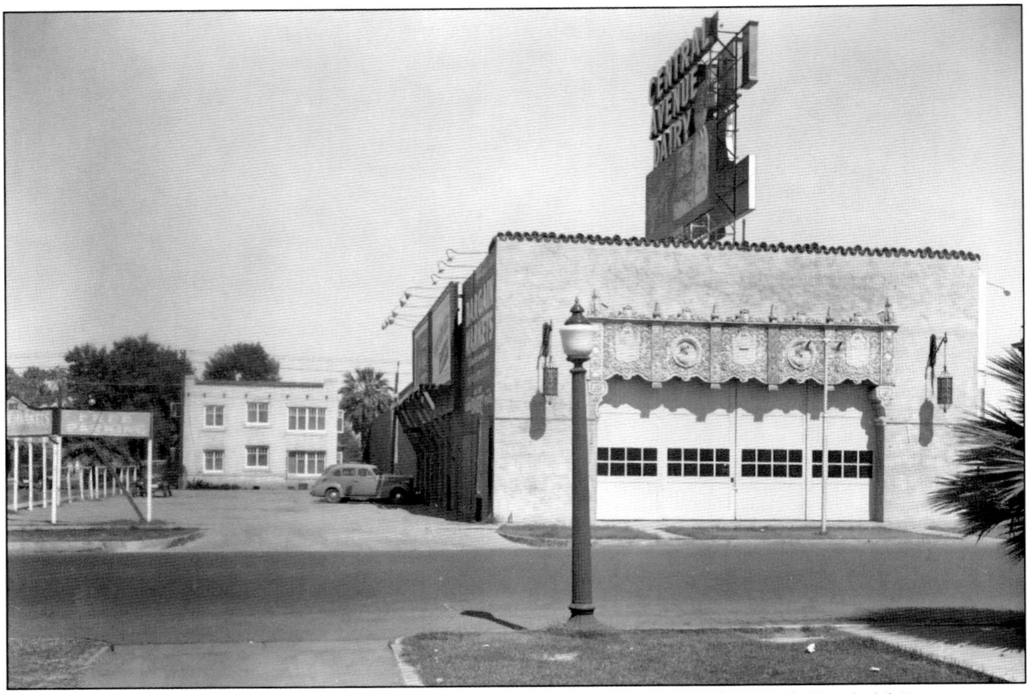

This building on the east side of Central Avenue, between McKinley and Garfield Streets, was the location of the Packard Phoenix Motor Company in the late 1920s. North of downtown, Central Avenue was the location of a number of auto dealerships. Packard was a luxury brand that lasted into the 1950s. Mardian Construction erected the building below at the southeast corner of Central Avenue and Garfield Street for A.S. Mehagian in 1940. Mehagian started in Phoenix as a rug and carpet dealer in 1928. With the opening of the new store, he expanded into furniture. Today, it is the office of HKS, Inc. (Both, courtesy of McCulloch Brothers Photographs, Herb and Dorothy McLaughlin Collection, Arizona State University Libraries.)

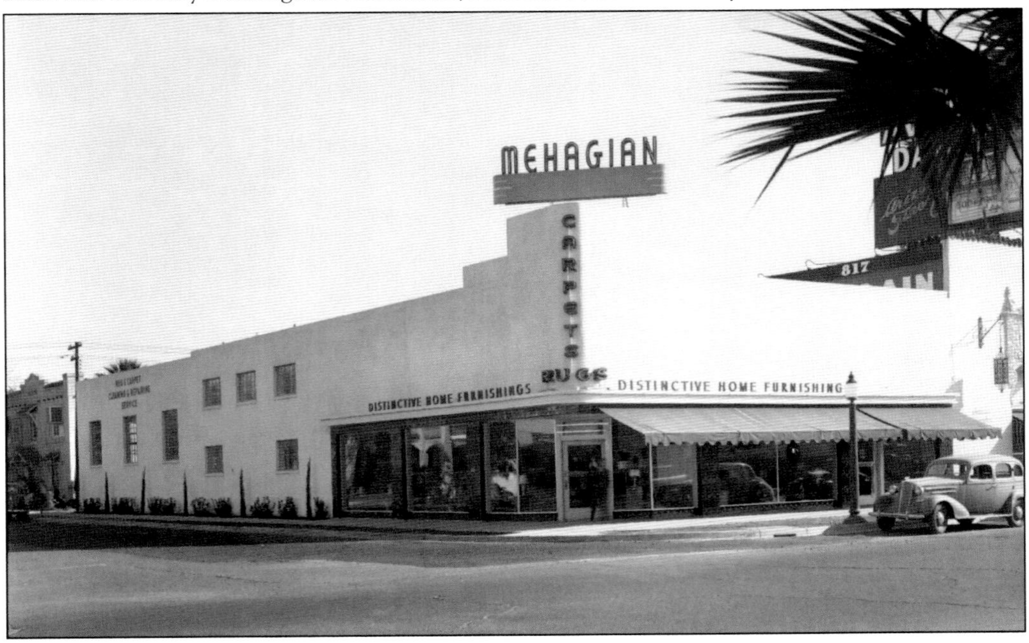

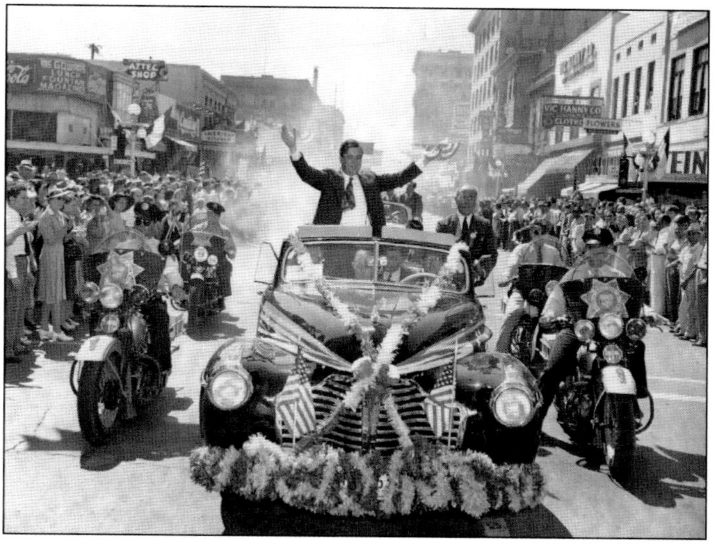

Businessman Wendell Wilkie ran for president on the Republican ticket in 1940. Wilkie campaigned in Phoenix on September 18 during a cross-country campaign tour. Here, he is shown in his car on Central Avenue north of Washington Street. The crowds in Phoenix looked large and friendly, but Wilkie lost both the state and the election to Pres. Franklin D. Roosevelt. (Acme Photograph; author's collection.)

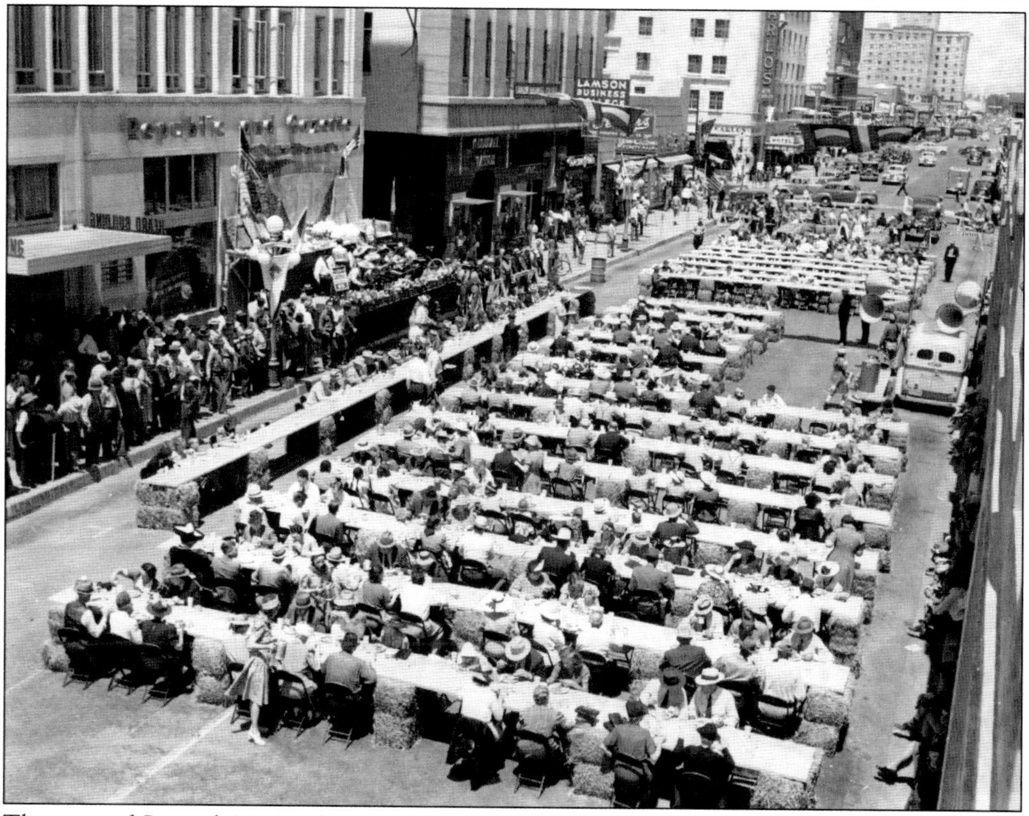

This view of Central Avenue, between Adams and Monroe Streets, shows a community barbecue for a water festival held on April 26, 1941, to celebrate the first time water had overflowed the Roosevelt Dam in 21 years. In the 1930s, drought gripped Arizona, but by 1941 there was sufficient rainfall to fill the reservoirs, including Roosevelt Lake. The wet years were short-lived, however. Drought returned in 1942 and lasted for over 20 years. The Heard Building, San Carlos Hotel, Security Building, and Westward Ho Hotel can all be seen on the left side of Central Avenue. (Acme Photograph; author's collection.)

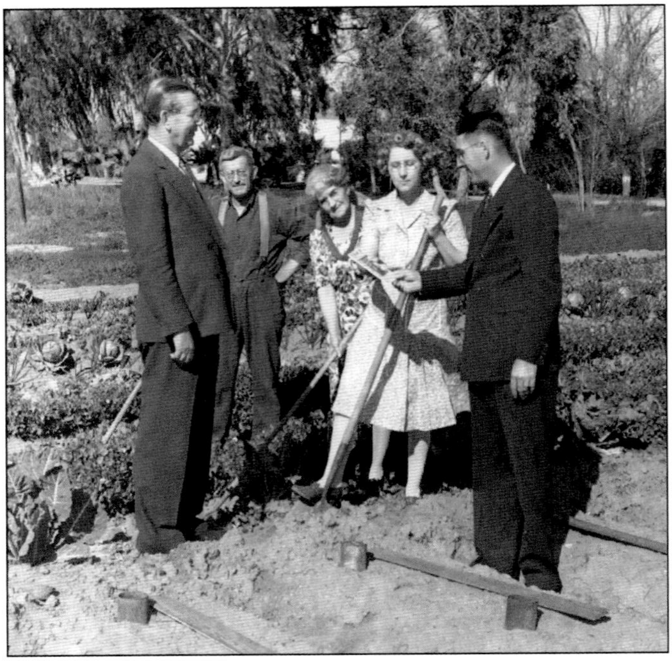

The United States' entry into World War II in 1941 effectively curtailed most construction for the duration with the exception of what was needed to meet wartime military and industrial demands. Commodities that consumers normally take for granted, such as gasoline and food, were rationed. Civilians were encouraged to grow their own food, and victory gardens sprung up on the urban landscape. Here, Gov. Sidney P. Osborn (left) visits a garden on Central Avenue. (Courtesy of Arizona State Library, Archives and Public Records, History and Archives Division, Phoenix, No. 14.9002.)

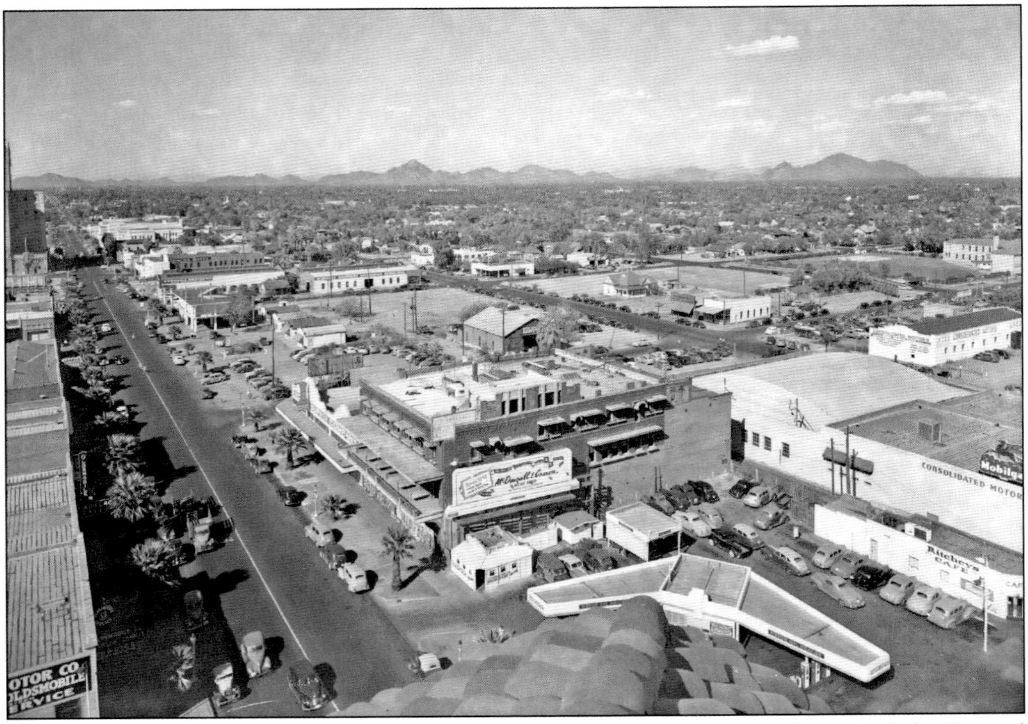

This view up Central Avenue from Van Buren Street was taken toward the end of the Second World War. It shows the continuing commercialization of the Corridor. A four-story hotel building begun by Hattie Mosher is in the center right. Her house, undergoing conversion to an office, can be seen farther up the street. The hotel structure was converted into an office in 1946. The small building in the foreground advertises "unrationed meat." (Courtesy of McCulloch Brothers Photographs, Herb and Dorothy McLaughlin Collection, Arizona State University Libraries.)

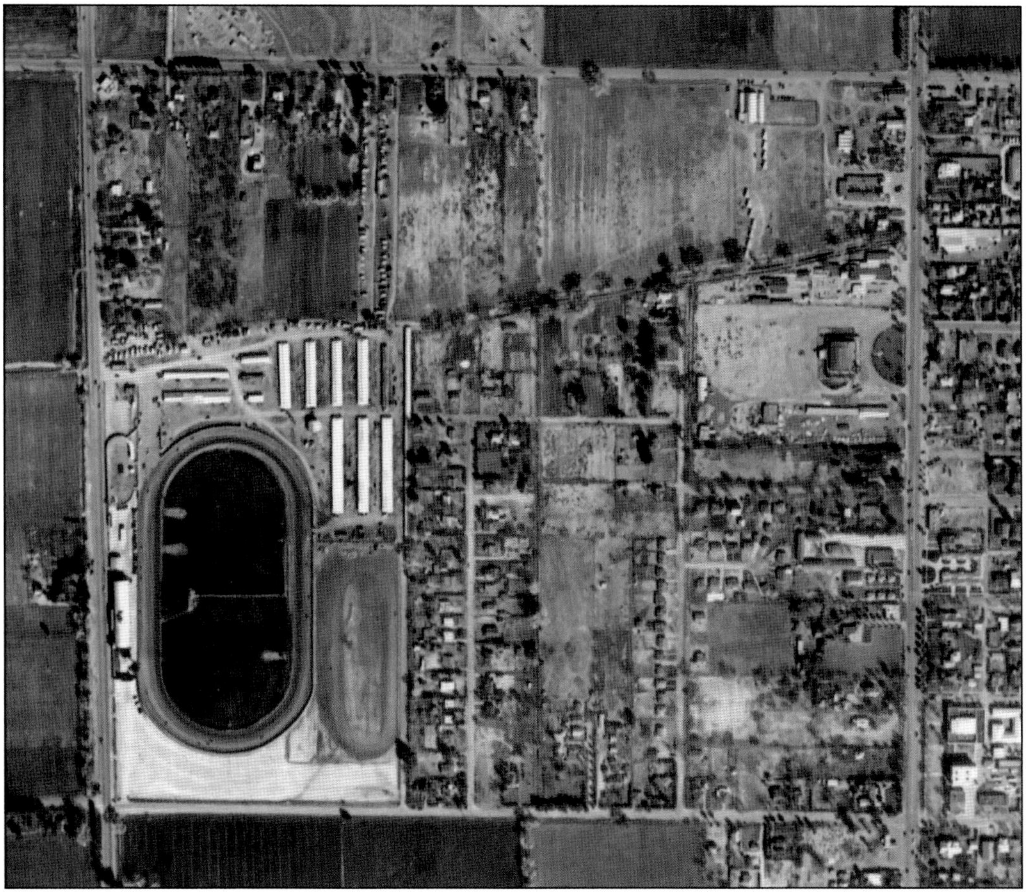

This 1949 aerial view shows the Sportsman's Park horse harness racetrack, which occupied a large parcel at the northeast corner of Osborn Road and Seventh Avenue. It was established in the early 1940s and held races into the early 1950s when it was demolished for commercial and residential development. (Courtesy of Maricopa County Flood Control District.)

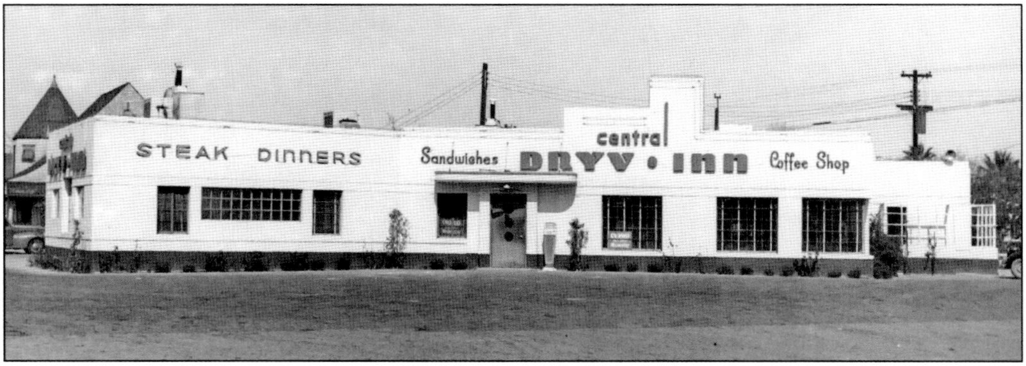

Central Dryv Inn occupied the northeast corner of Roosevelt Street and Central Avenue. It opened in February 1939 and boasted a soda fountain, lunchroom, and coffee shop service, as well as curb service for in-car dining. It advertised lunches between 25¢ and 35¢. In 1945, it was remodeled and redecorated, then went out of business in 1956. The Coronet Hotel (page 91) was constructed on its site soon after. (Courtesy of Del Webb Corporation Photographs, Arizona Collection, Arizona State University Libraries.)

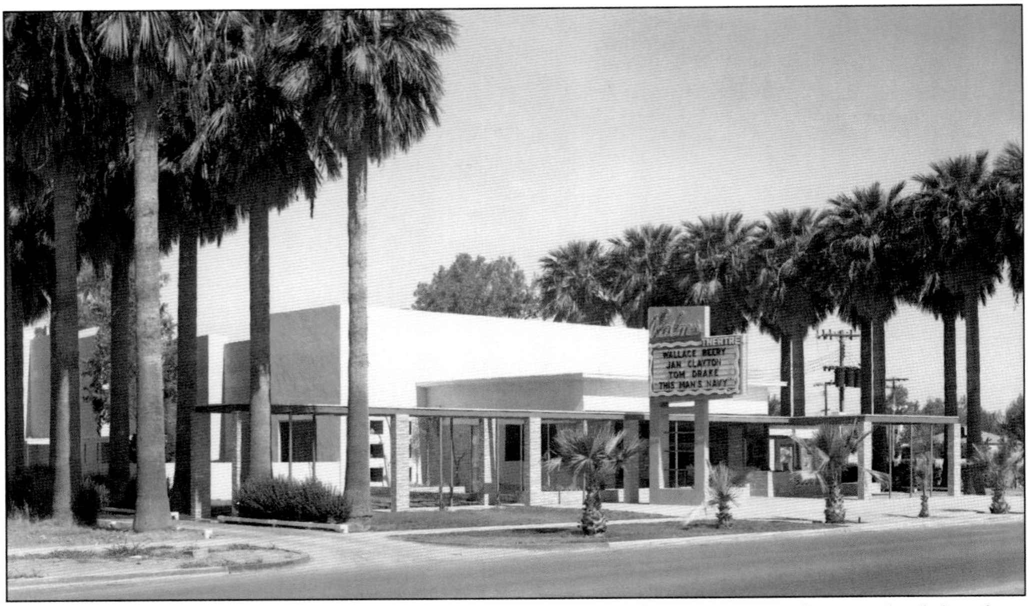

With the war nearly won, the reduction in requirements for wartime industries had freed up materials for civilian construction by early 1945. Publix, Rickards & Nace, Inc., which owned several local theaters, constructed the Palms Theatre on the northwest corner of Central and Virginia Avenues in 1945. It was designed in the modern architectural style by architects Pereira & Pereira of Chicago. This was the first movie theater outside of downtown. Above is the theater with its signature palm trees, and below is its organ being delivered. The Palms proved to be a popular location for Midtown moviegoers. It closed in the early 1980s and was torn down in 1982. The 2600 Building now occupies the site. (Above, courtesy of McCulloch Brothers Photographs, Herb and Dorothy McLaughlin Collection, Arizona State University Libraries; below, McLaughlin Associates Photograph, author's collection.)

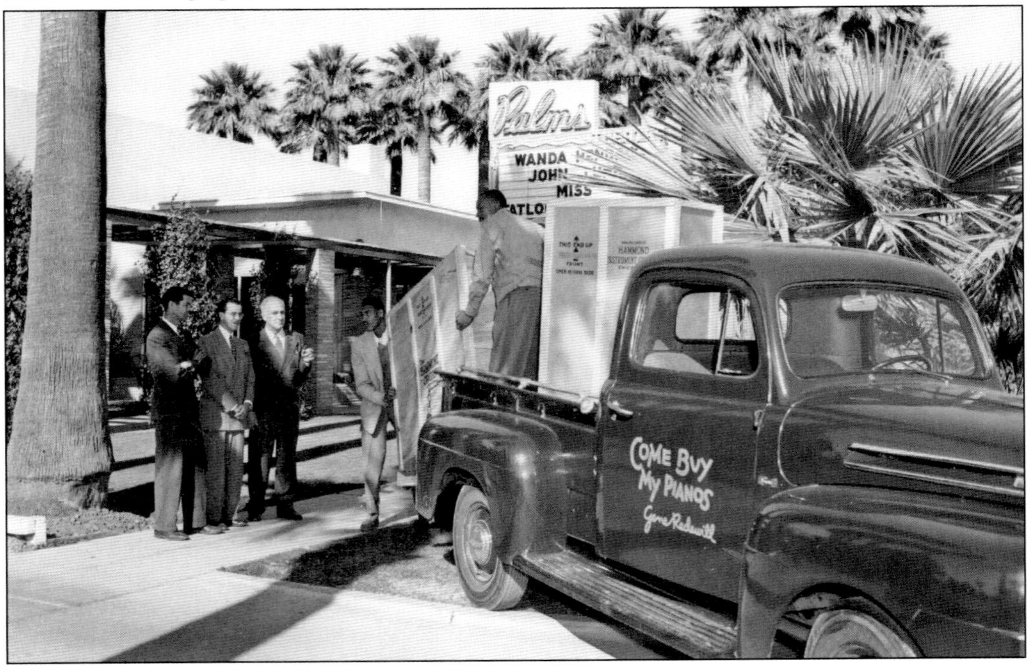

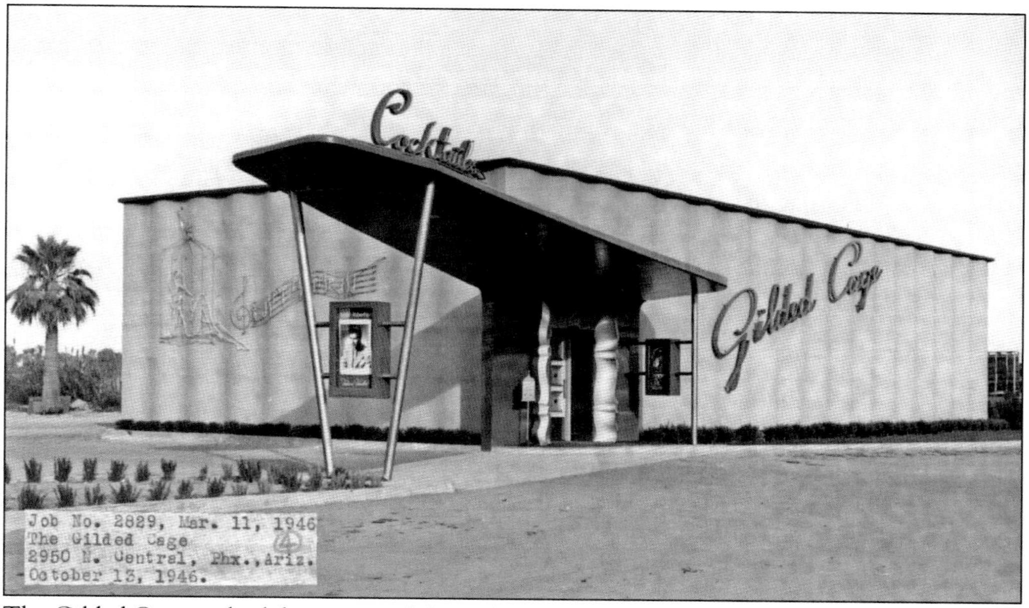

The Gilded Cage nightclub was one of the early postwar boom construction projects on Central Avenue. Established by C.E. "Teak" Baldwin in 1946 and located on the southwest corner of Central Avenue and Catalina Drive, it quickly became a popular nightspot. There were allegations that, in addition to dining, drinking, and entertainment, the Gilded Cage was also a location for high-stakes card and dice games. Baldwin was prosecuted for back taxes and other crimes. Another operator was arrested for illegal liquor storage. The Gilded Cage was demolished in 1956 for redevelopment. (Courtesy of Del Webb Corporation Photographs, Arizona Collection, Arizona State University Libraries.)

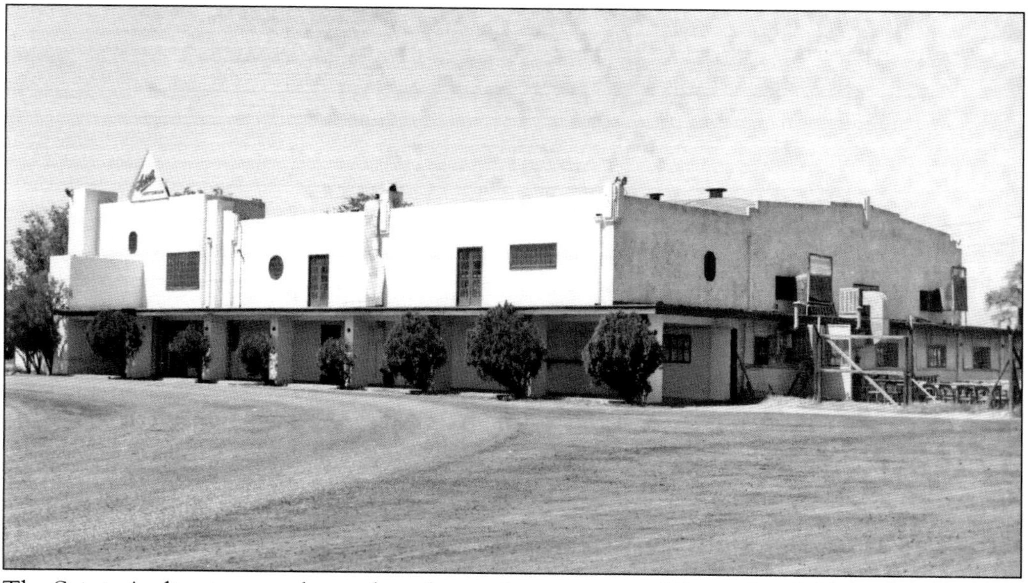

The Sciots Auditorium was located on the southwest corner of Central and Clarendon Avenues on land owned by the Rosenzweig family. Built in 1930 by Del Webb Construction as the Mirador Ballroom, it was the scene of dances, shows, and large meetings. Sciots lasted into the early 1960s, when Del Webb began construction on a large commercial center at the site. (Courtesy of Del Webb Corporation Photographs, Arizona Collection, Arizona State University Libraries.)

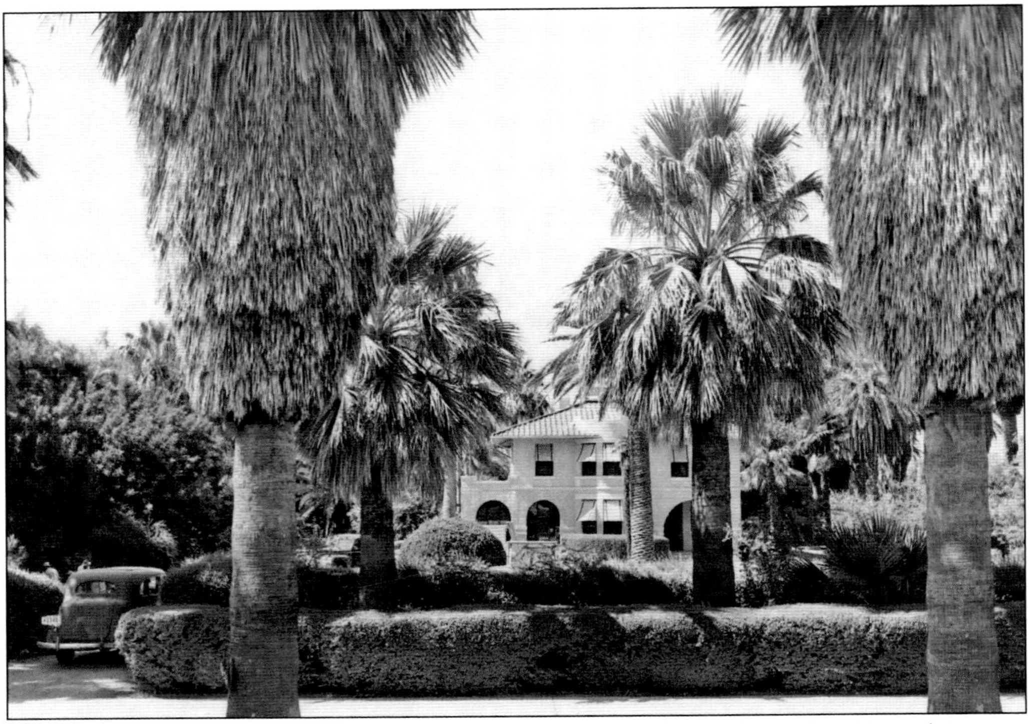

After the war was over, the change from residential to commercial accelerated on Central Avenue. In 1946, Del Webb constructed an office for Dr. L.D. Beck in front of his residence, north of McDowell Road. These photographs show the Beck house, where William Hartranft once lived (page 31), before (above) and after (below) the office construction. (Both, courtesy of Del Webb Corporation Photographs, Arizona Collection, Arizona State University Libraries.)

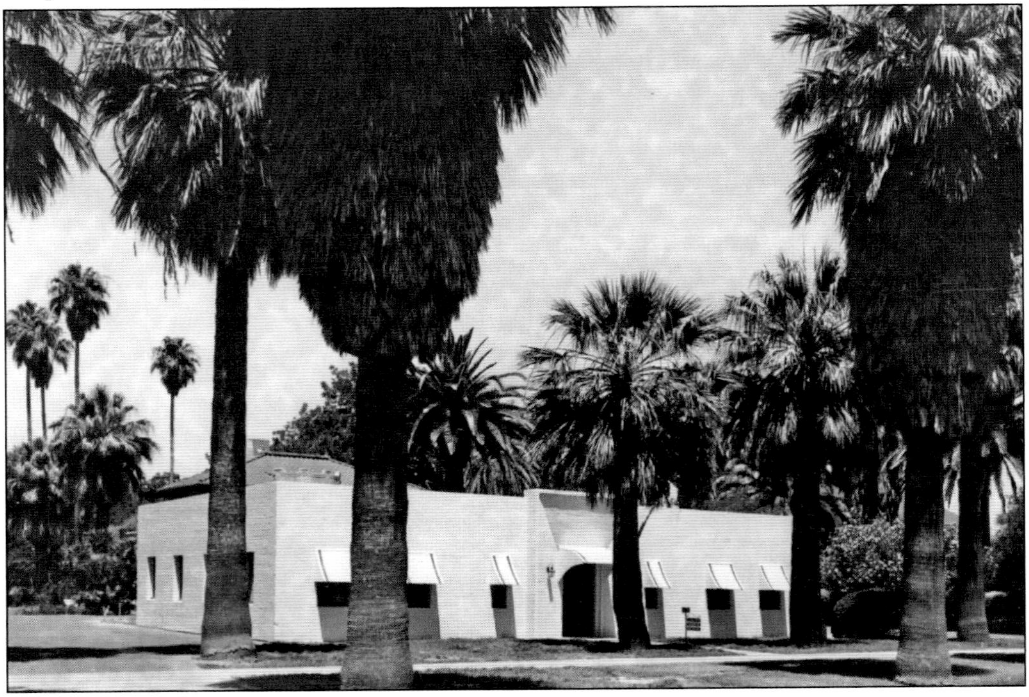

Four

The Boom Years 1945–1992

In the decades that followed the Second World War, the population of Phoenix exploded, and the Midtown area boomed with new construction. New industries, along with postwar prosperity, attracted workers, some of whom had served in the area during the war and were attracted by its climate and opportunity. Developers who had focused on wartime industries could again concentrate on civilian construction, and new residential neighborhoods sprung up where orchards and farmland had been. Most of the new homes had refrigeration air-conditioning, and many sported backyard swimming pools.

Over the next several decades, the large houses along Central Avenue were remodeled into shops, restaurants, and offices or knocked down for office buildings and shopping centers. Many of the homes and established neighborhoods east and west of Central Avenue survived the commercial onslaught, but by the 1980s, the character of Central Avenue itself had drastically changed as it displaced downtown as the city's premier commercial corridor.

During the 1960s, Midtown Phoenix between McDowell Road on the south and Indian School Road on the north saw intense construction activity as high-rise office towers popped up to support the demand for space. Many of these towers were designed by prominent local and national architects in the style now known as mid-century modern.

There was a downside. As the city continued to grow and spread ever outward into the desert, the character of Midtown started to change. Land parcels slated for development could remain vacant for years. Many left the established neighborhoods, and the shopping centers lost customers to new centers in the outlying areas.

Concerns about blight, neglect, and neighborhood destruction, along with a planned freeway slicing through Midtown, gave rise to a preservation movement that gained the support of prominent citizens in the 1970s. By the late 1980s, Midtown still had significant activity, but the nexus of development was moving away.

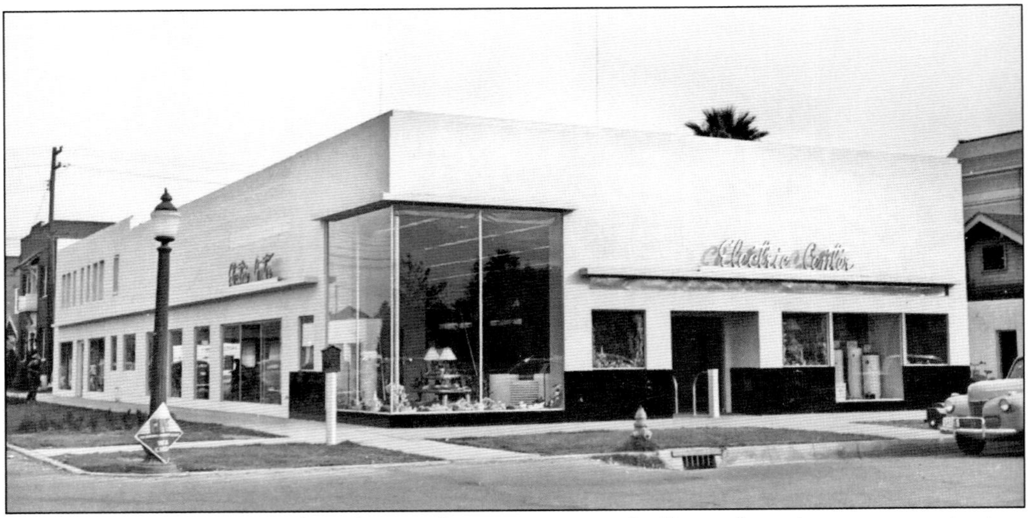

The end of the war released production for consumer goods. Years of wartime wages, rationing, and doing without created a pent-up demand for appliances, automobiles, and other wares. The Goldwater's Electric Center at the southeast corner of Central Avenue and McKinley Street was one of the new postwar commercial establishments in the Corridor that responded to this demand. (Both, courtesy of Del Webb Corporation Photographs, Arizona Collection, Arizona State University Libraries.)

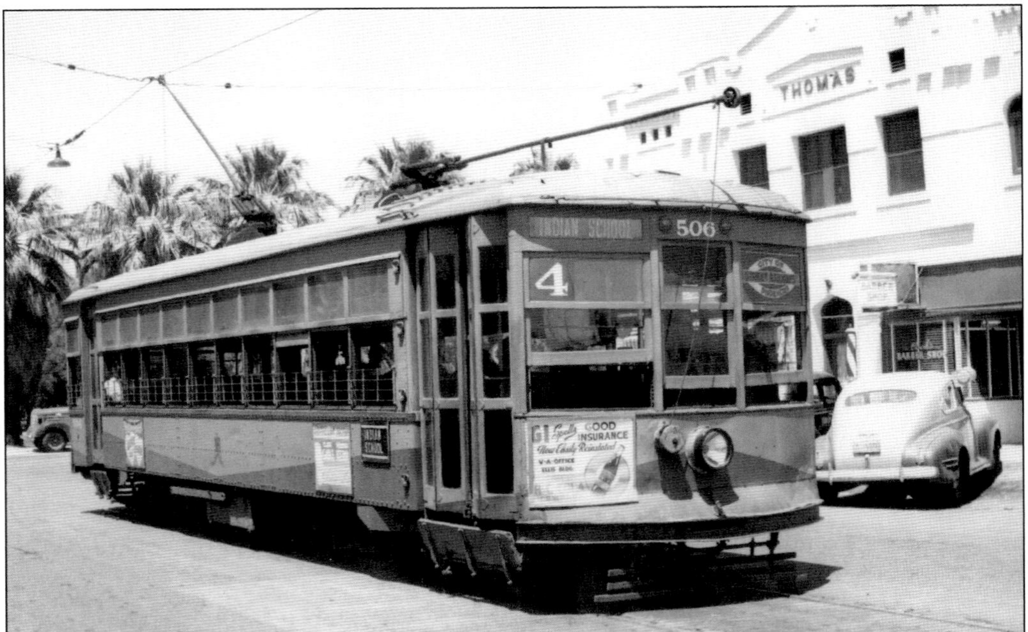

In this 1947 photograph, a Phoenix Street Railway streetcar is seen in front of the Thomas Building at the southeast corner of Indian School Road and Third Street. Developer H.C. Thomas created a subdivision called Thomas Place at this intersection in 1909 and constructed the building in 1914. Well outside the city limits at the time, this "streetcar suburb," and others like it, offered a suburban lifestyle at reasonable cost, as well as a transit link to businesses and shopping in downtown Phoenix. The following year, the streetcar system ceased operations. The building lasted into the 1980s. (Photograph by Fred Victor DeBrutz; author's collection.)

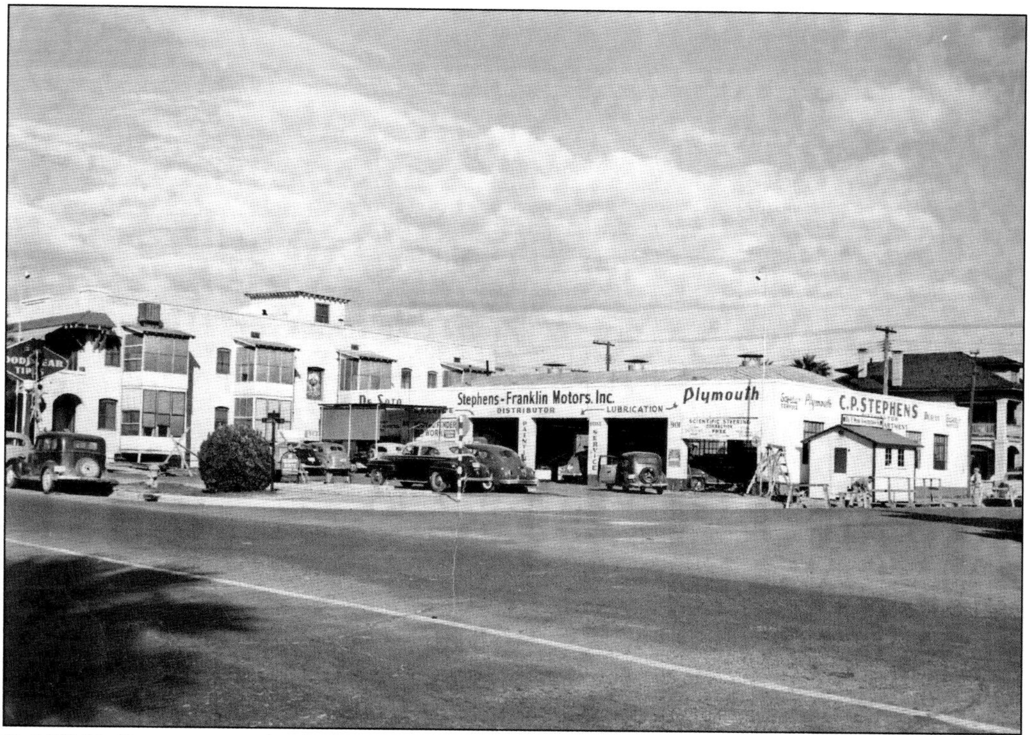

Del Webb Construction built the Stephens Lincoln Mercury at the northeast corner of Central Avenue and Garfield Street in 1947. Above is the site before construction. The Blenheim Apartments are in the background on the left, and the Garfield Apartments are on the right. Below is the dealership after construction. The building still exists. (Both, courtesy of Del Webb Corporation Photographs, Arizona State University Libraries.)

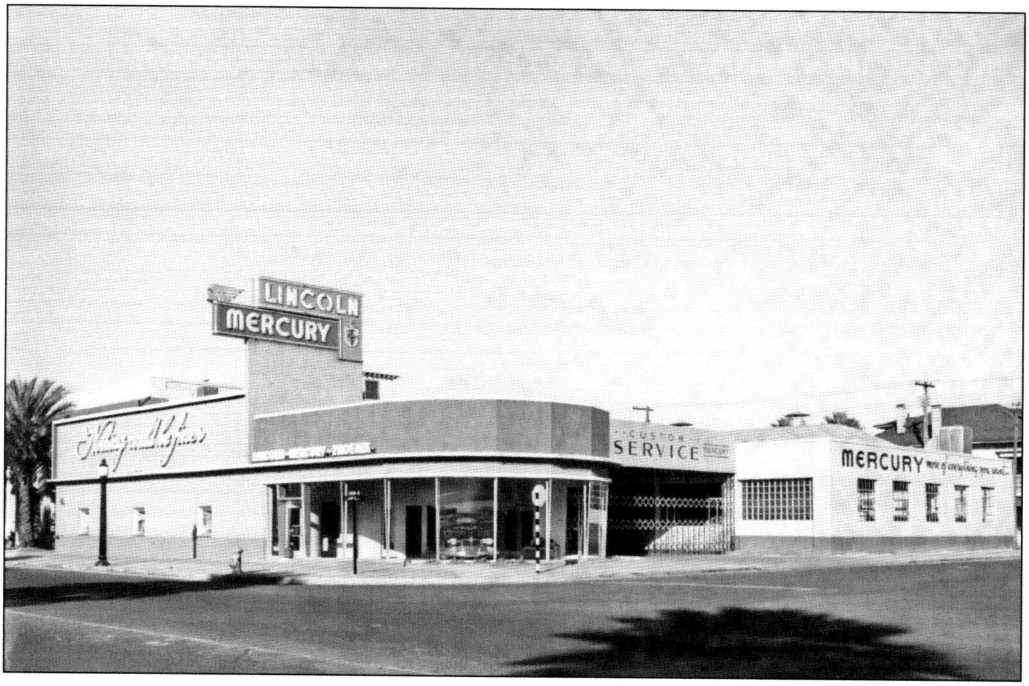

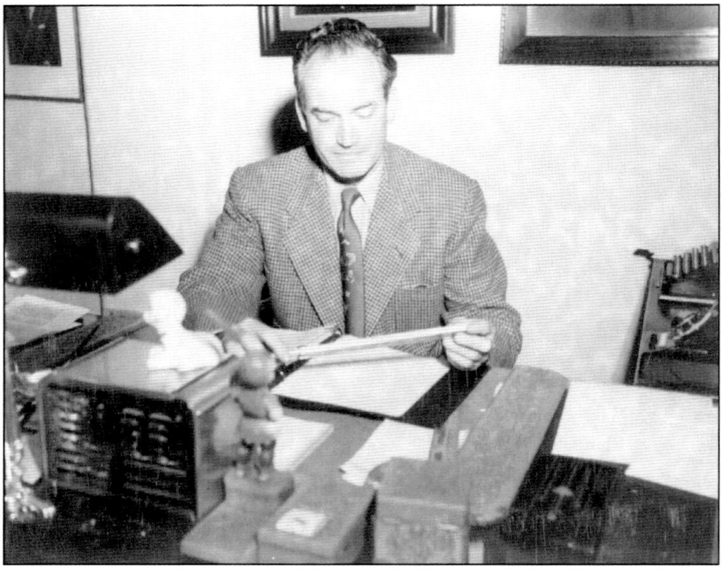

Before he was elected to the US Senate in 1952 and became a national figure, Barry M. Goldwater headed the Goldwater's department store chain and was active in local civic affairs. He grew up on Central Avenue, south of McKinley Street. Here he is at his desk in the 1940s. (Courtesy of Herb and Dorothy McLaughlin Collection, Arizona State University Libraries.)

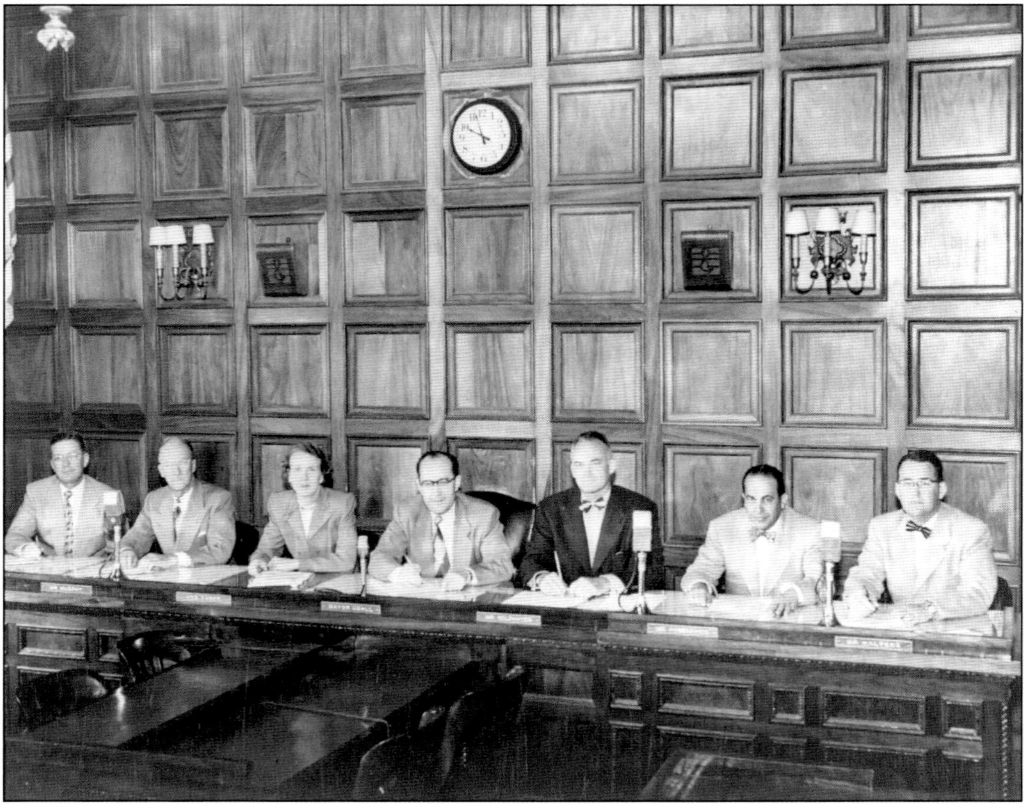

In the years before and during the war, Phoenix city government was plagued by corruption and incompetence. Local leaders worked to change this and realized success in 1948 when the electorate approved major reforms that became known as Charter Government. The first Charter city council, shown here, took office in 1949. It included Barry Goldwater as he began his career in government service. Charter Government heavily influenced city politics for the next three decades. (Courtesy of Herb and Dorothy McLaughlin Collection, Arizona State University Libraries.)

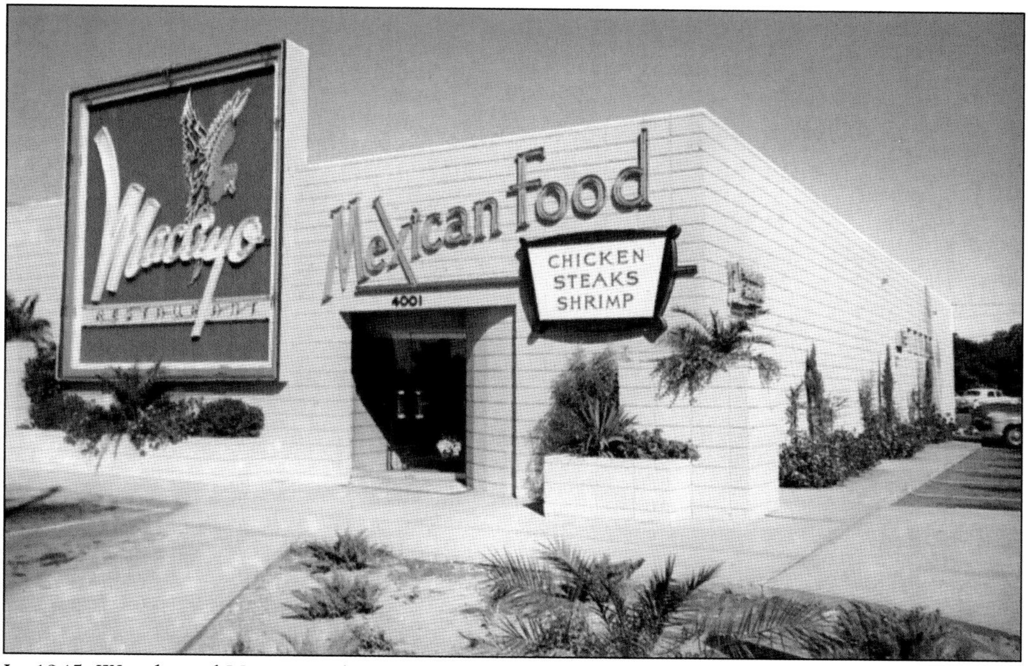

In 1945, Woody and Victoria Johnson established a restaurant called Valle del Sol at Sixteenth Street and McDowell Road. Later, they started Woody's El Nido at 1500 North Central Avenue. Their business grew, and in 1953, they opened Macayo on the northeast corner of Central and Clarendon Avenues. This 1950s photograph shows the building as it appeared before the Aztec facade was added in the 1960s. (Photograph by Jim Burke; author's collection.)

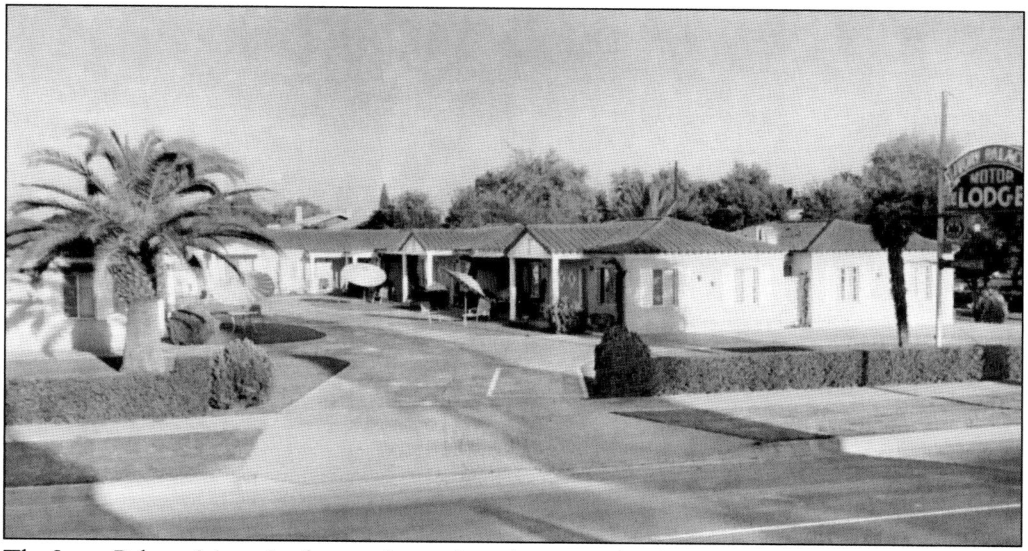

The Ivory Palaces Motor Lodge was located on the west side of Central Avenue, north of Osborn Road, between Columbus and Weldon Avenues. Constructed in the 1949, it advertised 21 refrigerated air-conditioned units in a quiet location. Later renamed the North Central Motor Hotel, it lasted into the 1970s. (Author's collection.)

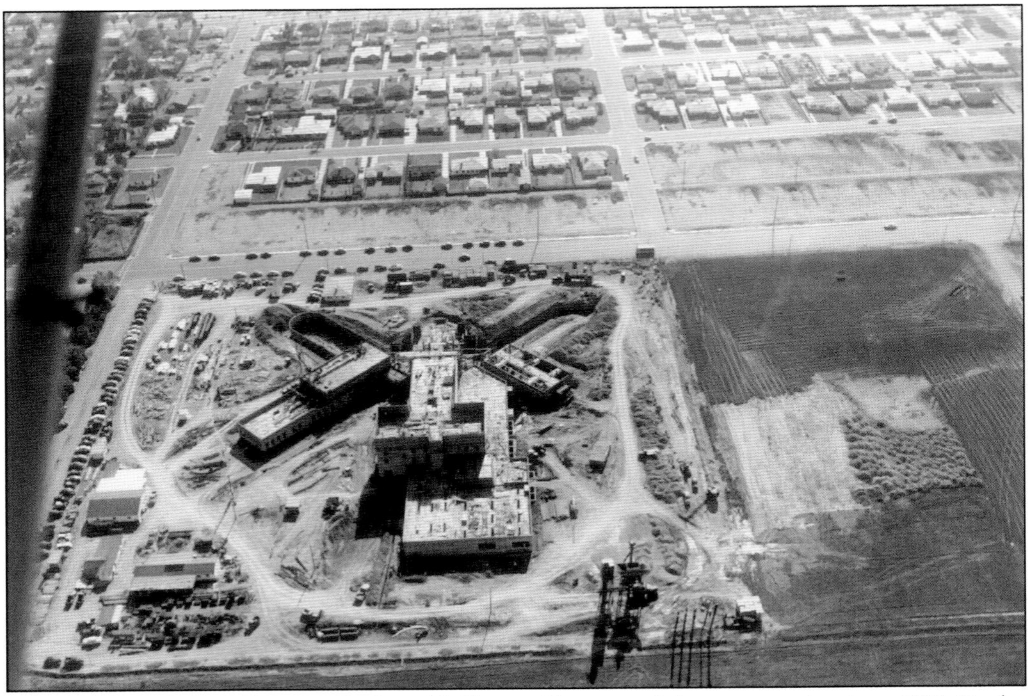

Started by the Sisters of Mercy, St. Joseph's Hospital has served the community since 1895. By the late 1940s, it had outgrown its facility at Fourth and Polk Streets (page 57). The sisters purchased land for a new hospital at the northwest corner of Third Avenue and Thomas Road in the 1940s. Designed by local architects Lescher & Mahoney and constructed by Del Webb, the new St. Joseph's opened in 1953. Above is view from the north with construction under way. Below is a view from the south in the mid-1950s. The hospital is on the right; the Park Central Medical Building is on the left. (Above, courtesy of Del Webb Corporation Photographs, Arizona Collection, Arizona State University Libraries; below, photograph by Don Keller, author's collection.)

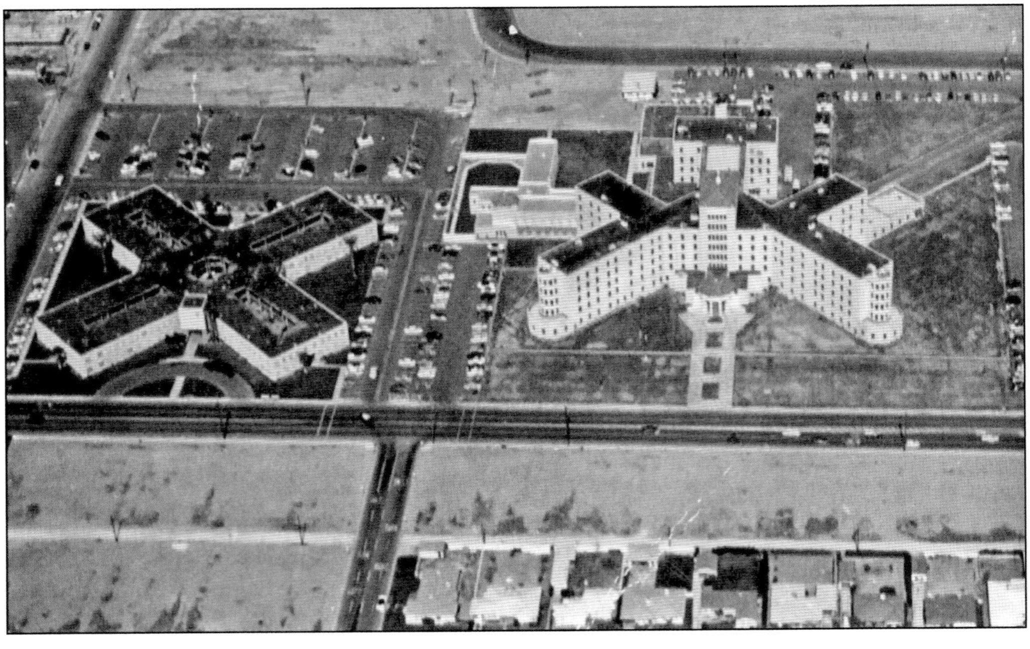

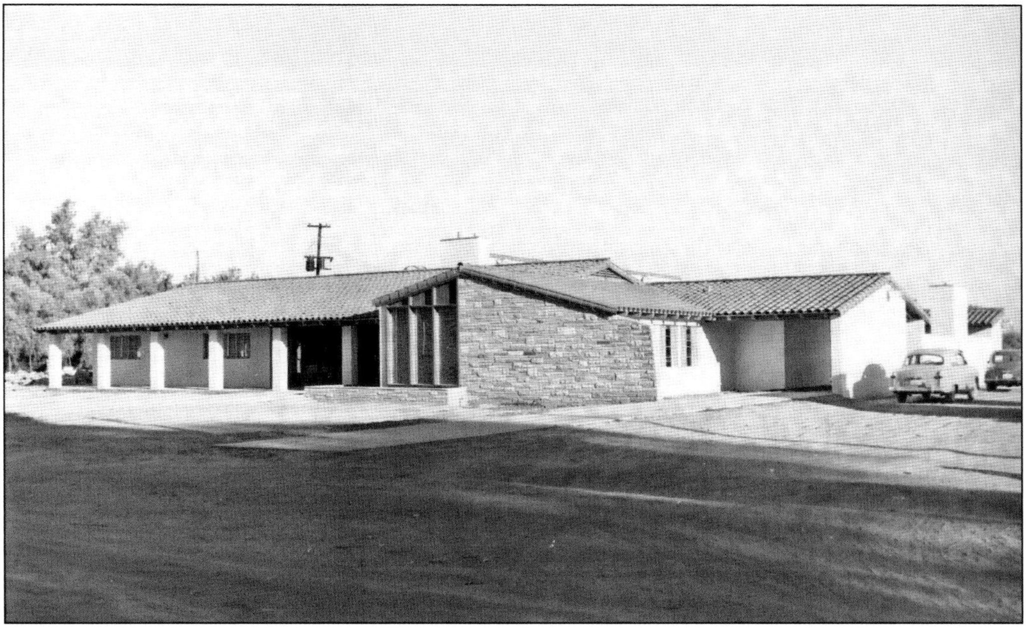

Built by Del Webb Construction in 1950, the Boy Scout Headquarters stood on the north side of Earll Drive at Second Street. This area east of Central Avenue was still residential and agricultural, but it quickly evolved into a commercial district in the years that followed. An office building now stands at that location. (Courtesy of Del Webb Corporation Photographs, Arizona Collection, Arizona State University Libraries.)

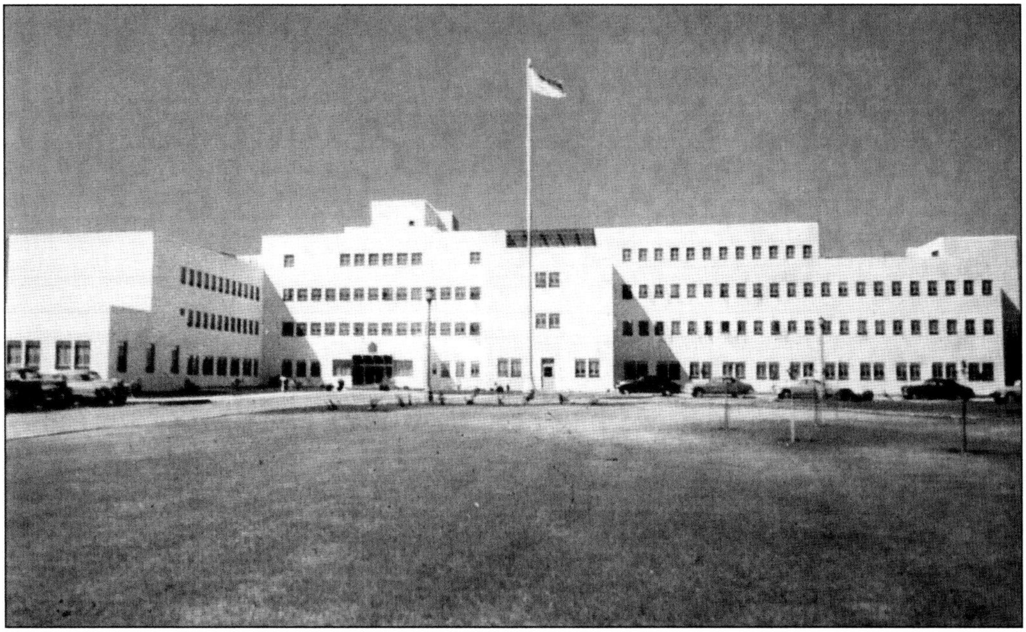

In 1951, Del Webb Construction built the Phoenix Veterans Hospital at the northwest corner of Indian School Road and Seventh Street. This view shows how it appeared as originally constructed. The facility has since been heavily modified. During the second decade of the 21st century, this hospital became a focal point in a nationwide scandal on the quality of health care for veterans. (Photograph by Bob Petley; author's collection.)

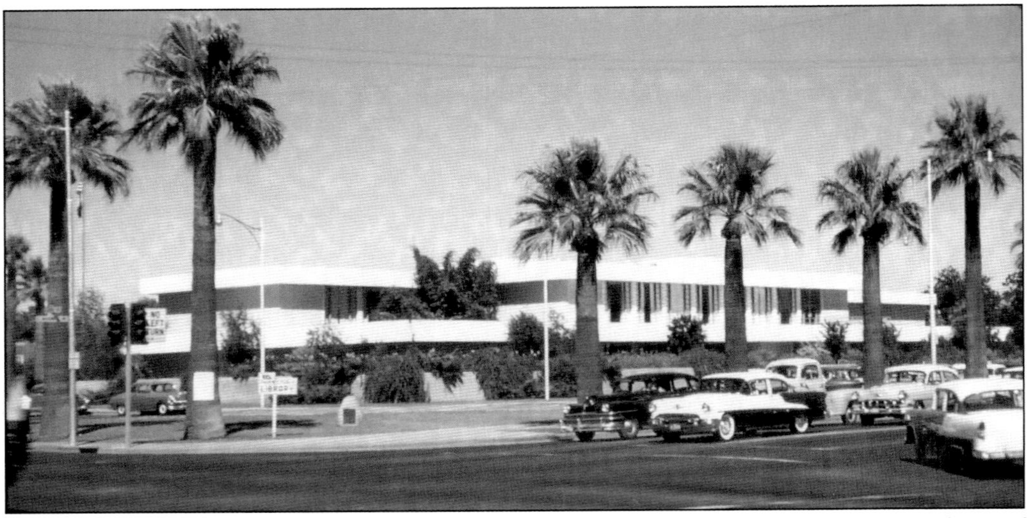

For years, the community worked to establish a new civic center on land donated by the heirs of Adolphus C. Bartlett, which included Maie Bartlett Heard, at the northeast corner of McDowell Road and Central Avenue. The planning and fundraising resulted in the new Phoenix Public Library, opened in August 1952, and the Phoenix Little Theatre. Above is the completed library in the 1950s. Below are the library and theater in 1955. Mrs. Heard did not live to see the result of their generosity. After decades of community leadership and philanthropy, she died the year before the library opened. (Above, author's collection; below, courtesy of Herb and Dorothy McLaughlin Collection, Arizona State University Libraries.)

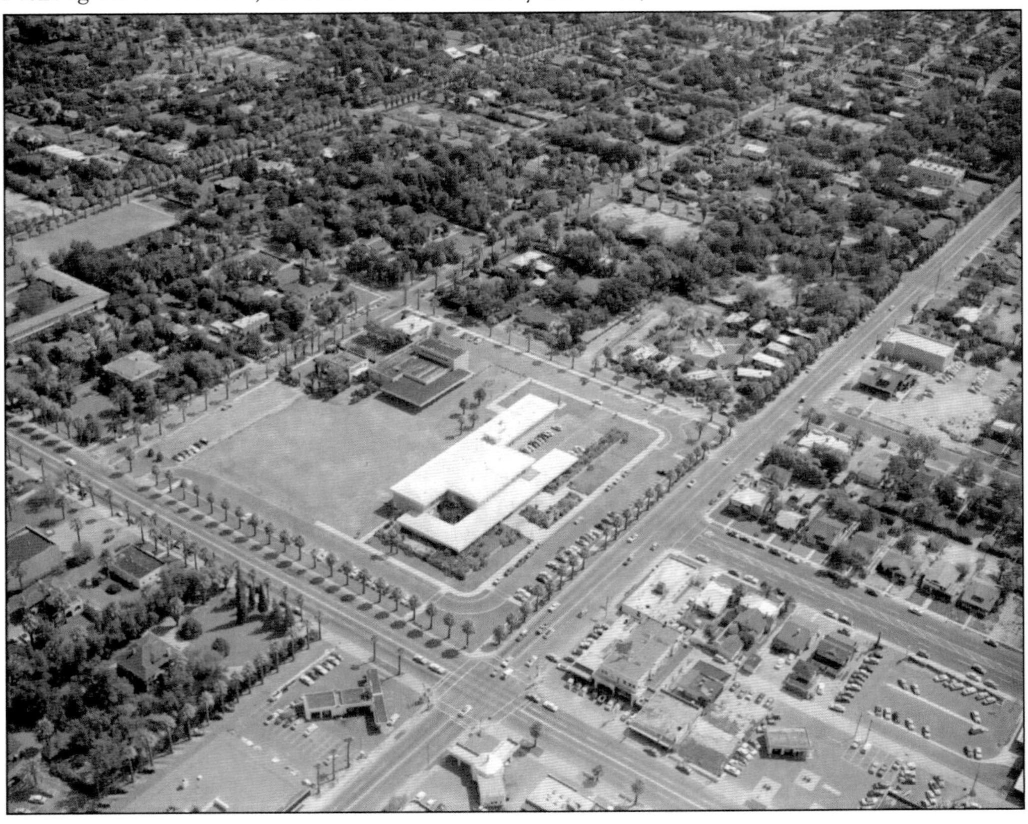

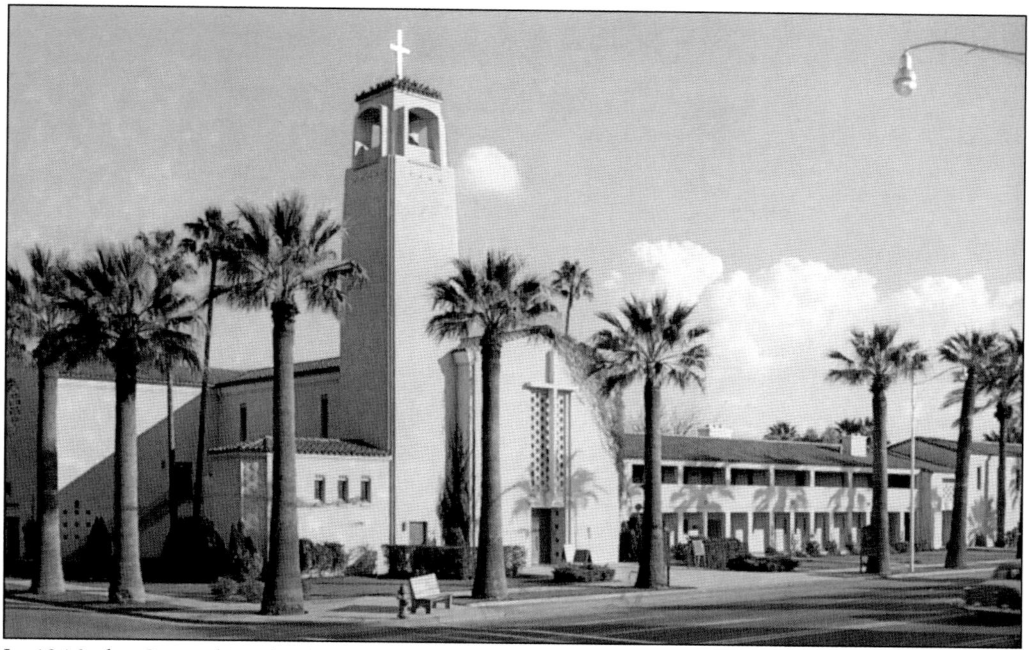

In 1946, the Central Methodist Church congregation purchased land at the southeast corner of Central Avenue and Palm Lane for a new church facility. In 1951, the facility was completed and the congregation moved into its new home (above). Their old facility at Central and Pierce (p. 53) lasted until 1954, when it was demolished (below). The site is now the location of the Phoenix Public Market and Farmers' Market. (Above, author's collection; below, courtesy of Herb and Dorothy McLaughlin Collection, Arizona State University Libraries.)

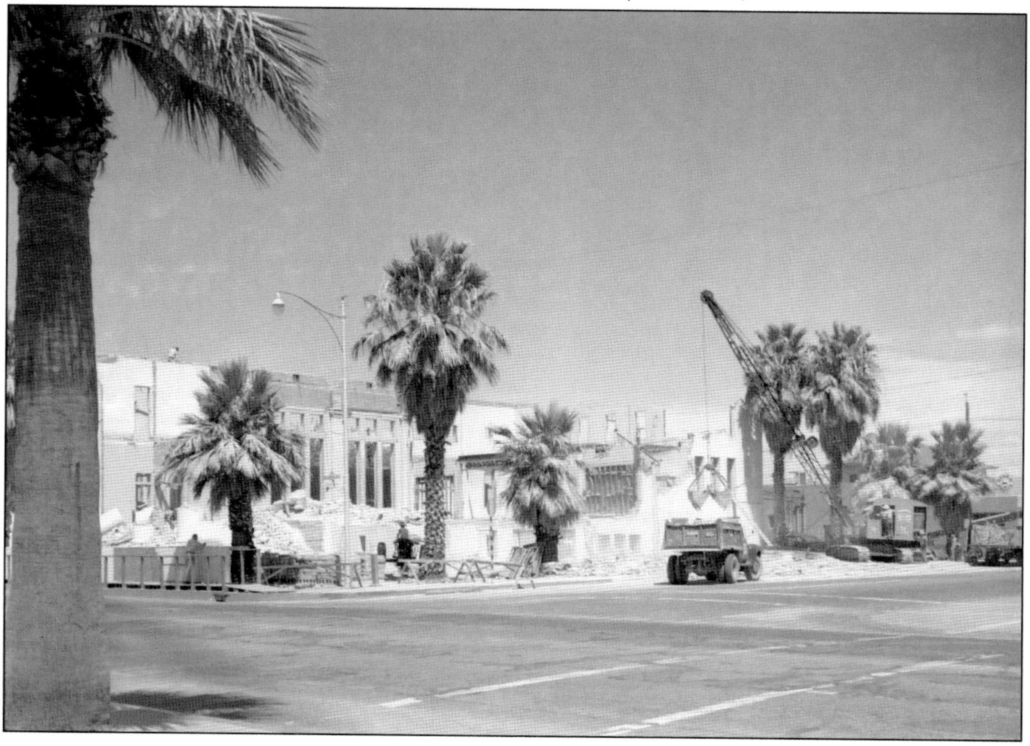

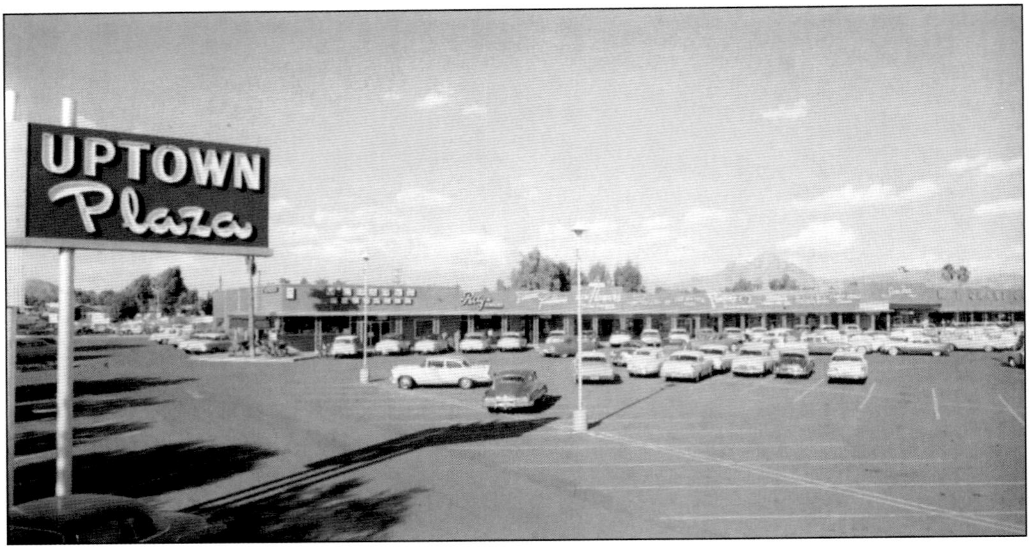

In August 1955, the Uptown Plaza opened at the northeast corner of Central Avenue and Camelback Road. Constructed by Del Webb, it housed a Piggly Wiggly supermarket, an elegant restaurant called Navarre's, and other shops (above). It was the first large shopping center located outside of downtown, but it would soon be superseded by another center south on Central Avenue. Webb also constructed Helsing's Coffee Shop on the corner for local restaurateur A.O. Helsing (below). Helsing's later became Lunt Avenue Marble Club before being demolished in the 1990s. (Both, author's collection.)

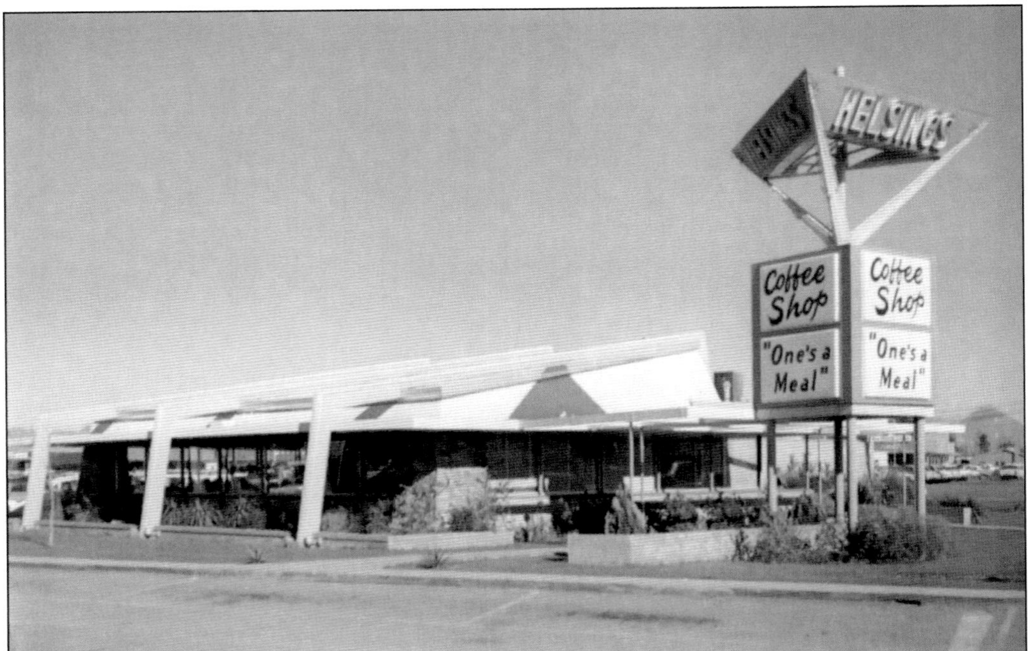

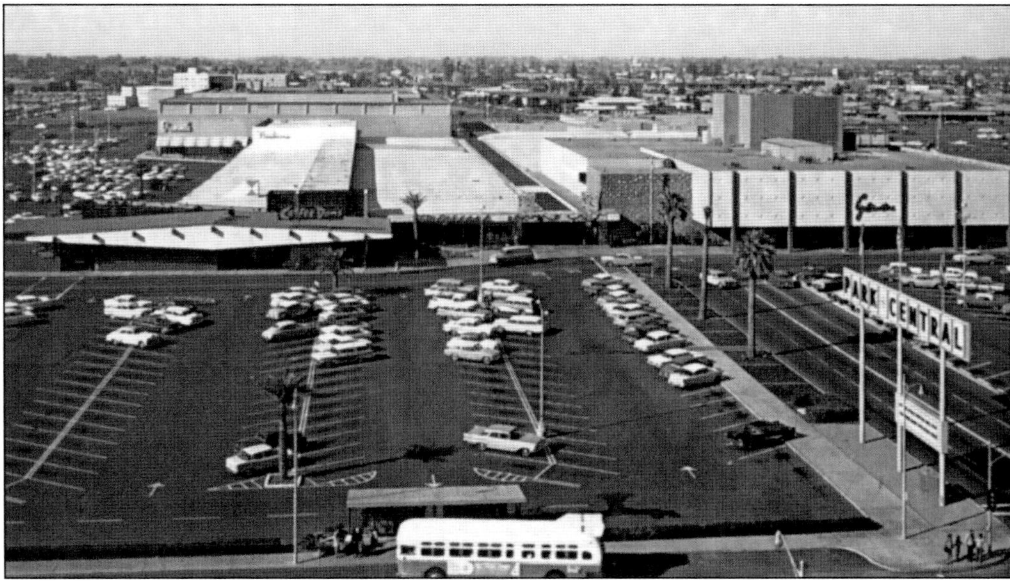

In 1950, big plans were announced to redevelop the Central Avenue Dairy property. During the next few years, the dairy would be turned into a housing development and the Park Central Shopping City, an outdoor shopping mall anchored with large local department stores, such as Goldwater's and Diamond's. Parking posed no problem, as the center was surrounded by over 5,000 spaces. Park Central was the second large shopping center outside of downtown and accelerated the movement of retail from downtown to the outlying areas closer to the customers. Above is Park Central soon after completion. Below is the area in 1959 when both the Mayer Central office building (page 96) and the Guaranty Bank tower (page 89) are under construction. The north tower of the Central Towers office building (page 101) is completed. (Above, author's collection; below, courtesy of Herb and Dorothy McLaughlin Collection, Arizona State University Libraries.)

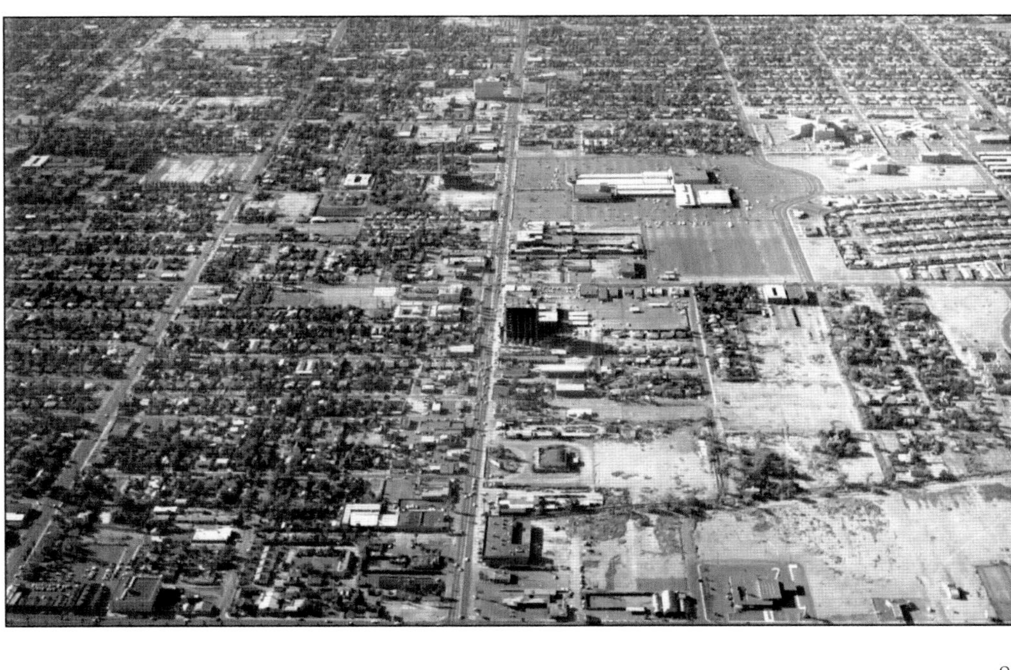

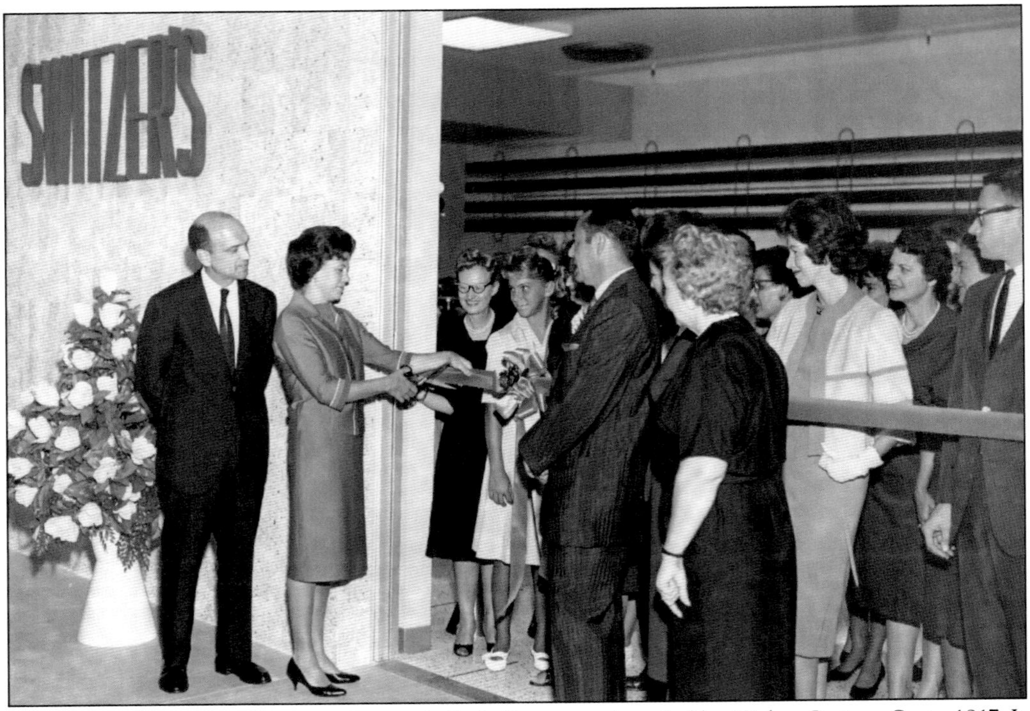

Located in downtown Phoenix, Switzer's Style Shop was founded by Walter Switzer Sr. in 1917. It eventually grew into a chain with locations in several states. Switzer's opened in its Park Central location in 1957. Here, Grace Switzer cuts the ribbon to open the store while husband Walter Switzer Jr. looks on. Daughter Jean (in white dress and shoes), along with Switzer employees, watch the event. (Courtesy of Jean Switzer.)

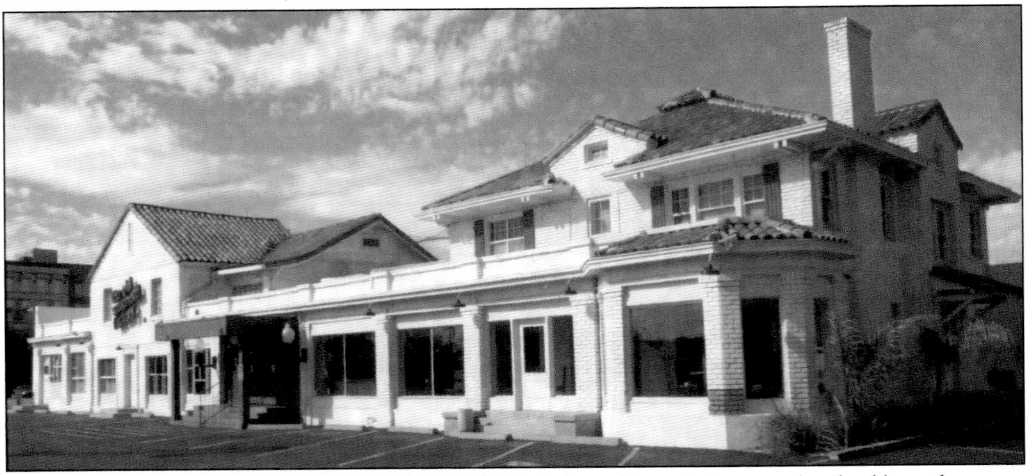

During the 1940s and 1950s, many of the residences along Central Avenue that had been home to the city's business and community leaders were remodeled into commercial establishments. These two houses at the southwest corner of Central Avenue and Lynwood Street were combined in 1946 for Coles Home Furnishings. The houses were a natural setting for furniture display. Owner Francis E. Coles also operated Dorris-Heyman Furniture. Coles made much of its own furniture and accessories in addition to selling china, silver, and crystal. The store offered complete home decorating services, as well as a popular bridal registry. It is now the location of the Old Spaghetti Factory restaurant. (Photograph by the author.)

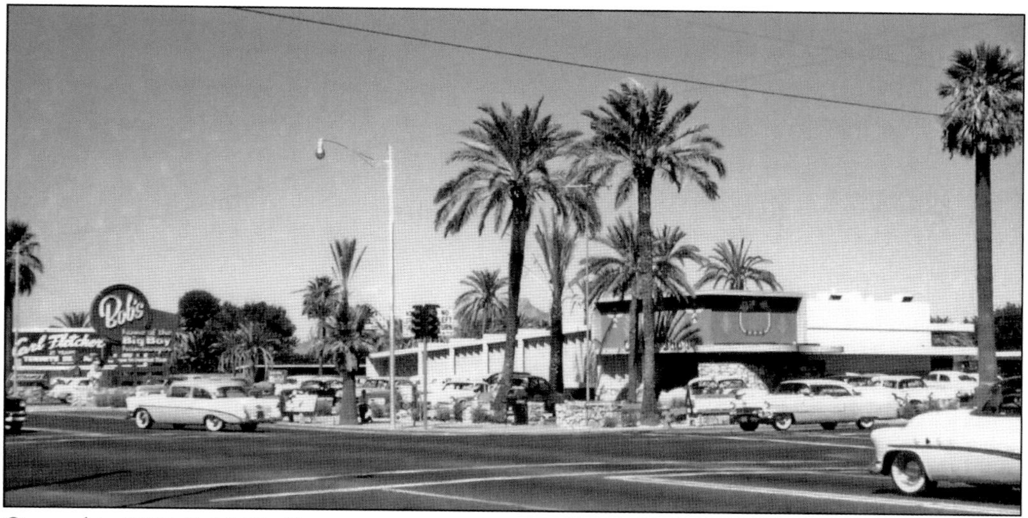

Opened in 1955, Bob's Big Boy restaurant replaced Palm Lodge (page 32) at the northeast corner of Central Avenue and Thomas Road. It quickly became very popular, as it offered both inside dining and carhop service. Bob's was in business for about 20 years. The building was torn down in the 1980s for redevelopment, and the Phoenix Plaza office complex now occupies the site. (Author's collection.)

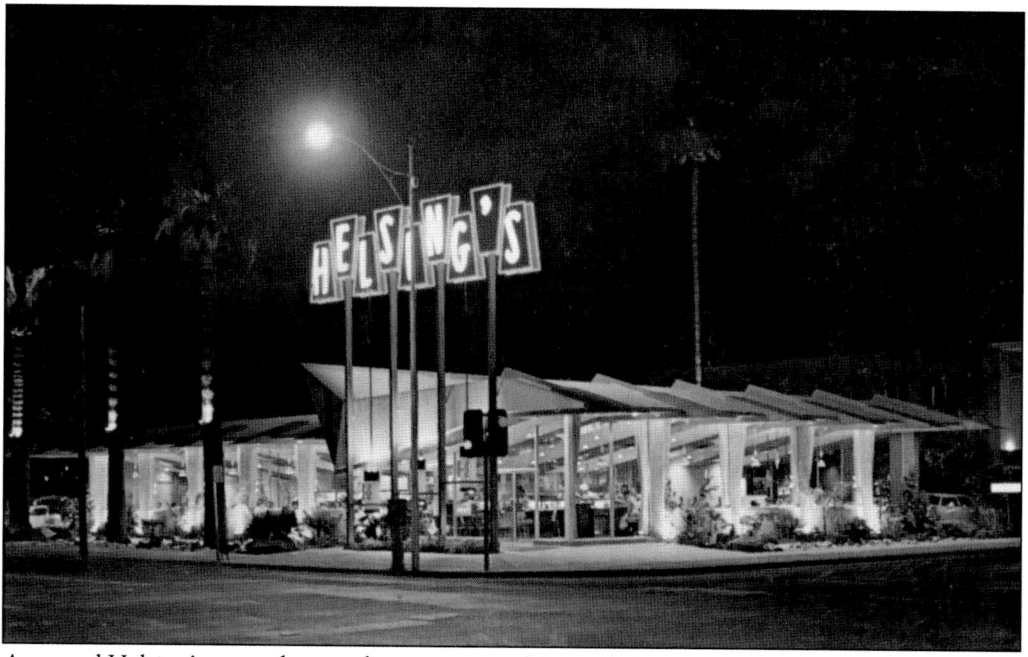

A second Helsing's opened at northwest corner of Central Avenue and Osborn Road in the mid-1950s. It was designed by architect John Sing Tang. This nighttime photographs shows off its unique architecture. (Photograph by Jim Sexton, author's collection.)

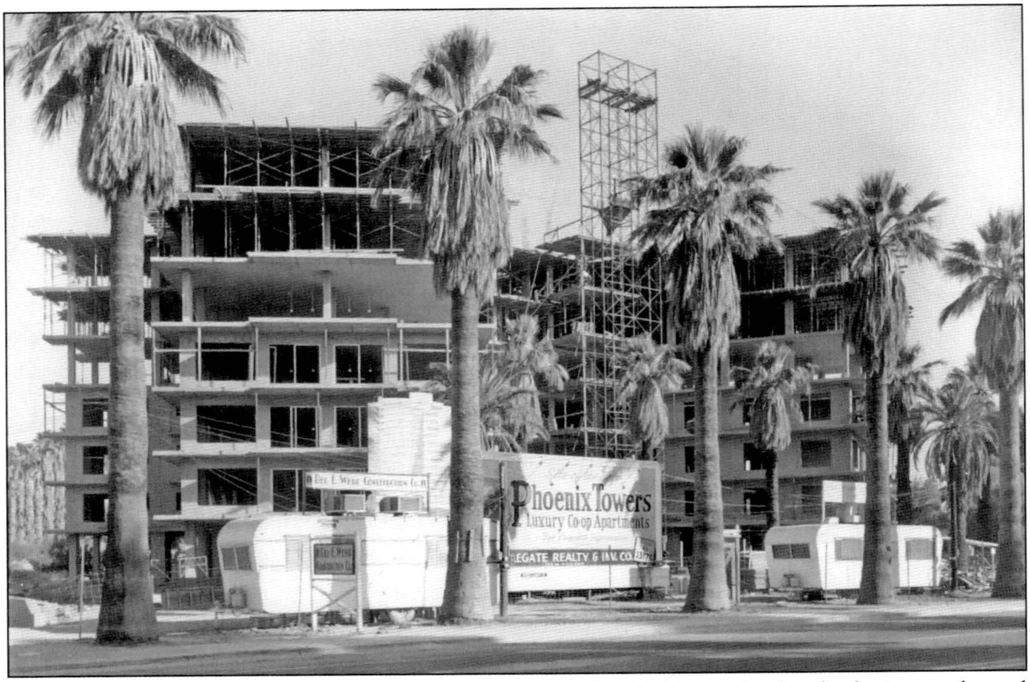

The Phoenix Towers cooperative apartments, completed in 1957, was the first high-rise residential tower in Phoenix. Constructed by Del Webb on the northeast corner of Central Avenue and Monte Vista Road, it replaced Casa Blanca, the Heard home (page 27). Above is a view from Central Avenue during construction of the concrete frame. Below are the towers after completion. When the first model opened, there was a line on Central Avenue to view it. Most units sold before the project was completed. The sign in the lower left corner points the way to the Heard Museum. (Above, courtesy of Del Webb Corporation Photographs, Arizona Collection, Arizona State University Libraries; below, author's collection.)

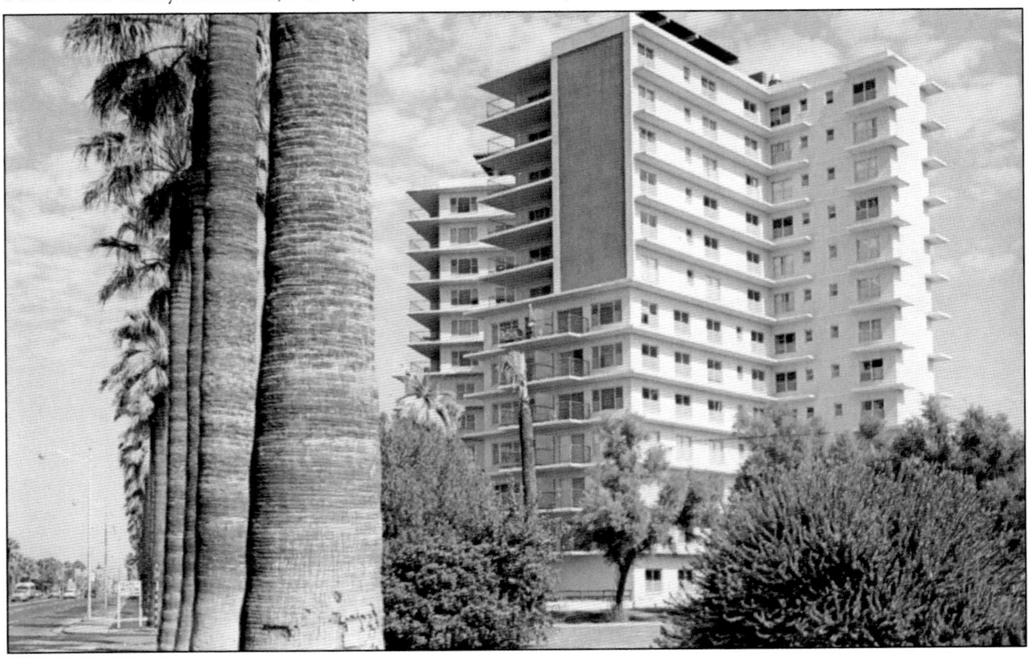

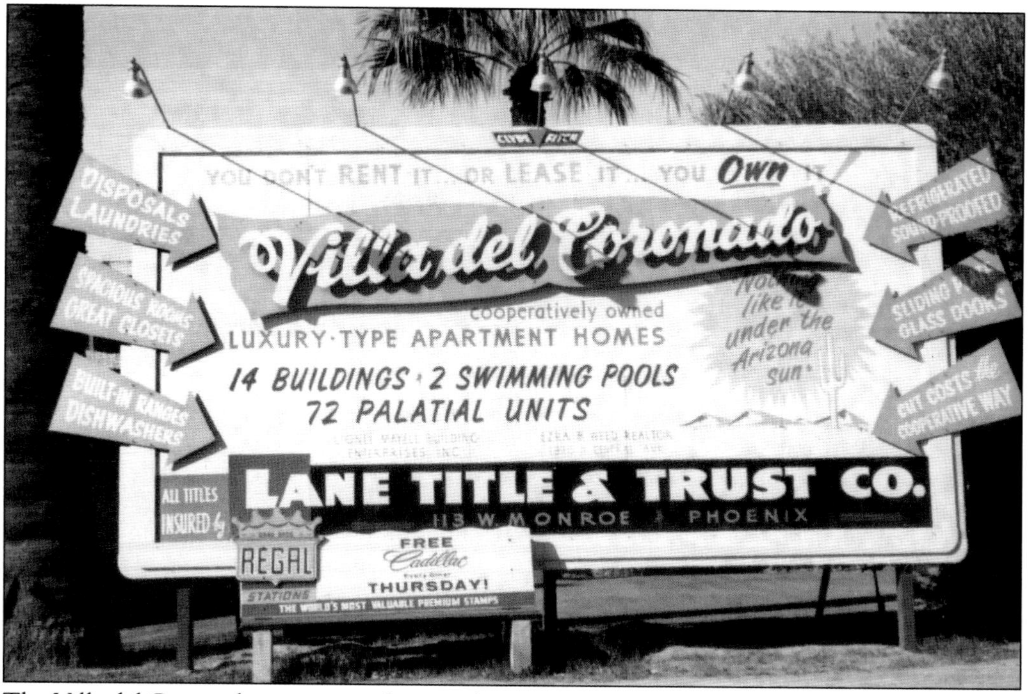

The Villa del Coronado cooperatively owned apartment complex was constructed between 1955 and 1957 at the northeast corner of Coronado and Alvarado Roads. Planned for the site were 14 buildings with a total of 72 apartments. The cost of an apartment was approximately $22,000, and monthly assessments for all utilities and maintenance could be as low as $41.46. Like the Phoenix Towers, the Villa del Coronado had significant presales. Above is a 1950s advertisement, and below are two of the apartment buildings. (Above, photograph by Alice Wagner, courtesy of Robert Russman; below, photograph by the author.)

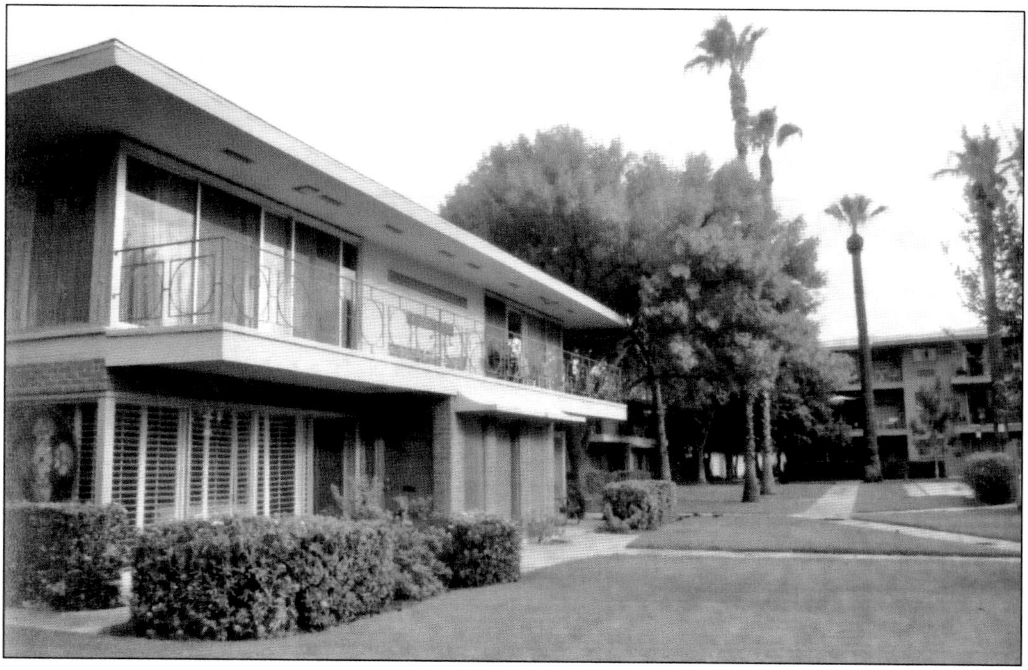

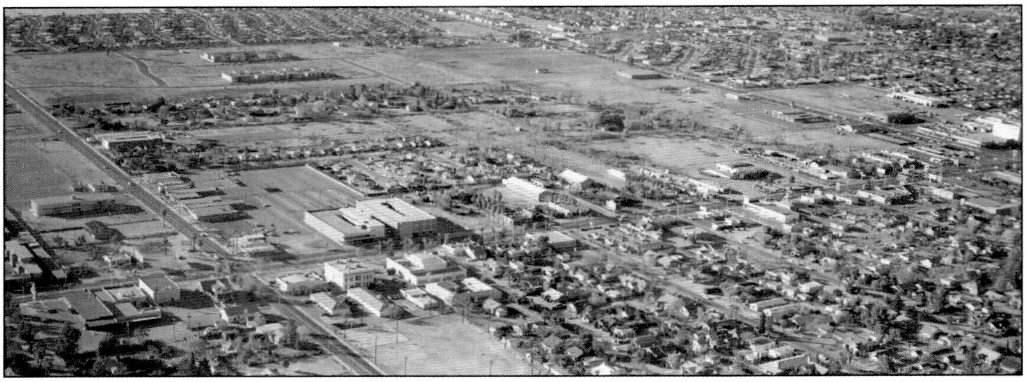

This aerial view from the late 1950s shows the Central Corridor between Osborn and Indian School Roads just before the high-rise boom. Central Avenue runs diagonally across the photograph, with Osborn intersecting on the left. Seen at the intersection are the Osborn School and Helsing's. Sciots Auditorium is farther up Central Avenue. Within a few short years, many of the buildings along this corridor would be swept away with new construction. (Courtesy of Herb and Dorothy McLaughlin Collection, Arizona State University Libraries.)

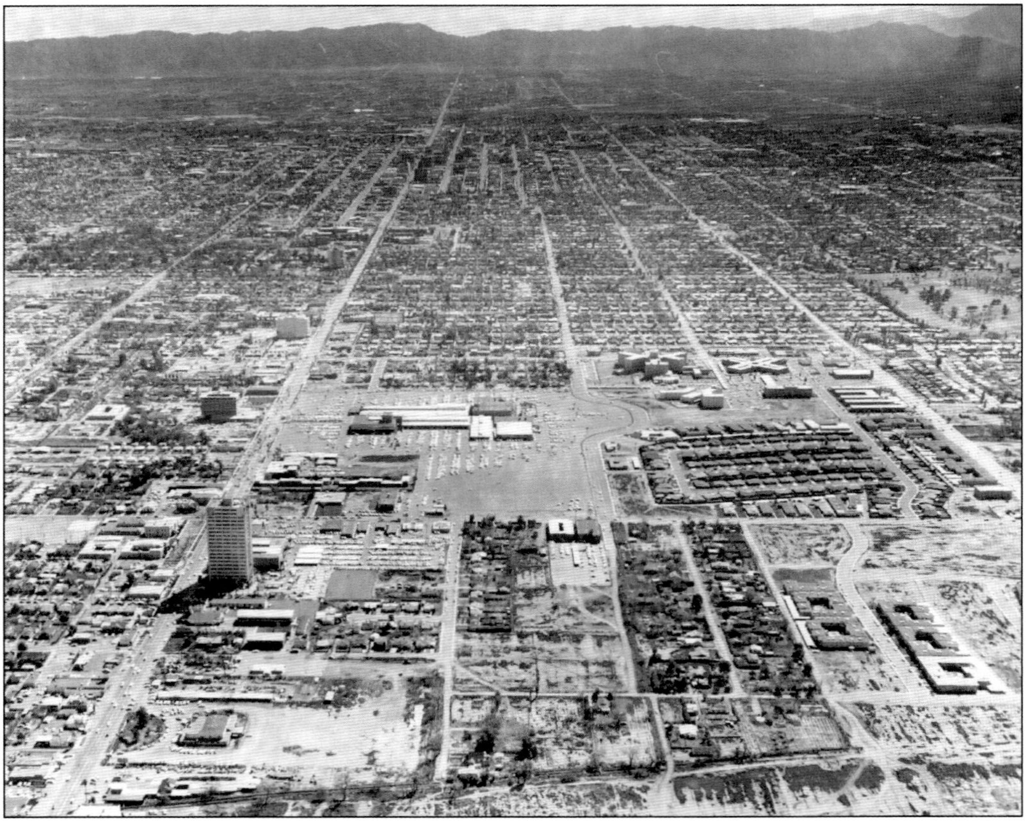

This 1960 view looks south on Central Avenue from Indian School Road and shows the beginning of the construction boom. The Guaranty Bank building (now 3550 North Central) and Sciots Auditorium are on the right side of Central Avenue. The Mayer Plaza office building (page 96), Central Towers office building (page 101), and Phoenix Towers apartments (page 86) are on the left side. Park Central and St. Joseph's Hospital can also be seen. (Courtesy of Herb and Dorothy McLaughlin Collection, Arizona State University Libraries.)

When completed in 1960, the Guaranty Bank building was the tallest in Phoenix at 20 stories. Built by developer David Murdock, it was known for its distinctive turquoise glass exterior. It was reported that Murdock wanted his new tower to have a bank. When the established banks were reluctant to move out of downtown, he started his own bank, the Guaranty Bank of Arizona. (Courtesy of Arizona State Library, Archives and Public Records, History and Archives Division, Phoenix, No. 05-6076.)

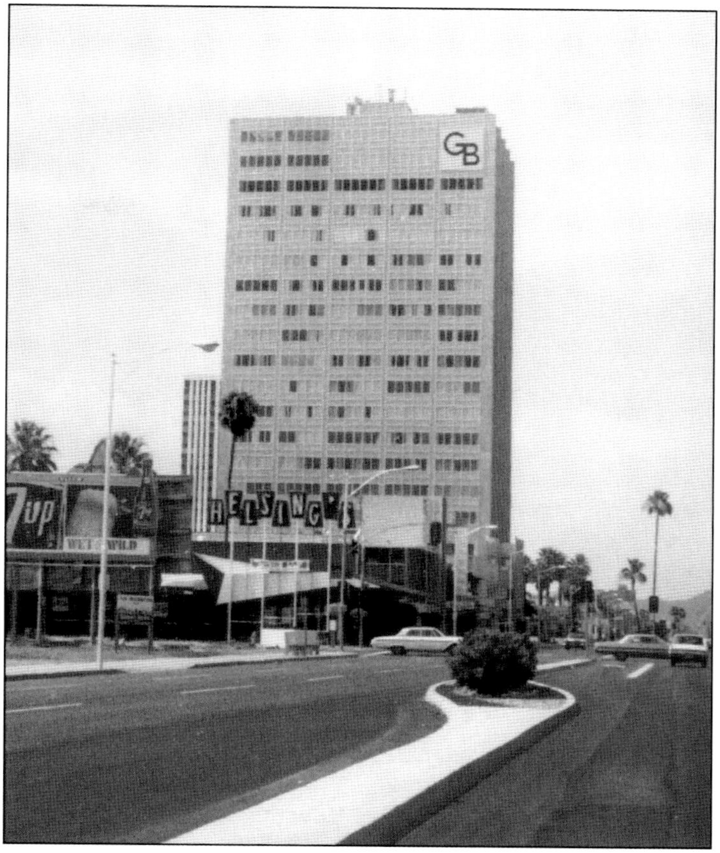

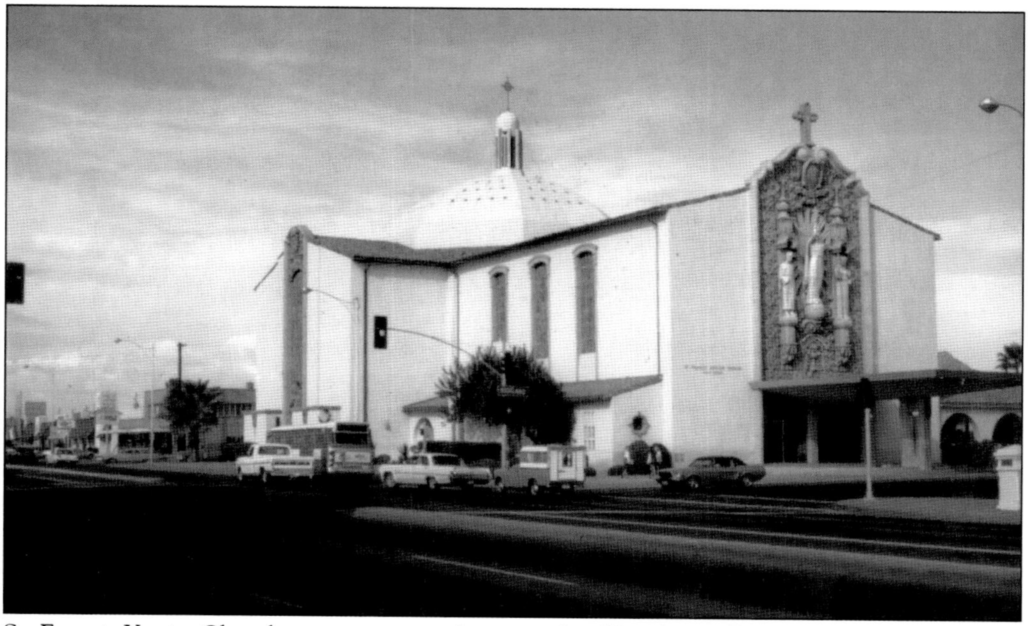

St. Francis Xavier Church was constructed just north of Brophy College Preparatory for the St. Francis Parish. Opened in 1959, it could seat over 1,500 people. This photograph from the mid-1960s showed how it appeared soon after completion. (Author's collection.)

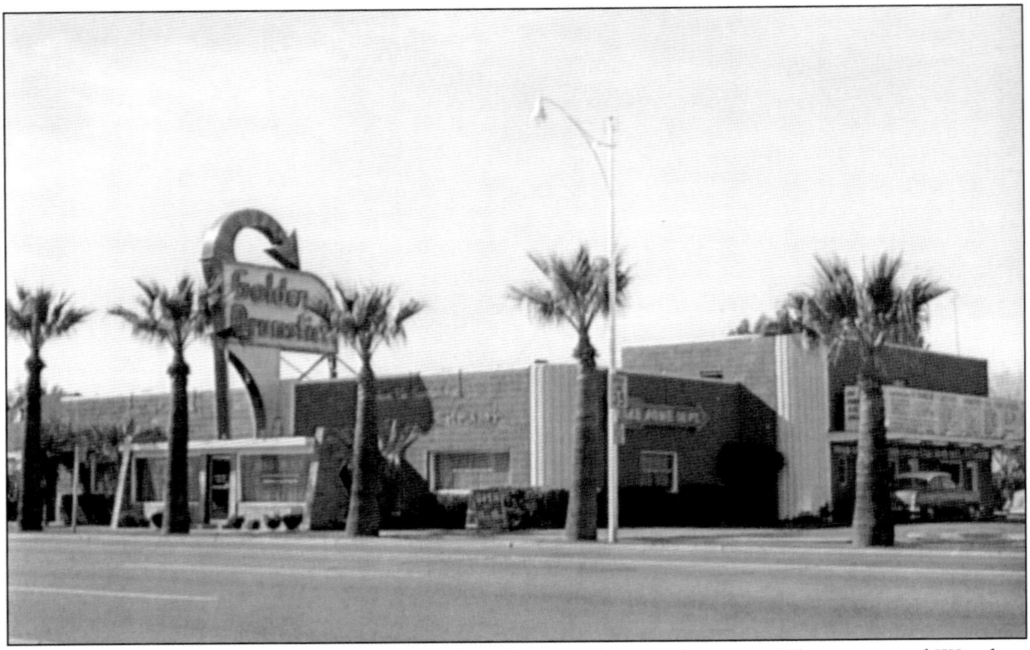

The Golden Drumstick Restaurant opened on Central Avenue between Edgemont and Windsor Avenues, in 1951. In 1959, a complete fried chicken dinner was $1.50, and a shrimp dinner was $1.19. In 1963, it became Kelly's. The building was demolished in the early 1980s, and an office tower now occupies the site. (Photograph by Dean Riggins; author's collection.)

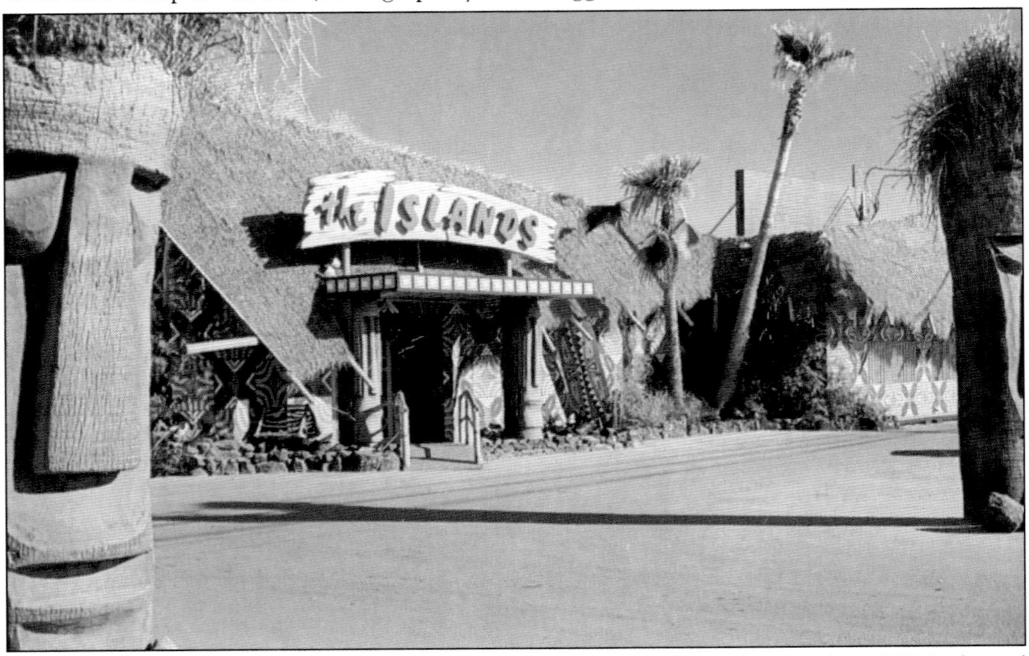

The Islands Restaurant on Seventh Street, just south of Camelback Road, opened in 1958. It plugged into the tiki craze of the 1950s, which was fueled by soldiers and sailors who had developed an interest in Polynesian ways while serving in the South Pacific during World War II. The Islands offered exotic rum drinks, Polynesian cuisine, and a South Seas atmosphere. The restaurant closed in the late 1970s. (Photograph by Jim Sexton; author's collection.)

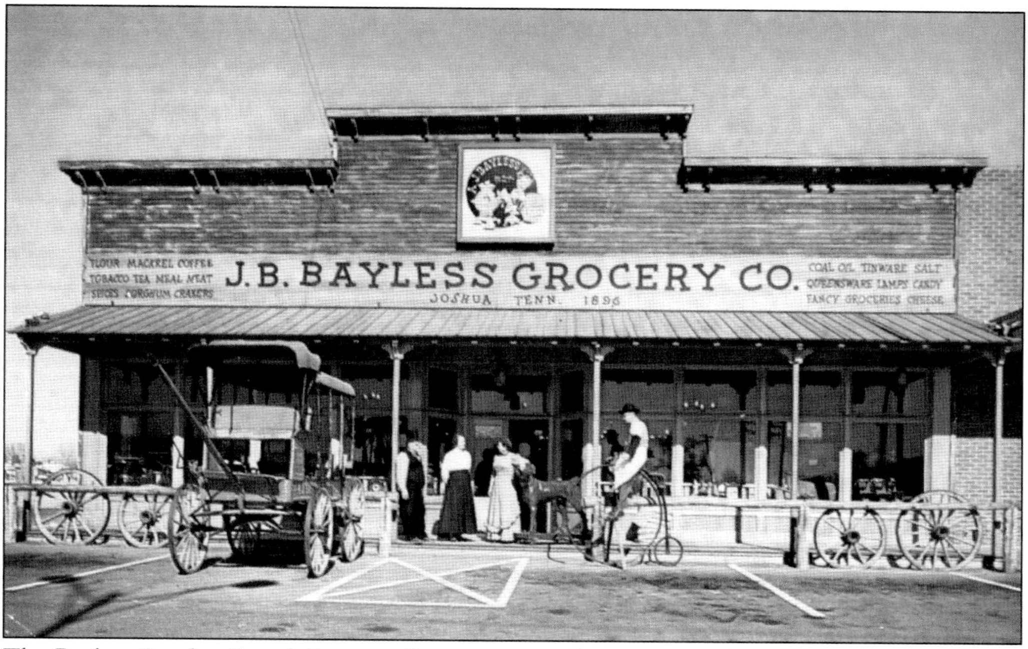

The Bayless Cracker Barrel Country Store was actually a museum designed to replicate a turn-of-the-century country general store. The A.J. Bayless Markets operated it as a way to show how much modern food marketing methods had advanced since the 1800s. Located next to one of their grocery stores, it operated from 1956 to 1987 in a modern shopping center on Indian School Road, just west of Central Avenue. (Photograph by Bob Petley; author's collection.)

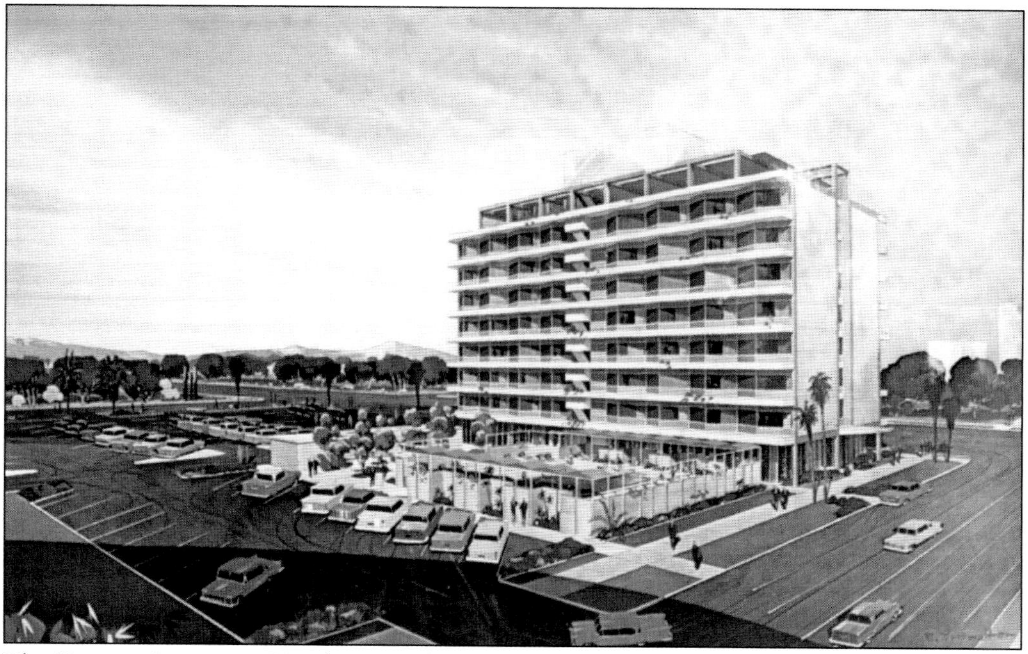

The Coronet Apartment Hotel rose on the site of the Central Dryv Inn (page 69) at the northeast corner of Central Avenue and Roosevelt Street. Completed in 1960, it had a unique sawtooth window wall design by architect Fred Guirey & Associates. During the early 1980s, its exterior was modified extensively. It is now an office building. (Author's collection.)

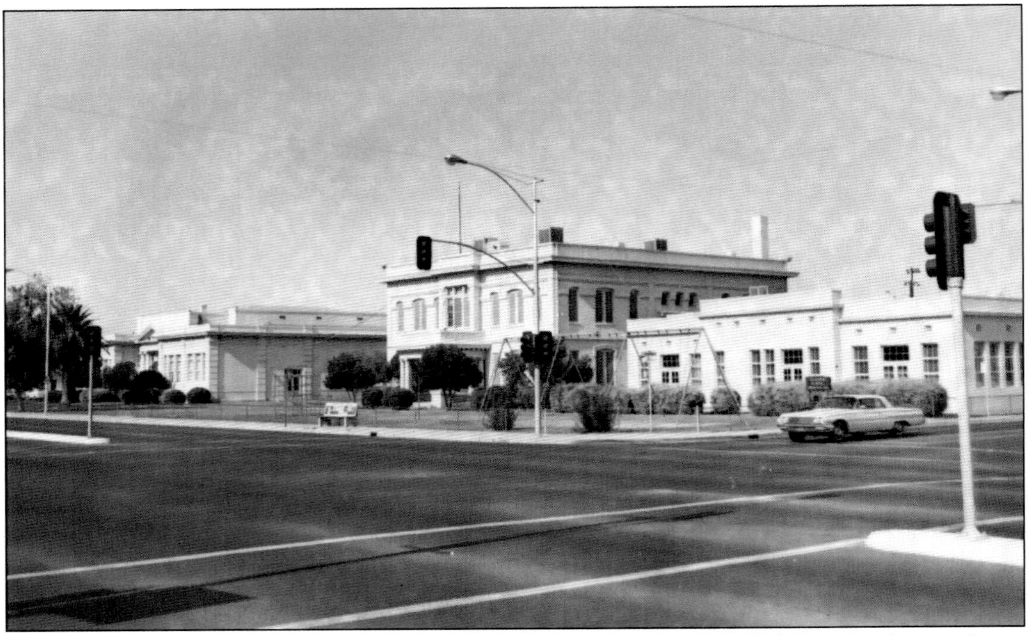

In the early 1960s, the Osborn School campus (page 12) still occupied the site at the northeast corner of Central Avenue and Osborn Road, as shown here. It had its peak enrollment of 1,000 students in 1949, but this had declined to less than 500 by 1962 when developer David Murdock purchased the property for redevelopment. (Courtesy of Herb and Dorothy McLaughlin Photograph Collection, Arizona State University Libraries.)

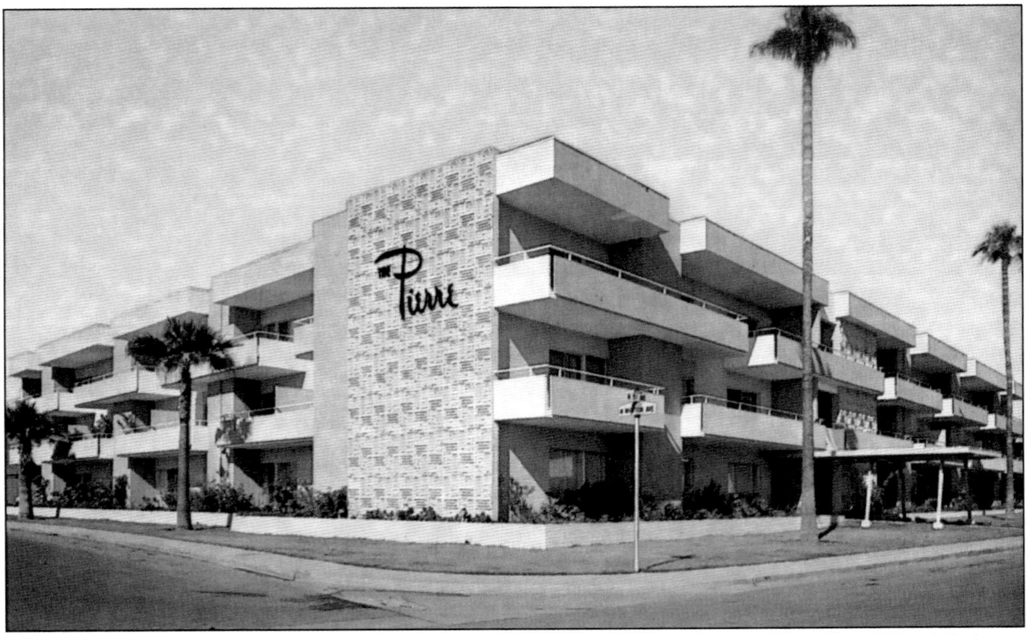

The Sportsman's Park harness racetrack (page 69) occupied the northeast corner of Osborn Road and Seventh Avenue, but by the mid-1950s, it had been closed and demolished. The land was redeveloped with a shopping center and apartments. Once part of the Sportsman's site, the Pierre apartments were constructed on Fifth Avenue, just north of Osborn Road, in 1961. (Author's collection.)

Into the 1960s, the Westward Ho Hotel (page 55) was a prime location for events and meetings. *Arizona Republic* publisher Eugene Pulliam chats with Vice Pres. Richard Nixon in this photograph taken at the hotel on October 15, 1960. His wife, Pat Nixon, is seen on the right. Nixon, who was running against Sen. John F. Kennedy for president, attended a breakfast in the Thunderbird Room of the hotel. Pulliam became publisher of the *Republic* in 1946 and was one of the most influential citizens in the community. In the 1970s, his opposition to the elevated Papago Freeway through Midtown was a major factor in its defeat at the polls. (Courtesy of Arizona State Library, Archives and Public Records, History and Archives Division, Phoenix, No. 11-0025.)

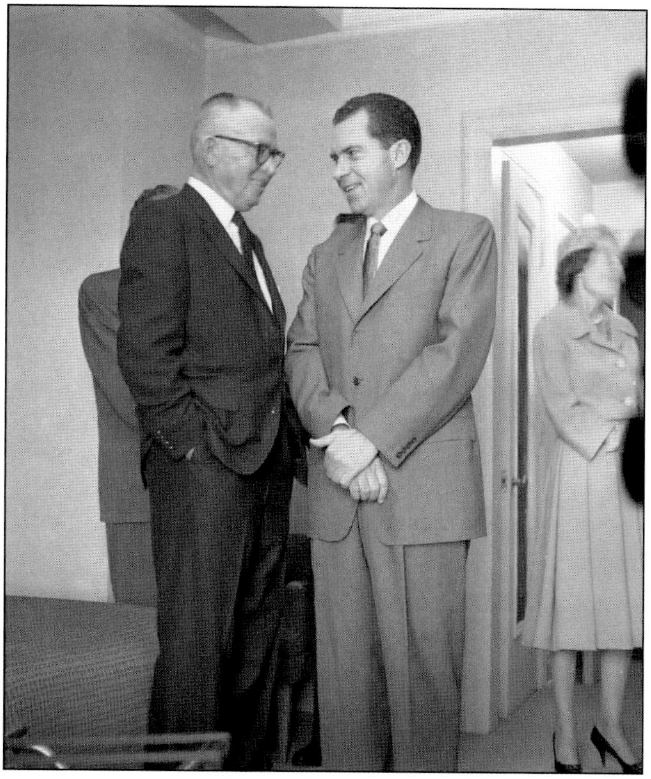

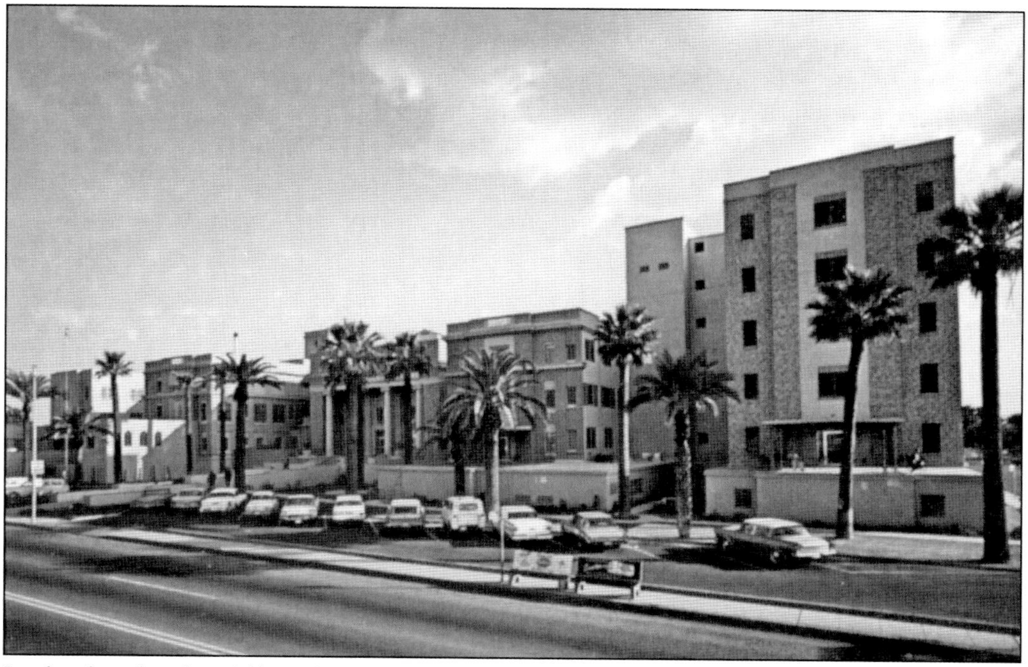

In the decades that followed its construction, Good Samaritan Hospital grew steadily. This photograph from the early 1960s shows the expansion up to that time, but the original 1923 Neoclassical facade (page 46) still survived. The original structure would eventually disappear as the campus grew. It is now the Banner – University Medical Center. (Author's collection.)

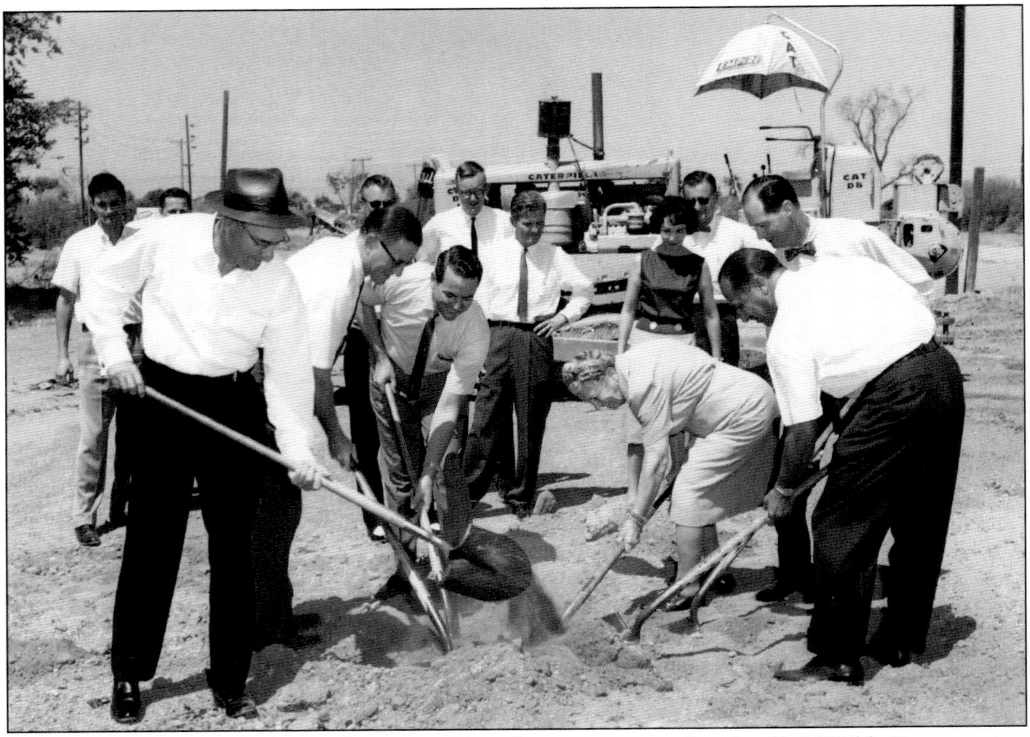

This 1961 photograph shows the ground-breaking ceremony for the Del Webb Corporation headquarters building at the southwest corner of Central and Clarendon Avenues—the first structure in the Rosenzweig Center (now City Square). From left to right in the foreground, Del Webb (in fedora) is joined by L.C. Jacobson and Richard Wartes of Del Webb Corporation, Rosa Rosenzweig, and sons Harry and Newton Rosenzweig. The Rosenzweig family, who owned the property, were longtime business and community leaders. They were instrumental in forming Charter Government (page 76). (Courtesy of Del Webb Corporation Photographs, Arizona Collection, Arizona State University Libraries.)

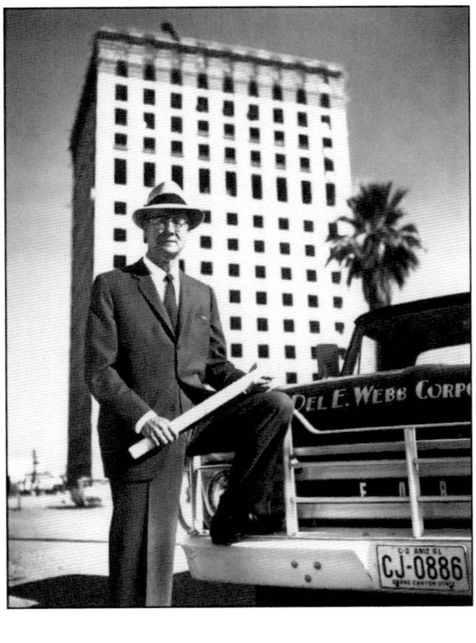

Starting in 1928, Phoenix contractor Del Webb had built his construction firm from a local operation into a large national builder with projects in many states by the 1950s. While now better known for developing the Sun Cities retirement communities, Webb constructed many Midtown buildings during his career until his death in 1974. He is pictured here in 1963 by the office tower that bore his name. (Courtesy of Del Webb Corporation Photographs, Arizona Collection, Arizona State University Libraries.)

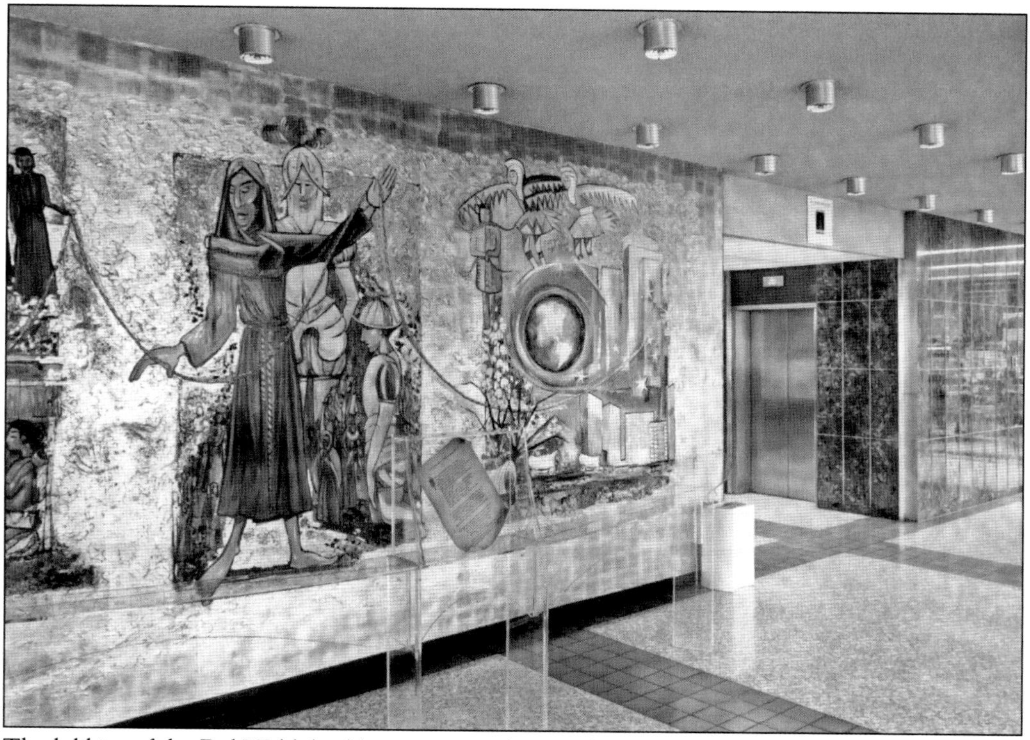

The lobbies of the Del Webb building contained artwork depicting the history of Arizona. In the main lobby, artist Elaine S. Michelson created this mural featuring the prehistoric period and early history of the state. (Courtesy of Del Webb Corporation Photographs, Arizona Collection, Arizona State University Libraries.)

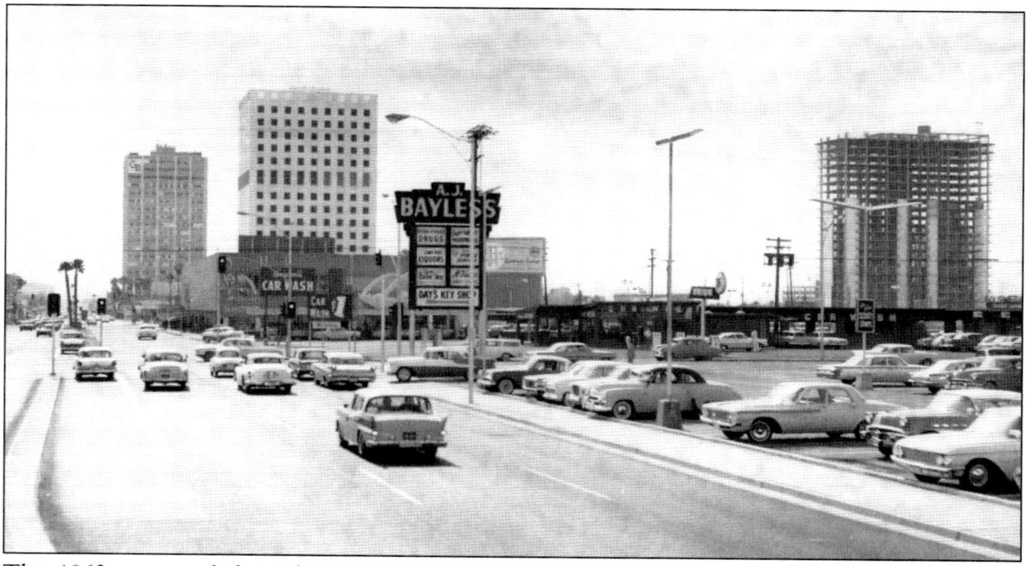

This 1963 view south from the intersection of Central Avenue and Indian School Road shows the newly completed Del Webb building and the Guaranty Bank building. To the right, the Executive Towers apartments (page 98) are under construction. A McDonald's, one of the first with the iconic Golden Arches, occupied the southwest corner of the intersection. (Courtesy of Del Webb Corporation Photographs, Arizona Collection, Arizona State University Libraries.)

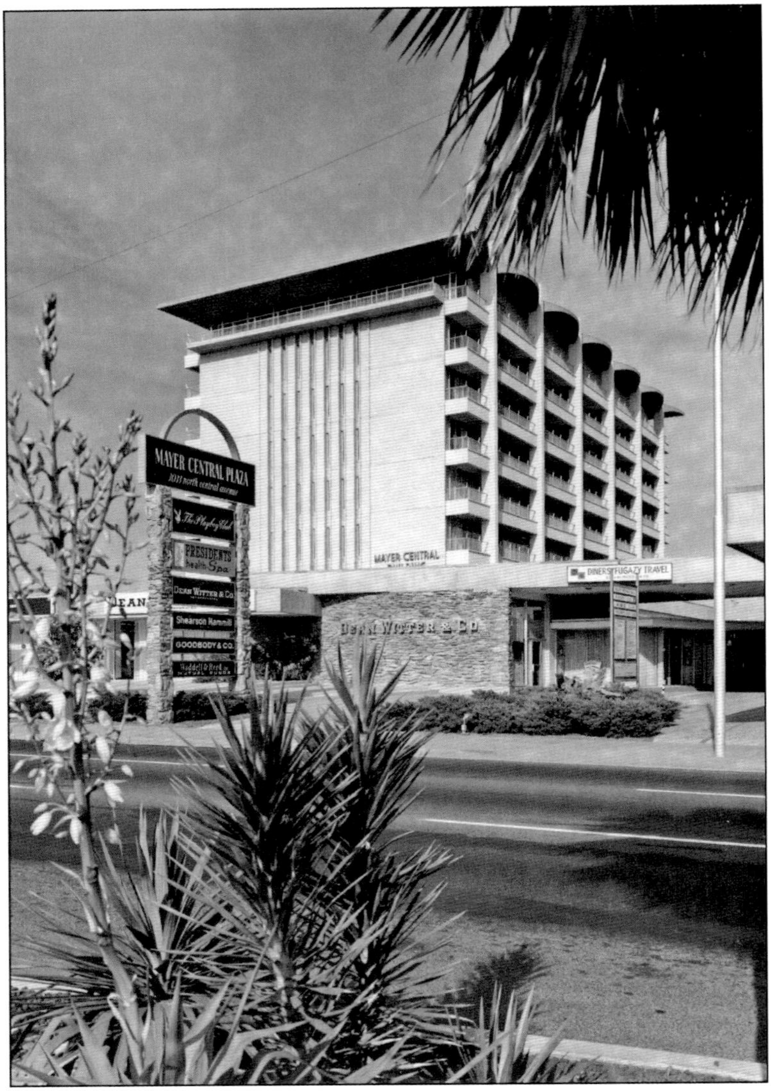

The Mayer Central office building was constructed by the Mayer Development Company at the southeast corner of Central Avenue and Earll Drive in 1959. This photograph shows the building in the mid-1960s. One of the tenants listed on the sign is the Playboy Club. (Courtesy of Del Webb Corporation Photographs, Arizona Collection, Arizona State University Libraries.)

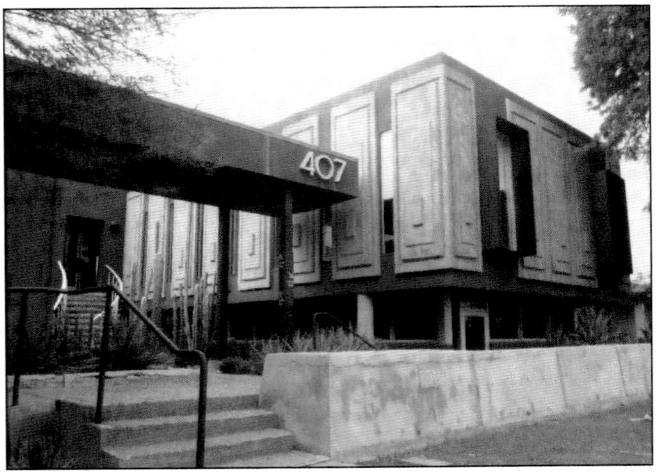

Royal Lescher and Leslie Mahoney established their architectural partnership in 1917. For many years, it was the go-to firm in Phoenix and Arizona for many public and private buildings. They built this office building on Osborn Road, west of Central Avenue, for their firm in 1963. The firm remained there until Mahoney's retirement in 1974. (Photograph by the author.)

The Phoenix Playboy Club opened in December 1962 and occupied the entire top floor of the Mayer Central office building. From 1966 to 1972, it was managed by Webb Ellis, shown at right with some friends in the lobby of the club. Members bought keys that gave them access to every club. Not only was the club a popular place, but it was also involved in various charities to assist veterans and Native Americans. Below, Ellis receives an award on behalf of the Playboy Club from Howard Adams for service to disabled veterans. The club closed in 1983. (Both, courtesy of Webb Ellis, Phoenix Playboy Club Manager, 1966–1972.)

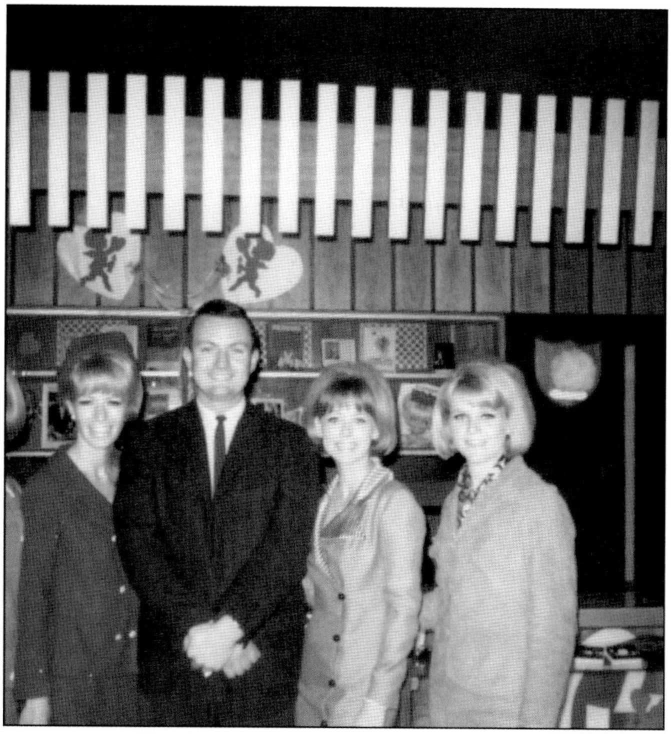

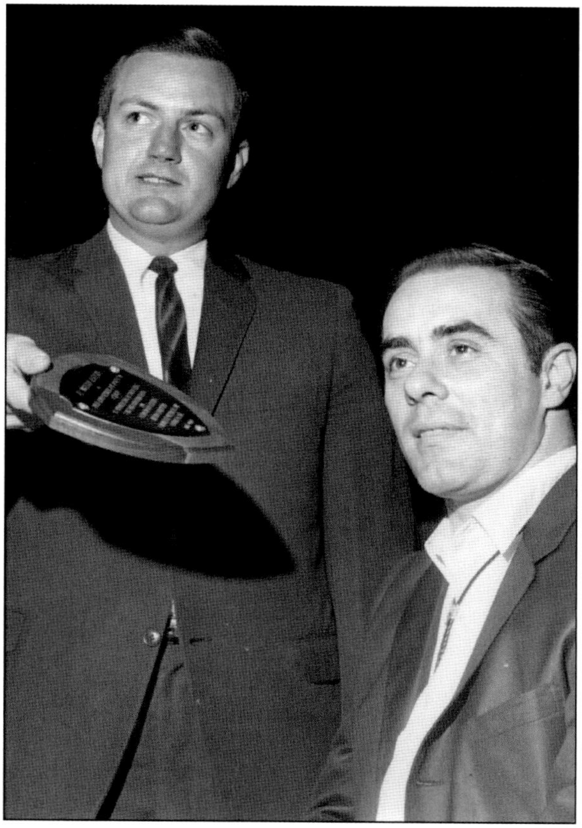

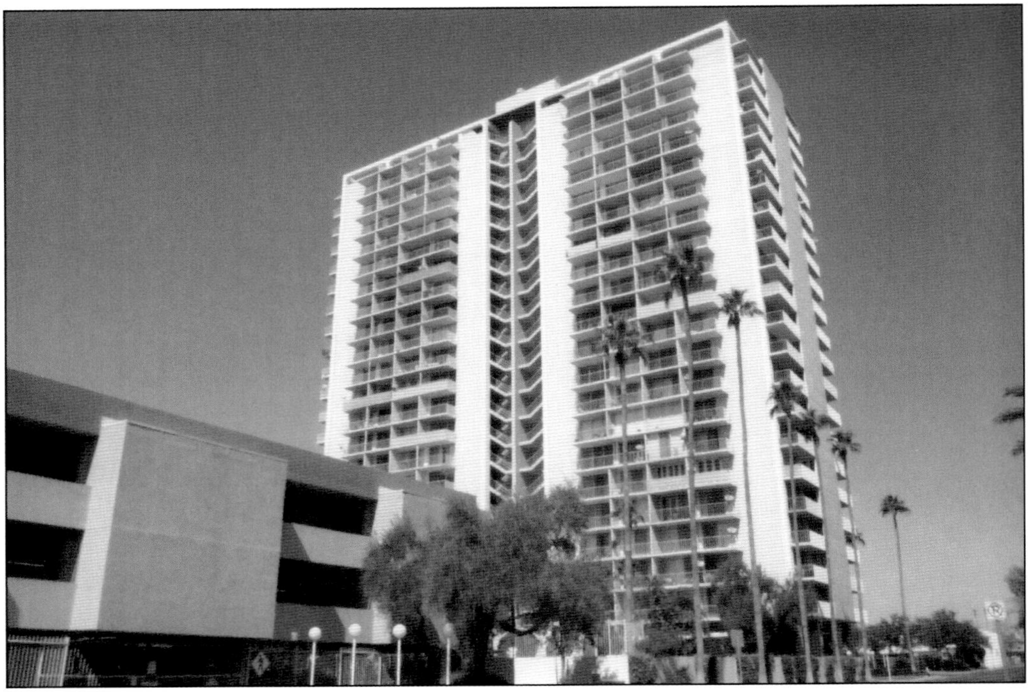

Located at the southwest corner of Clarendon and Second Avenues, the Executive Towers apartment building was the immediate neighbor of the new Rosenzweig Center that was under way to the east. Designed by architect Alfred Newman Beadle and completed in 1963, the 22-story tower had 160 apartments. The developers had planned a second tower, to be called the Imperial Towers, just to the west, but it was never built. (Photograph by the author.)

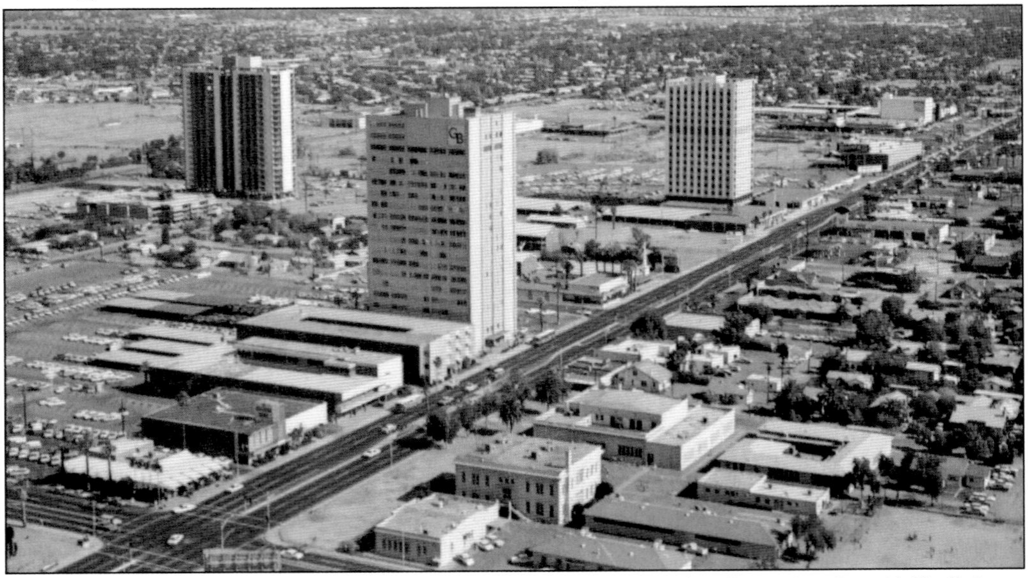

This photograph shows the intersection of Central Avenue and Osborn Road in 1963. Osborn School, at the corner, is about to be demolished. From left to right are the newly completed Executive Towers apartments, David Murdock's Guaranty Bank building, and Del Webb's headquarters. Helsing's restaurant (page 85) is seen at the intersection opposite the school. The changes can be compared with the photograph on page 88. (Photograph by Mike Roberts; author's collection.)

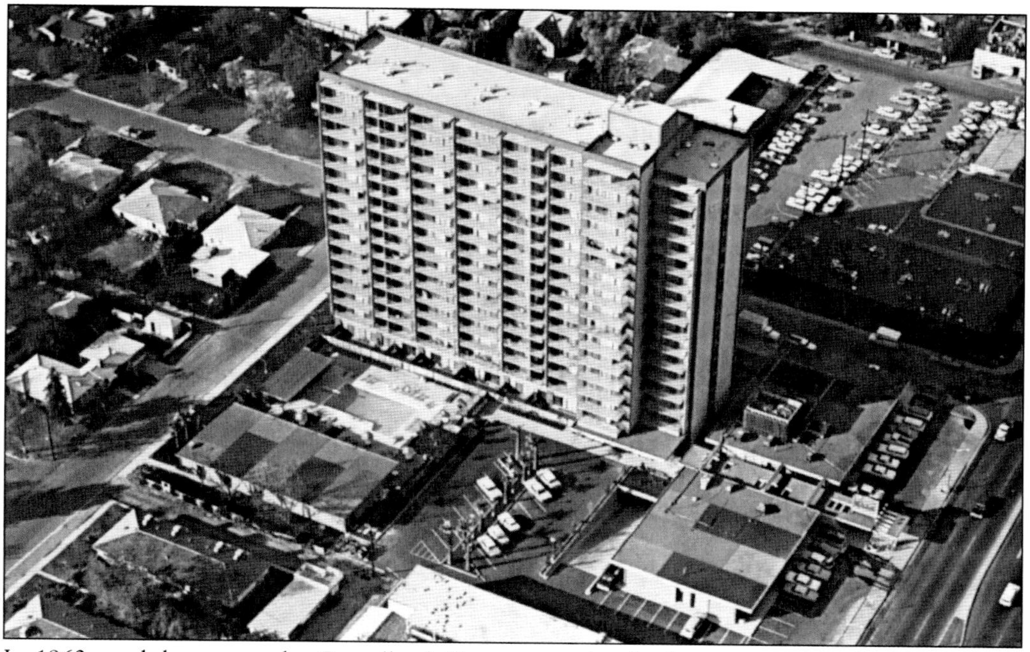

In 1963, work began on the Camelback Towers, another high-rise apartment building in the Central Corridor. Located on the west side of Central Avenue, just south of Camelback Road, it had 17 floors and 254 apartments. Rental rates started at $106 per month. It is now the Landmark on Central condominiums. (Author's collection.)

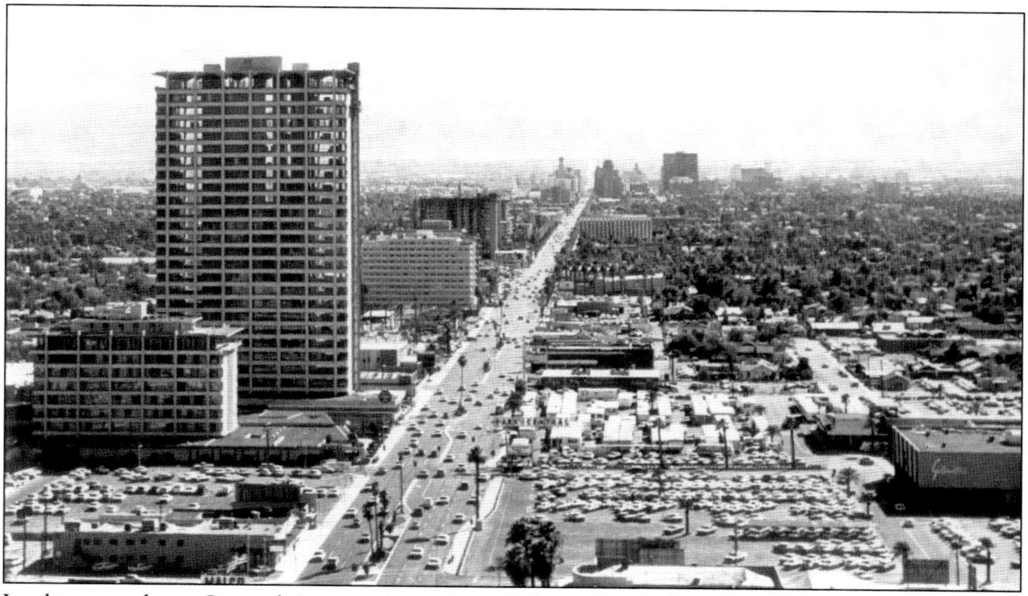

Looking south on Central Avenue from about Osborn Road, this 1964 photograph shows some of the major buildings in the Central Corridor. From left to right are (left of Central) the Mayer Central office, First Federal building (Phoenix Corporate Tower) under construction, Central Towers with the new south tower, and the Royal Towers (Regency on Central) under construction; (right of Central) the new Lawyers Title building (2200 North Central), Palms Theatre, and Park Central shopping mall. (Courtesy of William Dinwiddie Photographs, Arizona Collection, Arizona State University Libraries.)

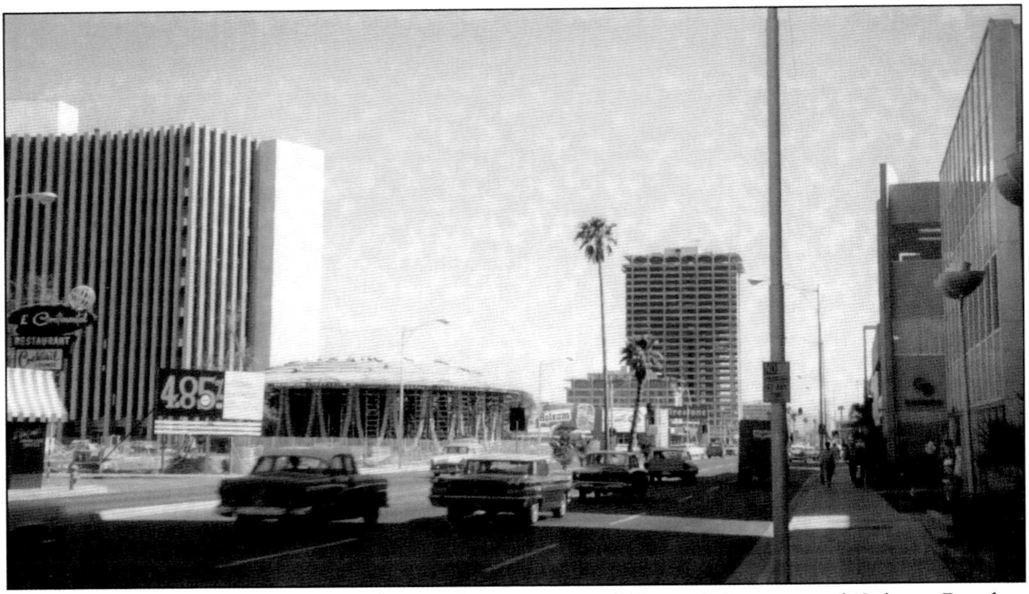

Above is the Financial Center at the northeast corner of Central Avenue and Osborn Road as it is nearing completion in 1964. The tower is fully enclosed, the southern rotunda still has its scaffolding, and the northern rotunda is just getting started. Designed by W.A. Sarmiento, it replaced the Osborn School (page 92). Farther to the south, the First Federal building (Phoenix Corporate Tower) is nearing completion. Below is the Financial Center as completed in 1964. Although the complex was originally envisioned with two towers along the Central Avenue frontage, only the south tower was built. (Above, author's collection; below, courtesy of Arizona State Library, Archives and Public Records, History and Archives Division, Phoenix, No. 98-1658.)

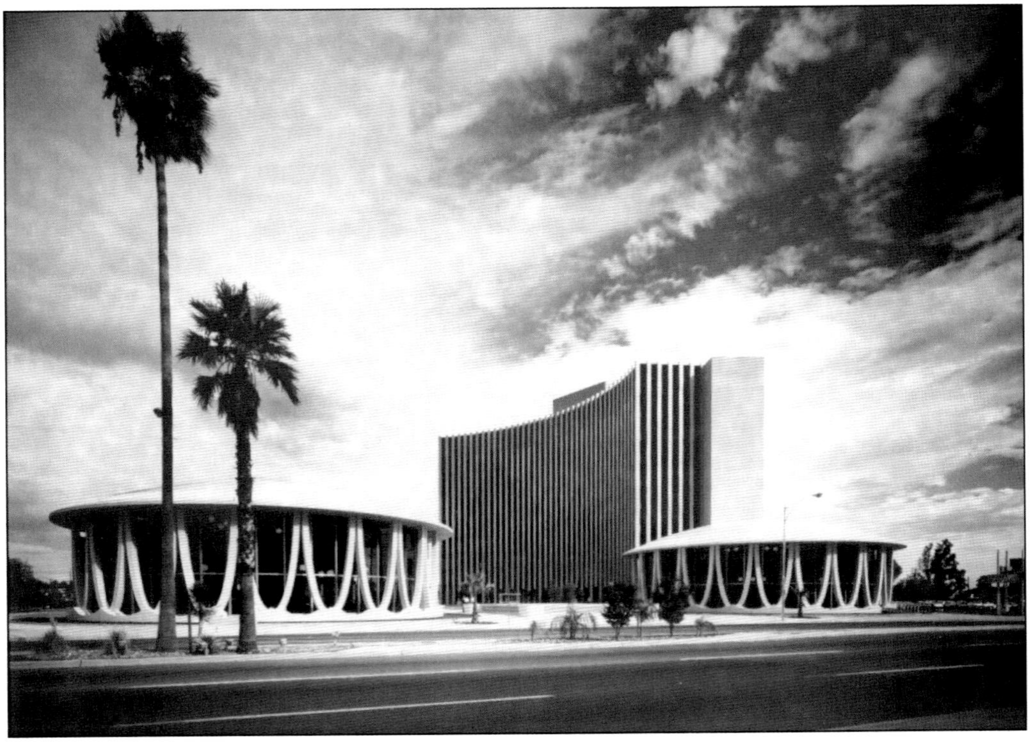

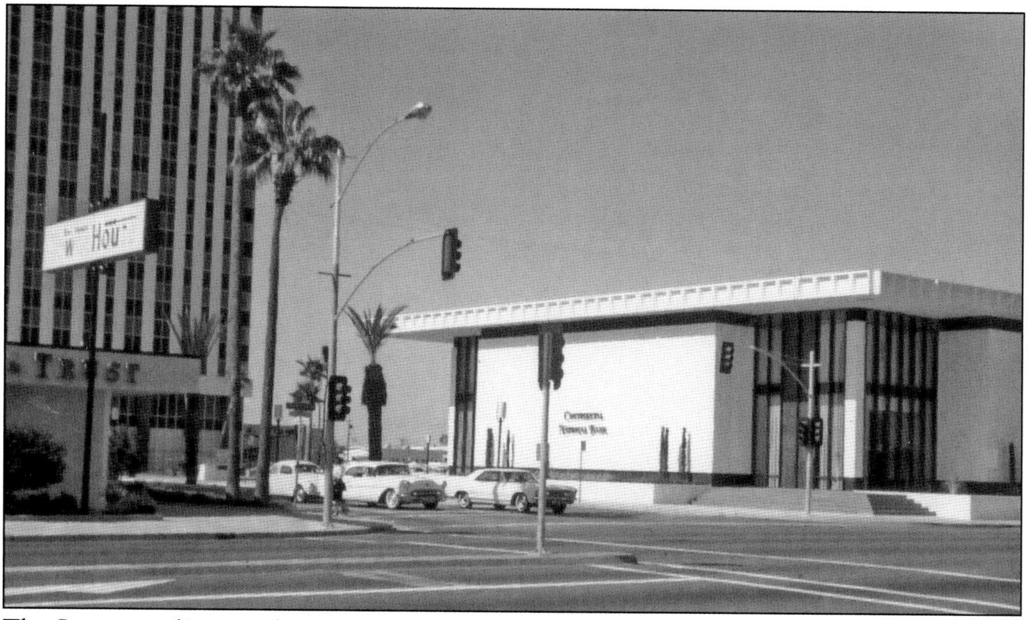

The Continental National Bank building stood at the northwest corner of Central and Clarendon Avenues. Designed by Flatow, Moore, Bryan & Fairburn and constructed in 1965, this structure was built by the Del Webb Corporation and stood at the gateway to the Rosenzweig Center. It was demolished in the late 1990s. (Author's collection.)

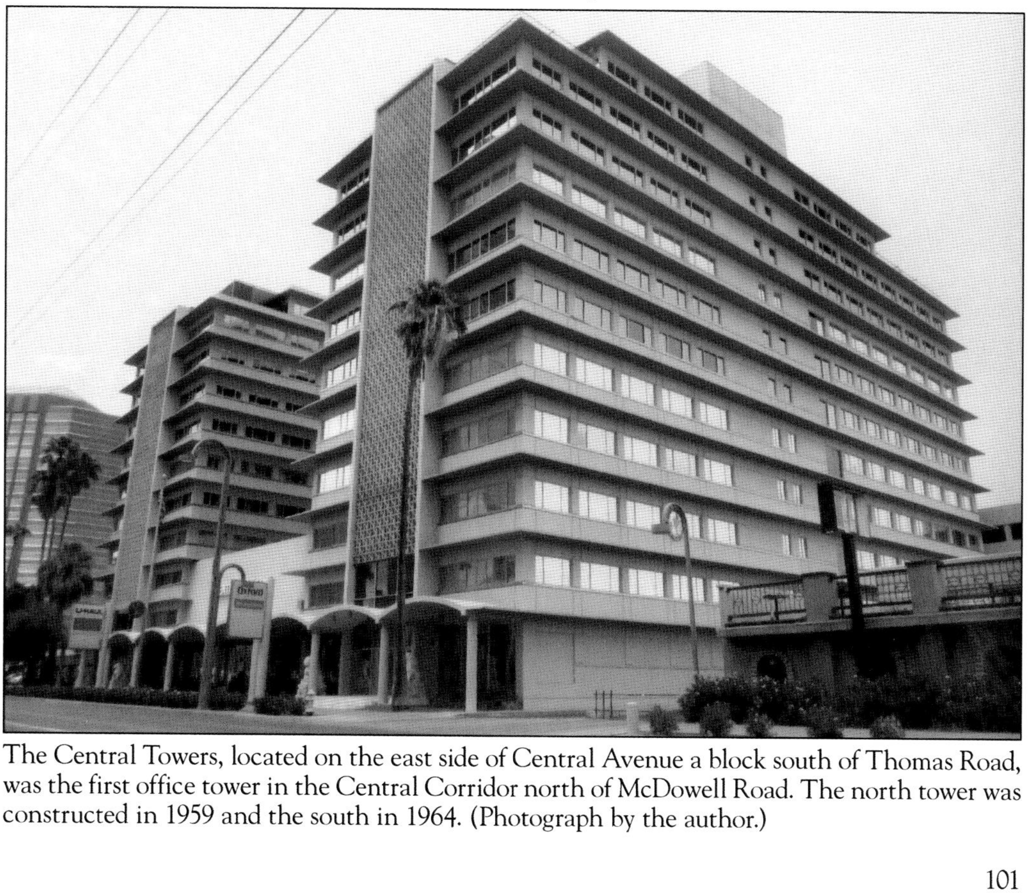

The Central Towers, located on the east side of Central Avenue a block south of Thomas Road, was the first office tower in the Central Corridor north of McDowell Road. The north tower was constructed in 1959 and the south in 1964. (Photograph by the author.)

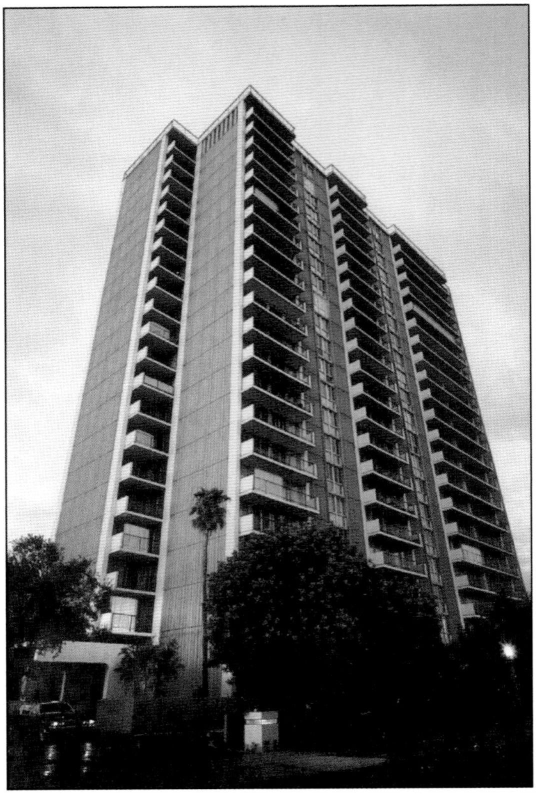

The Royal Towers complex (left), later Regency House, has been a fixture on North Central Avenue since 1965. This mid-century landmark at the northeast corner of Central and Hoover Avenues was designed by architect George Schoneberger and developed by Royal Properties. It was originally planned as condominiums, but an economic downturn forced its seizure by the lender shortly after completion. The new owners converted it into a rental apartment building. Then, in the early 1980s, it was converted back into condominiums. Royal Properties and Schoneberger also developed the Royal Willetta East apartments (below) on Willetta Street at Fifth Street at the same time. Both responded to a growing demand for luxury apartments in the central city. (Left, courtesy of Regency House Association; below, photograph by the author.)

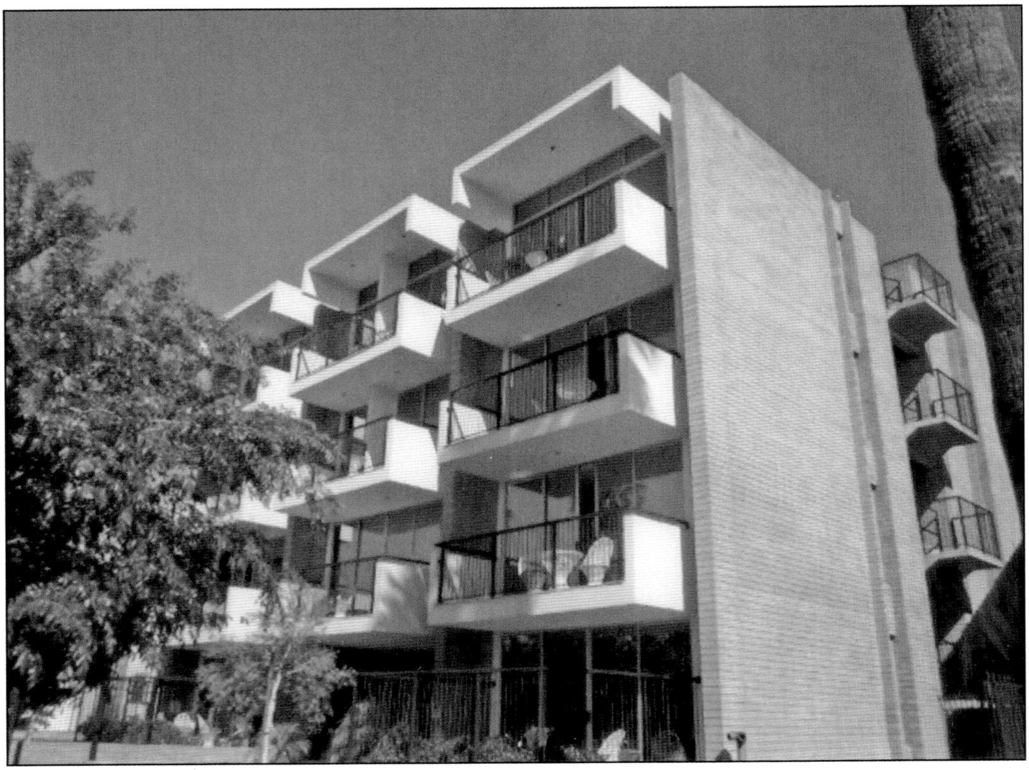

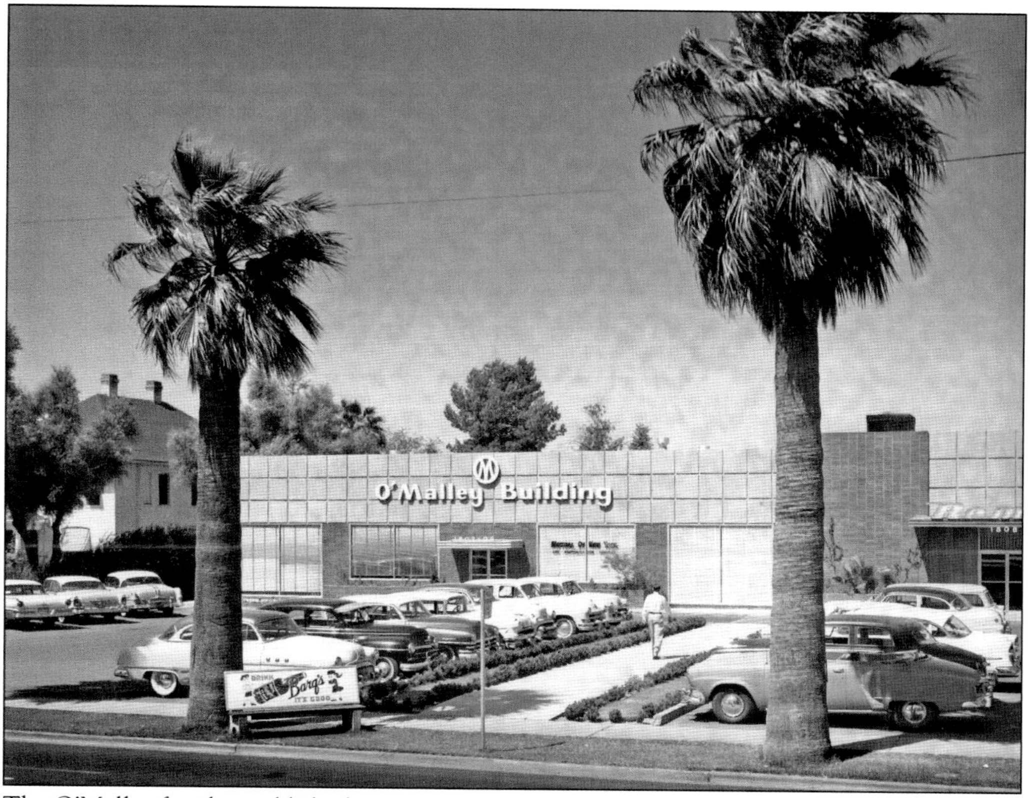

The O'Malley family established themselves in Phoenix at the turn of the 20th century. Originally from Missouri, they built an enterprise centered on building materials and rapidly established themselves as community and business leaders. The O'Malleys developed property on the west side of Central Avenue, just north of McDowell Road, for the O'Malley Lumber Company and their other businesses. Their first building (above), located at 1802 North Central Avenue, was constructed around 1954 to house their offices. In 1964, they constructed an office tower (right) at 1800 North Central Avenue, next to their existing building. Known as the O'Malley Building, it would stand on Central Avenue until the early 1990s. The Flinn Foundation and Arts Plaza Tower now occupy the sites of both buildings. (Both, courtesy of Timothy J. O'Malley.)

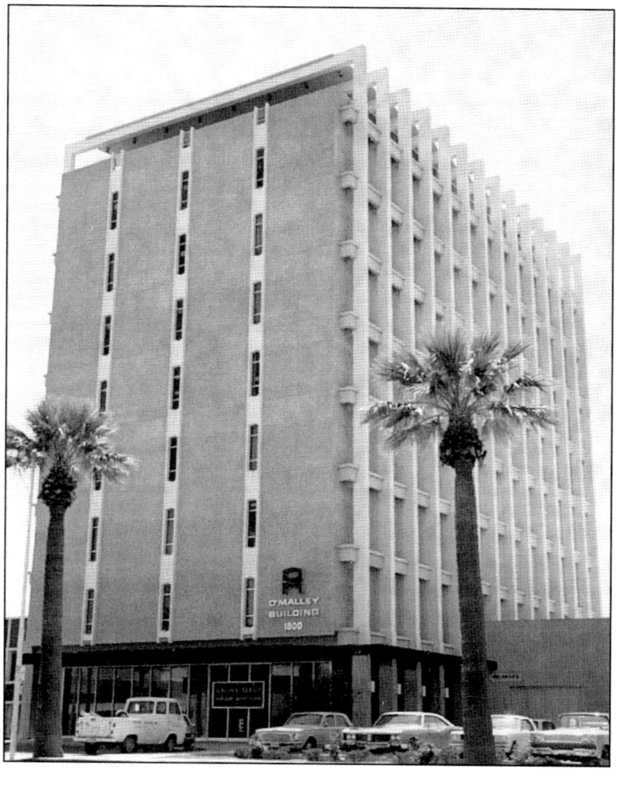

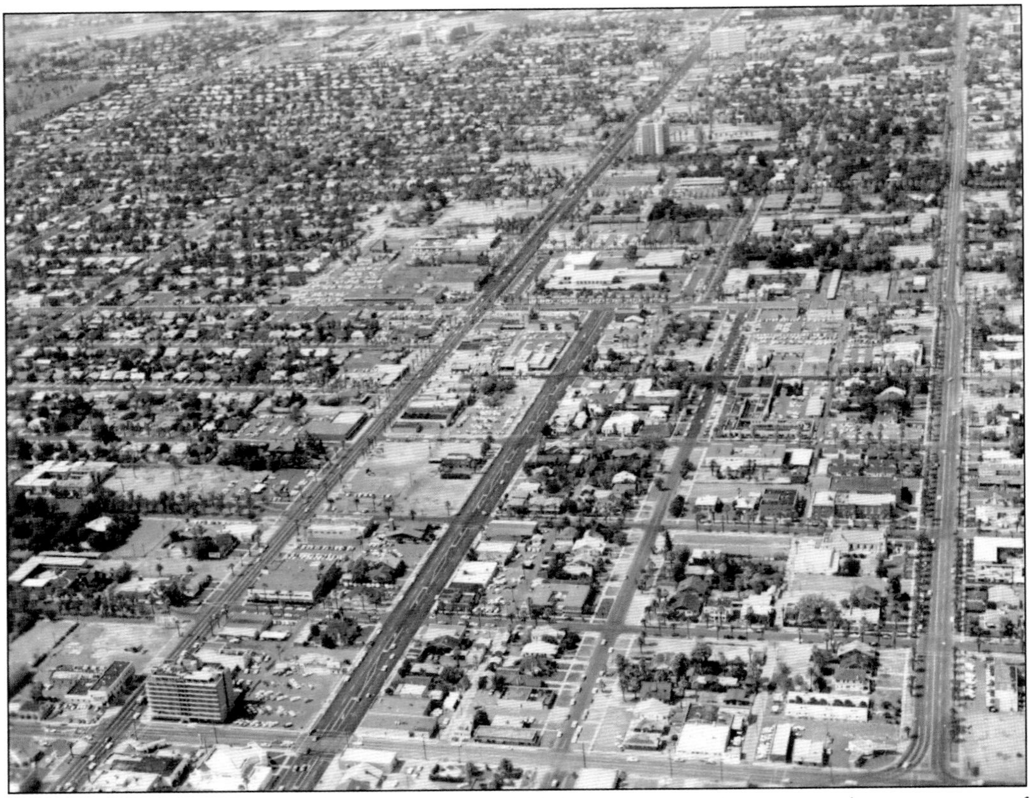

One of the most controversial issues that faced Midtown was the location and construction of the Papago Freeway. A freeway north of downtown had been planned since the mid-1940s. By the mid-1960s, the path of the elevated roadway had been proposed to run along Moreland Street, just south of McDowell Road. The aerial view above shows the affected area in the early 1960s. Central Avenue runs diagonally from the lower left corner. Also visible is the vacant land where homes and business had already been razed for future freeway construction. The photograph below shows a freeway hearing at the Arizona Highway Commission in the 1960s. The freeway route through established neighborhoods, along with the destruction of vintage buildings, generated passionate community opposition and neighborhood activism that was supported by Eugene Pulliam's *Arizona Republic*. (Both, courtesy of Arizona State Library, Archives and Public Records, History and Archives Division, Phoenix; above, No. 02-1835; below, No. 02-2580.)

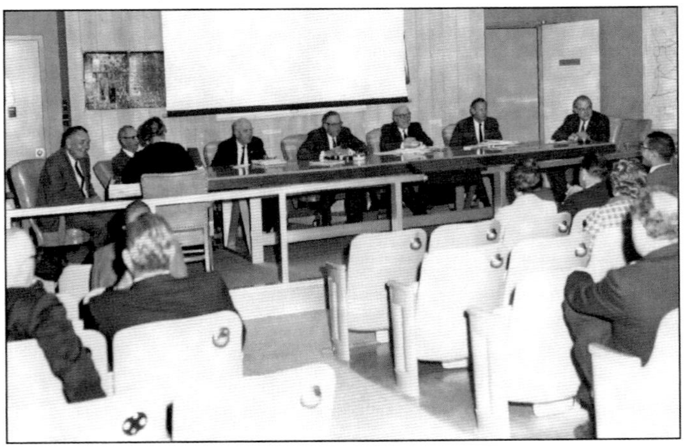

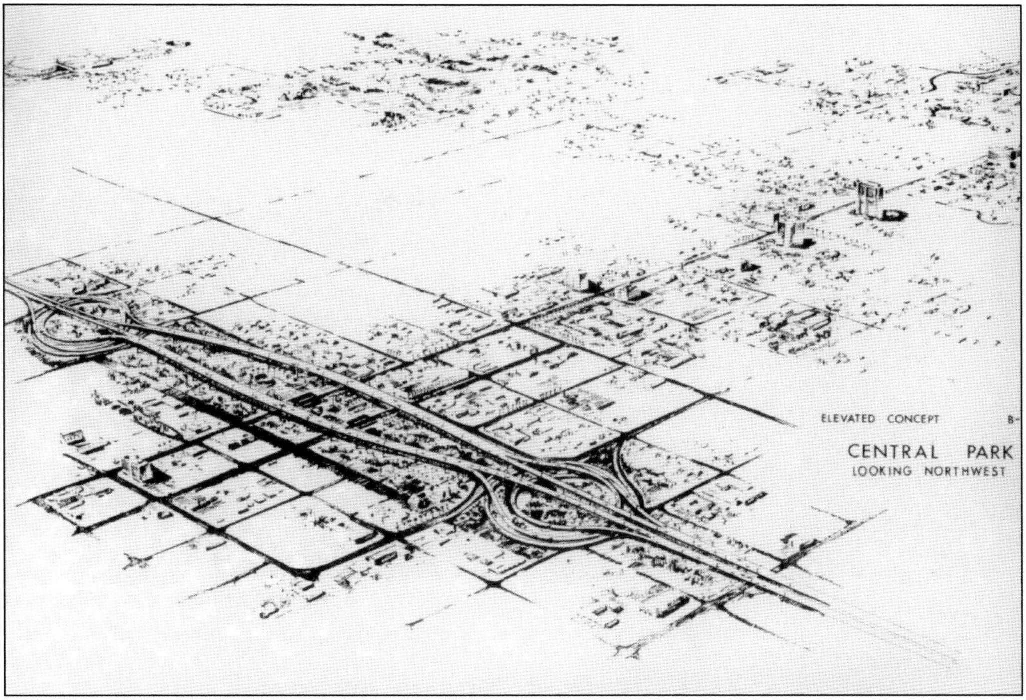

The plan for the Papago Freeway called for an elevated roadway about 100 feet tall over the Central Corridor with access from helicoid interchanges at Third Street and Third Avenue, as shown in the artist's rendering above. A public park was planned for the space underneath. The rendering below depicts how the freeway could appear as viewed south from Central Avenue and Willetta Street. The drawings show a benign situation, but there is little doubt the elevated freeway would have had a major negative impact on the area. The debate raged for years and spurred many residents of the area to get involved in the fight to save their homes and neighborhoods. The freeway opposition eventually won a referendum in 1973 that killed the overhead scheme. The Papago would be completed years later in 1990, but as an underground freeway with a park on top. (Both, courtesy of Encanto Citizens Association.)

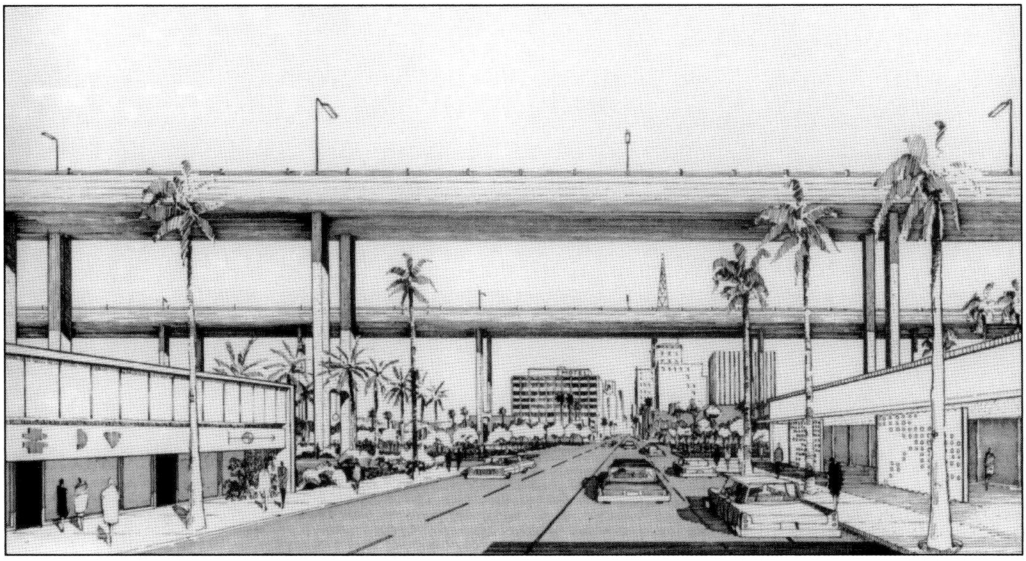

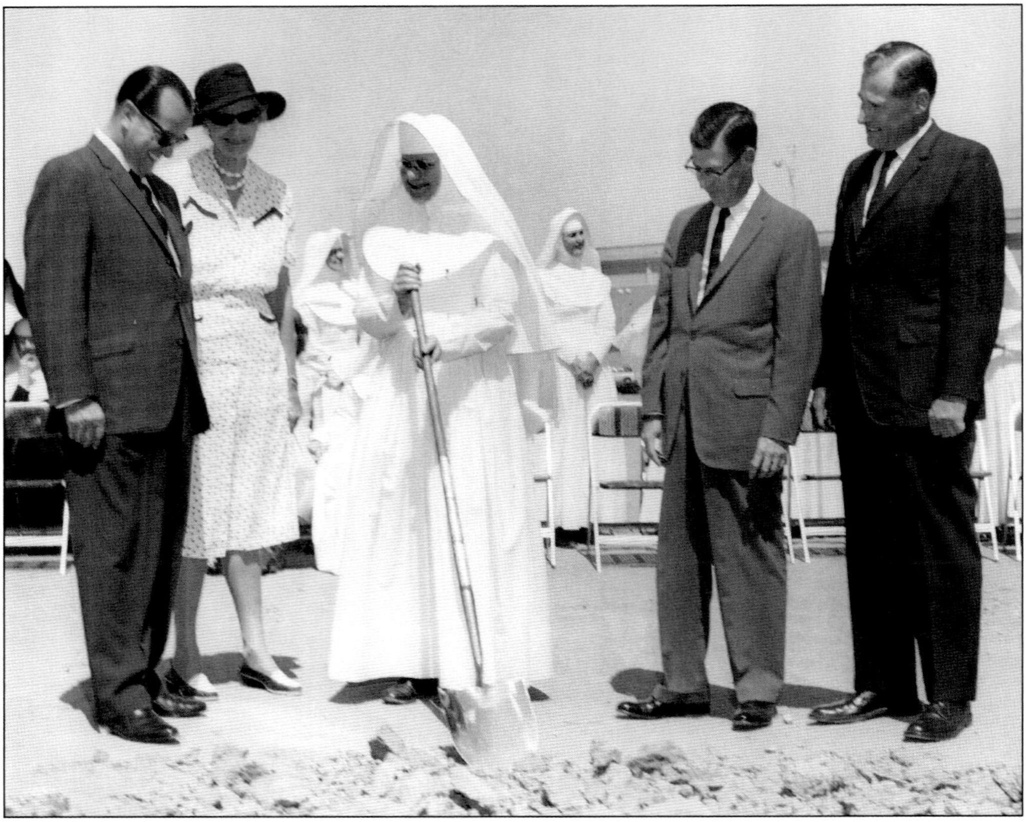

St. Joseph's Hospital (page 78) has steadily expanded since its opening in 1953. This 1964 photograph shows hospital administrator Sister Mary Placida breaking ground for a new long-term care unit at Third Avenue and Catalina Drive. Phoenix mayor Milton Graham (far left) and builder John Dickmann of Manhattan-Dickmann (far right) are also in attendance. Over the years, Dickmann was involved in many major construction projects throughout the valley, including some in Midtown. (Courtesy of Marilyn Dickmann Barrows.)

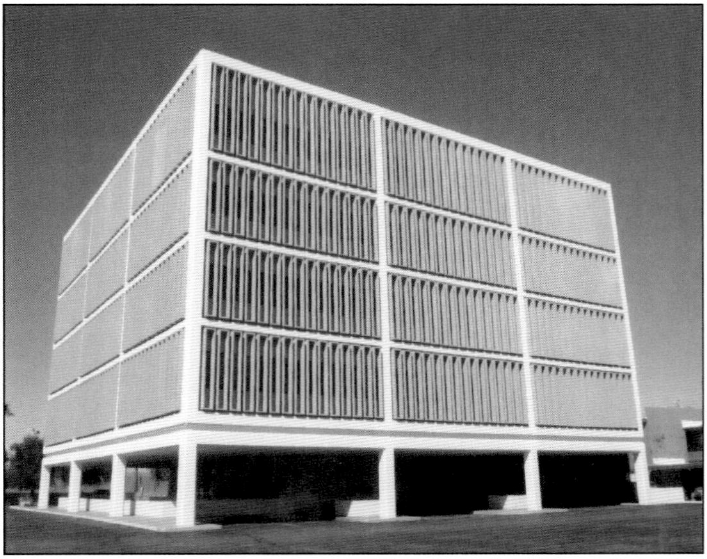

In 1967, the Fifth Avenue Medical Office Building went up just north of Osborn Road on land once occupied by the Sportsman's Park (page 69). It was designed by Alfred Newman Beadle, a prominent architect of the mid-century modern movement known for his work in glass, steel, and concrete. The Central Corridor is home to a number of buildings designed by Beadle. (Photograph by the author.)

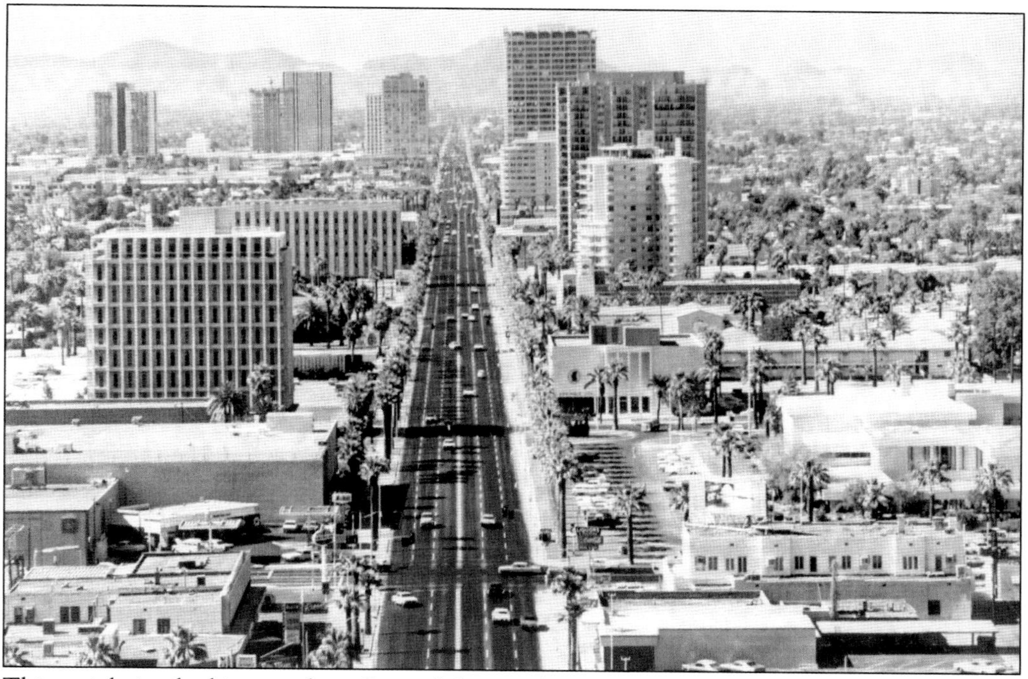

This aerial view looking north on Central Avenue from McDowell Road shows the Midtown area around 1970. When compared with the aerial photograph taken in 1948 (page 8), tremendous change can be seen over two decades. While it appears heavily built up, more high-rises would go up in the Central Corridor during the next two decades. (Courtesy of Herb and Dorothy McLaughlin Collection, Arizona State University Libraries.)

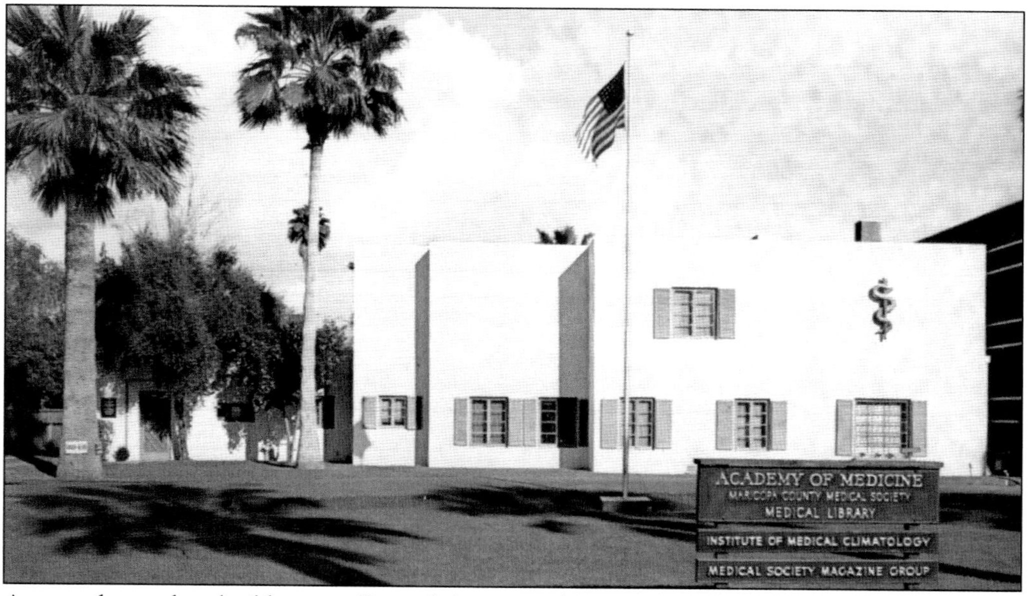

Among the modern buildings on Central Avenue, a few remnants of earlier times remained. The Academy of Medicine occupied a converted house on the east side of Central Avenue, south of Palm Lane. As commercialization moved north from downtown, many houses on Central Avenue were converted to commercial use before being torn down for redevelopment. This building survived into the late 1980s. (Author's collection.)

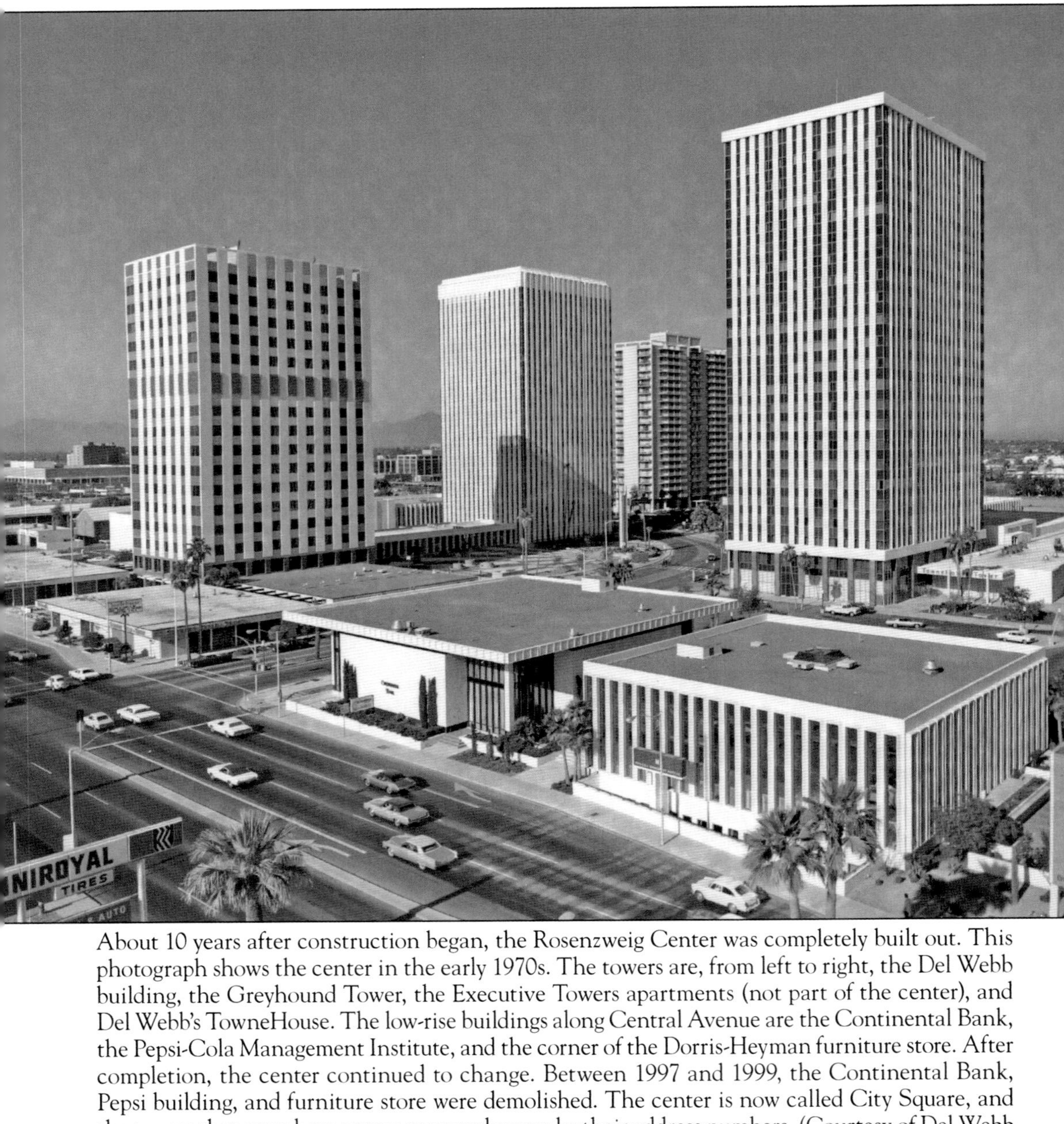

About 10 years after construction began, the Rosenzweig Center was completely built out. This photograph shows the center in the early 1970s. The towers are, from left to right, the Del Webb building, the Greyhound Tower, the Executive Towers apartments (not part of the center), and Del Webb's TowneHouse. The low-rise buildings along Central Avenue are the Continental Bank, the Pepsi-Cola Management Institute, and the corner of the Dorris-Heyman furniture store. After completion, the center continued to change. Between 1997 and 1999, the Continental Bank, Pepsi building, and furniture store were demolished. The center is now called City Square, and the towers that once bore names are now known by their address numbers. (Courtesy of Del Webb Corporation Photographs, Arizona Collection, Arizona State University Libraries.)

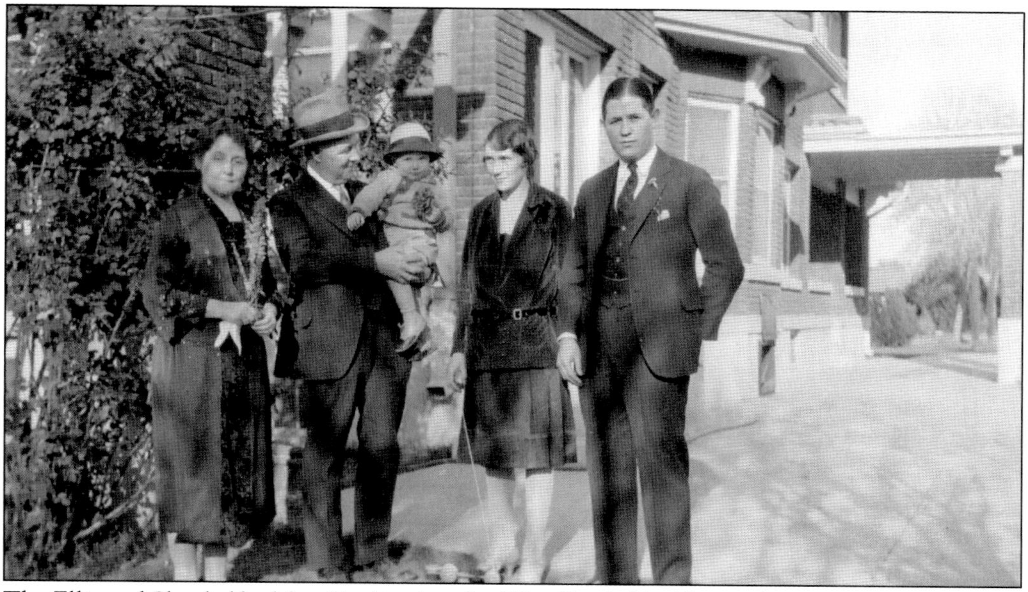

The Ellis and Shackelford families lived in the Ellis-Shackelford house (page 41) until 1964. The above photograph, taken in front of the house in 1926, shows, from left to right, Reba Blount Ellis and Dr. William Ellis holding grandson James Shackelford. With them are daughter Helen Ellis Shackelford and son-in-law Dr. J. Gordon Shackelford. Even though it was condemned for construction of the Papago Freeway (page 104), it was not demolished. Instead, it became a home for boys, then later the offices and museum for the Arizona Historical Society. Mirroring the 1926 group, the below photograph from the 1972 dedication ceremony shows, from left to right, Dr. J. Gordon Shackelford, Phoenix mayor John Driggs, Helen Shackelford, and son James Shackelford. The Ellis-Shackelford house is the only unaltered survivor of the mansions that once occupied Central Avenue in Midtown. Today, it is owned and preserved by the City of Phoenix and is the home of Arizona Humanities. Mayor Driggs was an early, active, and effective proponent of historic preservation. (Both, courtesy of the Shackelford family.)

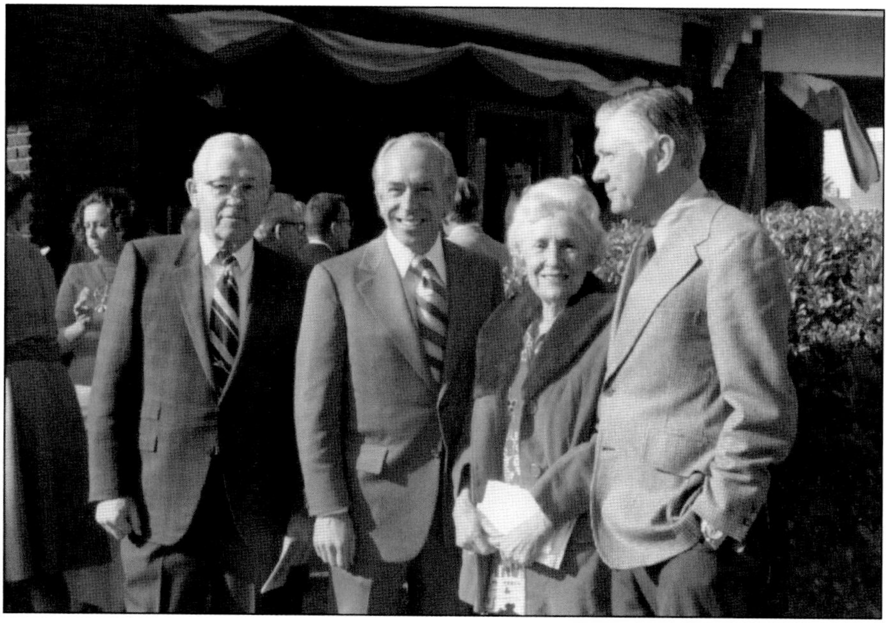

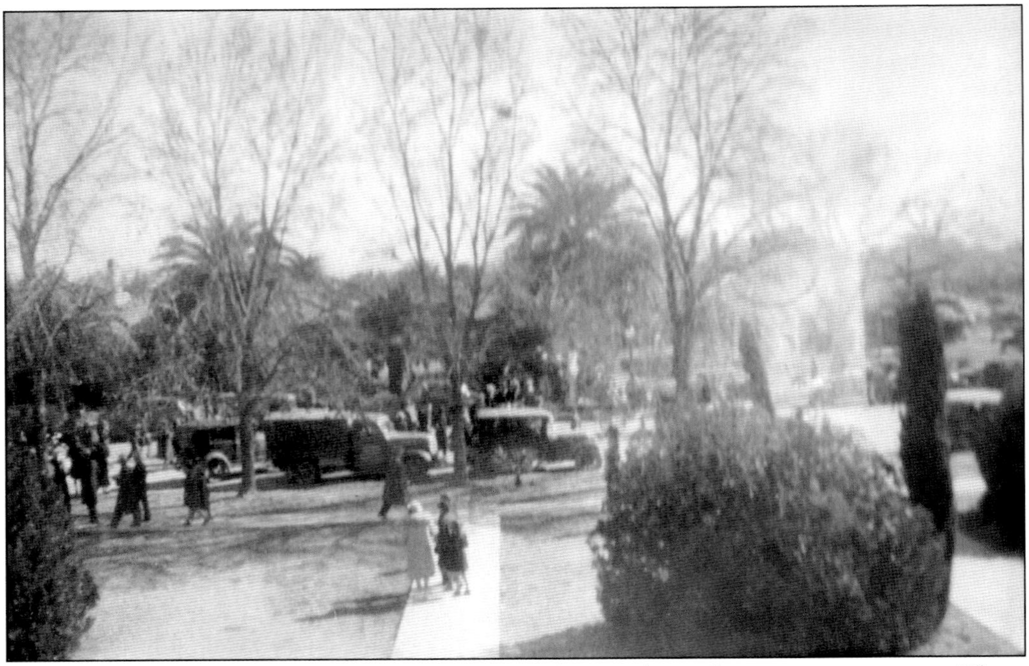

For many years, Central Avenue was the location for parades and various street events. These photographs show parades from different eras. Above is a Fiesta de Sol parade in front of the Ellis-Shackelford house in the 1930s. Below is a Fiesta Bowl parade on Central Avenue, just north of McDowell Road, in the late 1970s. Among the visible landmarks are the Central Methodist Church (page 81), Phoenix Towers (page 86), Regency House (page 102), and the First Federal tower (page 100). (Above, courtesy of the Shackelford family; below, courtesy of the Arizona State Library, Archives and Public Records, History and Archives Division, Phoenix, No. 03-0375.)

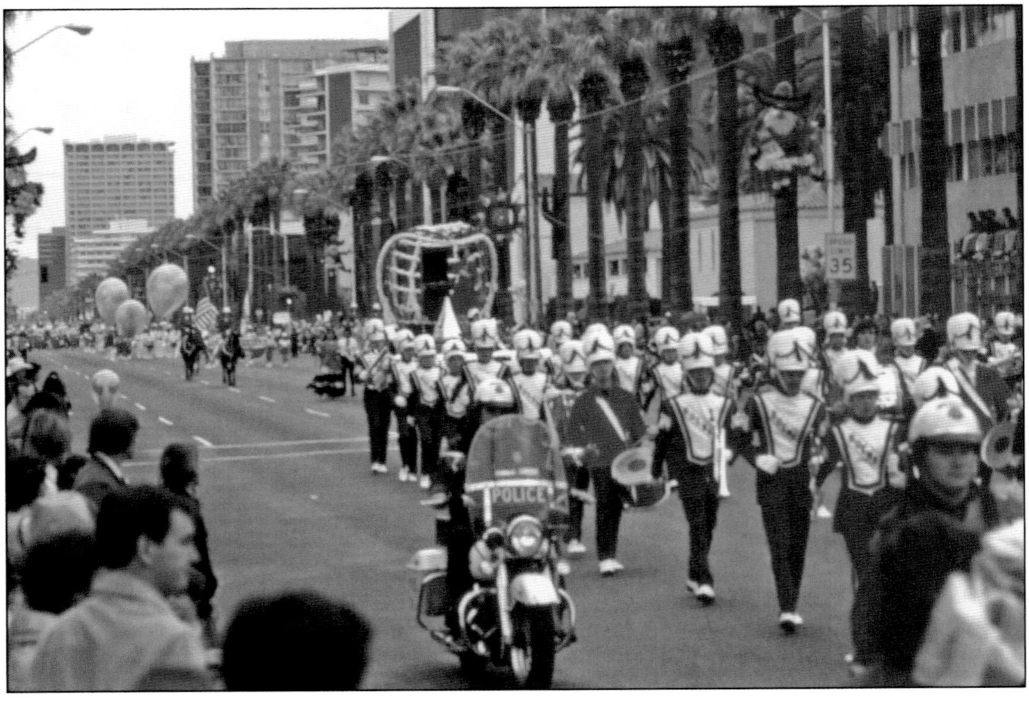

In 1970, an additional eight floors were added to the Financial Center tower. This photograph from the mid-1970s shows the addition. The difference can be contrasted with the images on page 100. (Author's collection.)

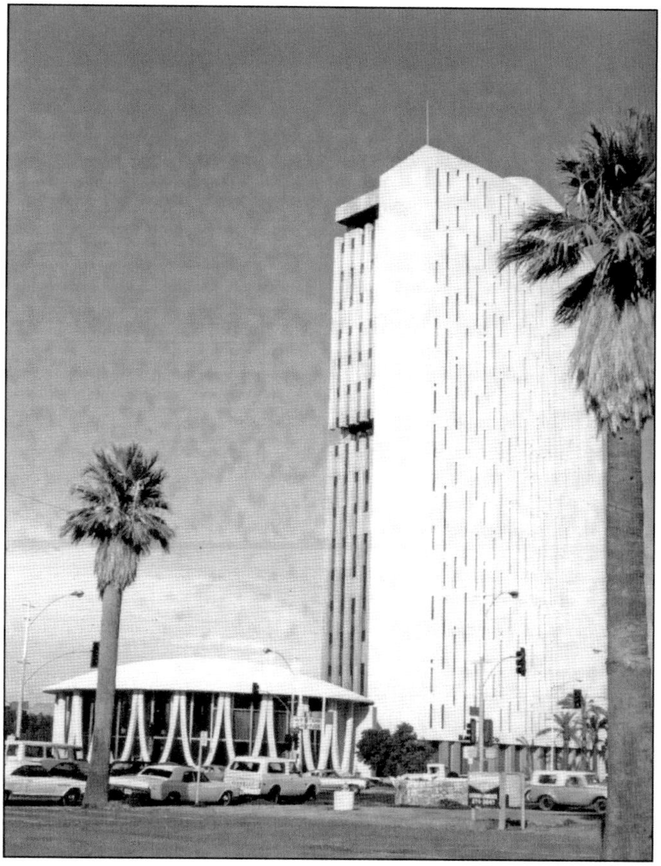

This house at the southeast corner of Central and Ashland Avenues was built around 1915 and became the last unaltered house on Central between McDowell and Thomas Roads. For a number of years, it was a rental then an art studio before being moved to a new location. It is pictured here in 2005 shortly before relocation. (Courtesy of City of Phoenix Historic Preservation Office, Planning and Development Department.)

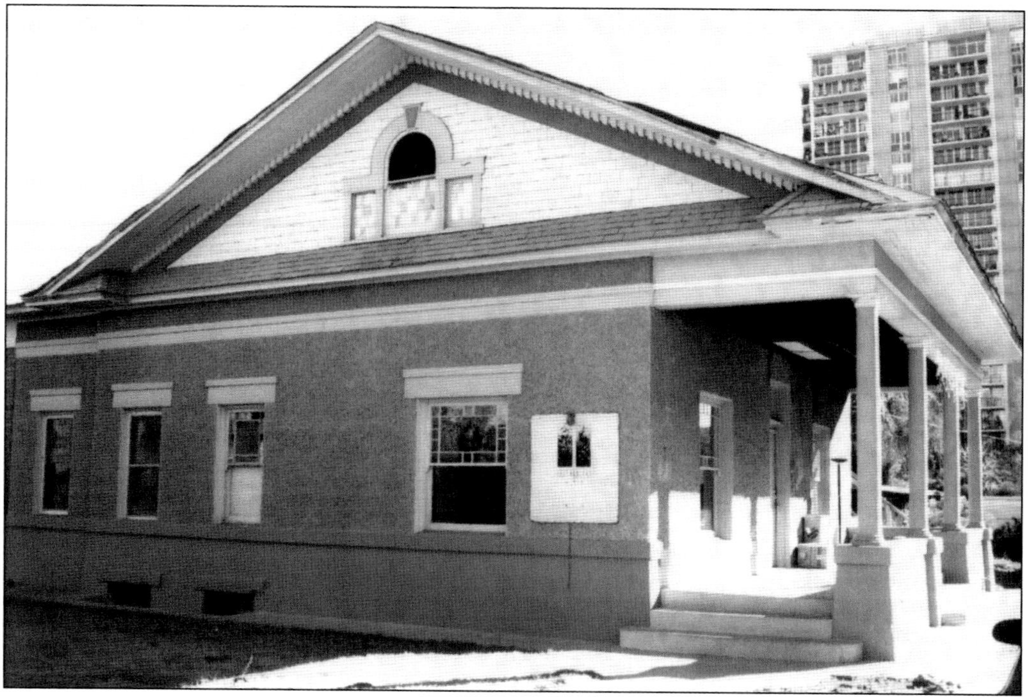

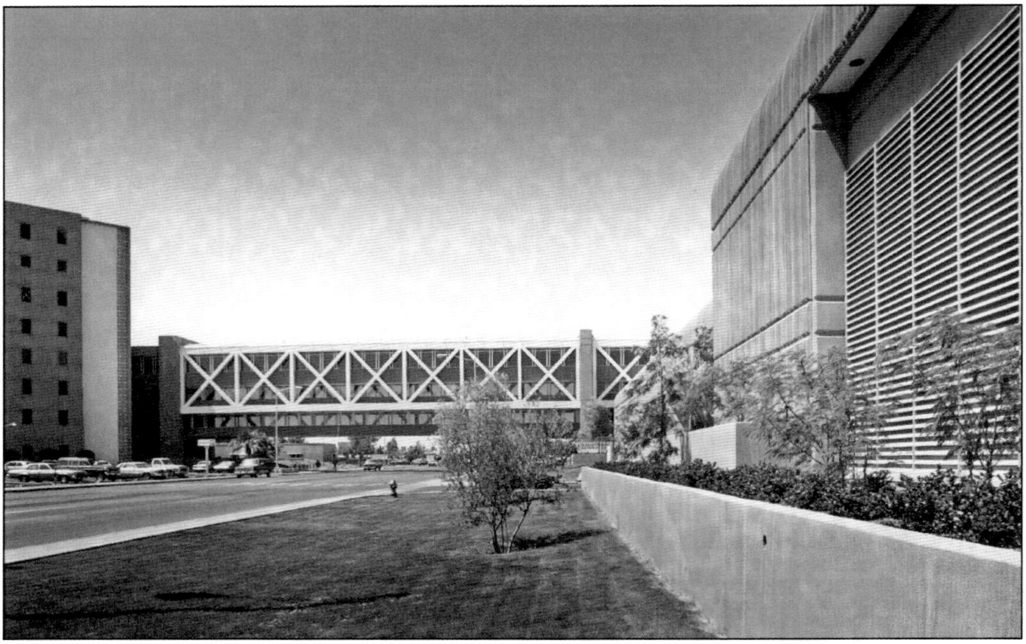

St. Joseph's Hospital and Medical Center continued expansion into the 1980s. While the original building has remained, other architects have added their own approach to the facility as the campus has grown. Architect Reginald Sydnor, AIA, of Varney Sexton Sydnor Architects, designed the major expansion, which included the outpatient facility on Third Avenue and the three-story pedestrian bridge that connected the new facilities to the parking structures to the east. Both were constructed in a 1981 expansion. Above is the bridge, which utilized the first private air rights over a Phoenix right-of-way. Below is the interior of the admitting lobby in the outpatient facility and its impressive use of space and light. (Both, photograph by Koppes Photography, Inc., Varney Sexton Sydnor Architects, Inc.)

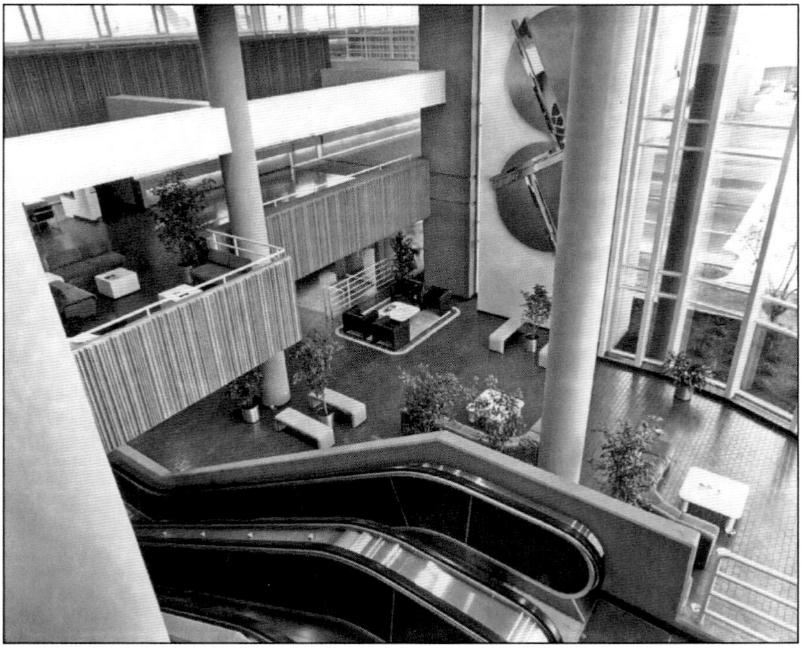

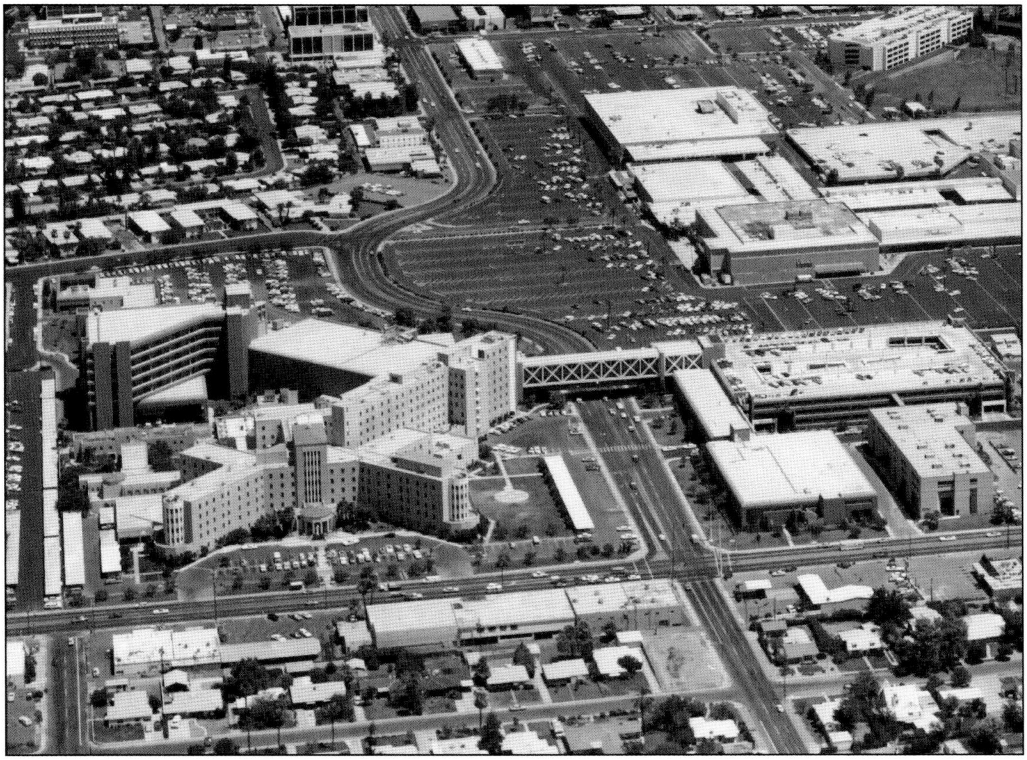

This aerial view of St. Joseph's Hospital shows the expansion into the mid-1980s from the original campus seen on page 78. The pedestrian bridge connects the hospital to new buildings on Catalina Drive. The frontage along Thomas Road (foreground), vacant in the early 1950s, has been built out with commercial buildings. Park Central Mall is in the background. (Courtesy of Douglas Sydnor, FAIA.)

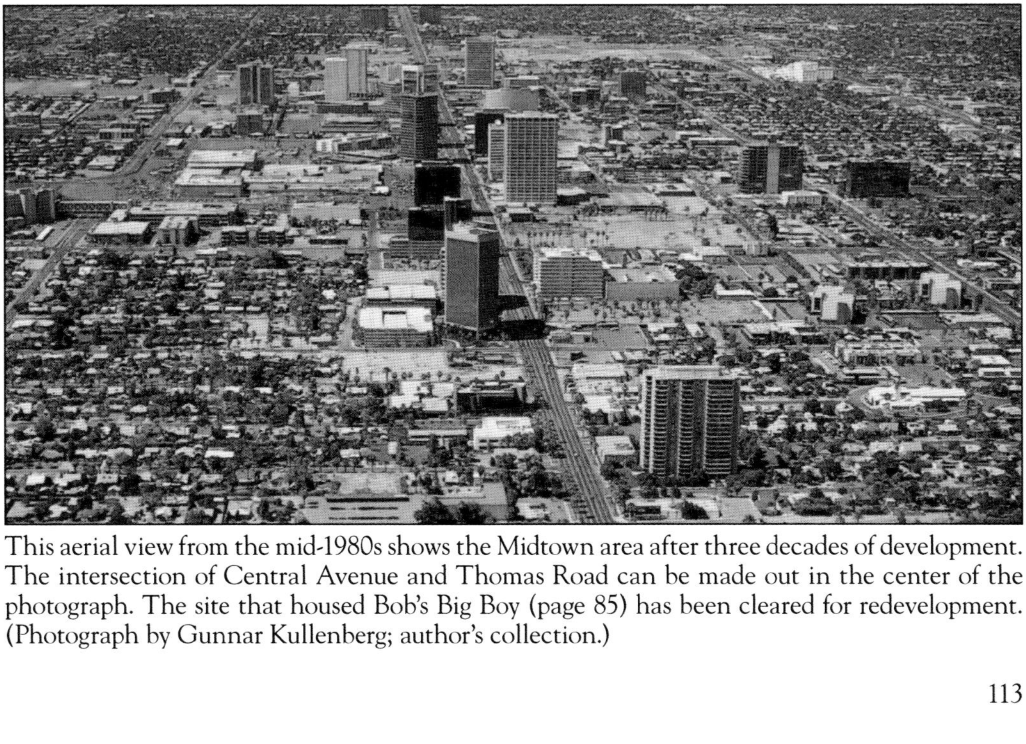

This aerial view from the mid-1980s shows the Midtown area after three decades of development. The intersection of Central Avenue and Thomas Road can be made out in the center of the photograph. The site that housed Bob's Big Boy (page 85) has been cleared for redevelopment. (Photograph by Gunnar Kullenberg; author's collection.)

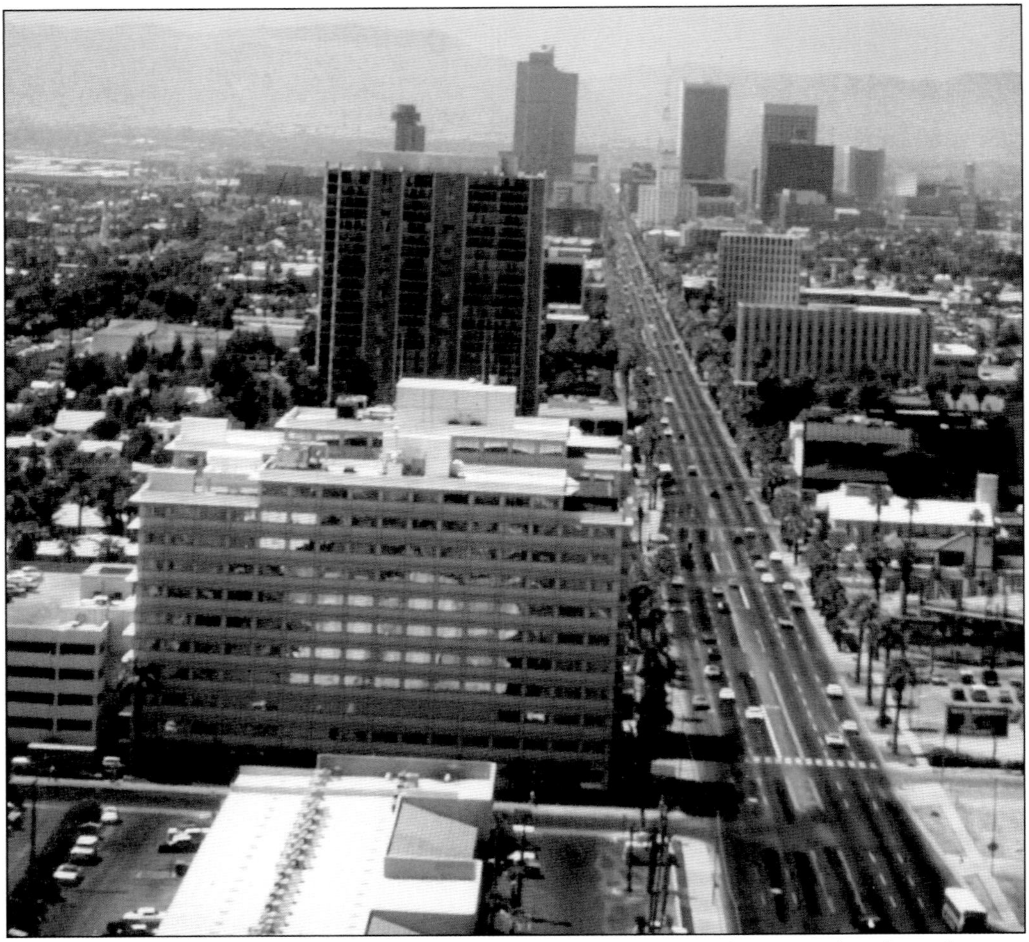

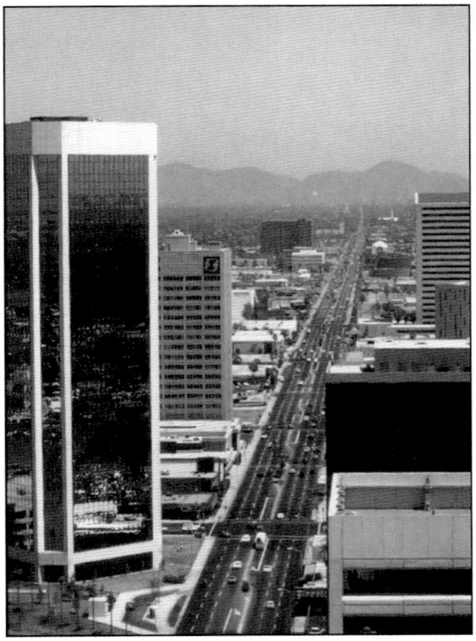

These 1982 photographs were taken from the Phoenix Corporate Tower. The above photograph looks south on Central Avenue across Thomas Road. On the left are the Central Towers and the Regency House. Downtown is in the background. On the right are the Westward Ho Hotel, the O'Malley Building, the 2200 Building, and the Central Baptist Church. The Palms Theatre has just been demolished, and the Phelps Dodge tower, now the 2600 Building, is under construction in its place. The left photograph looks north on Central Avenue from the same location. On the left side of the street are the 3300 Tower, the First Interstate (former Guaranty Bank, now 3550 North Central) building, and Camelback Towers (now Landmark on Central). On the right are the CBIZ Plaza, Century Plaza (now One Lexington condominiums), Financial Center, Central Plaza tower, and the dome of St. Francis Xavier. (Both, photograph by Paul Reitmeir; author's collection.)

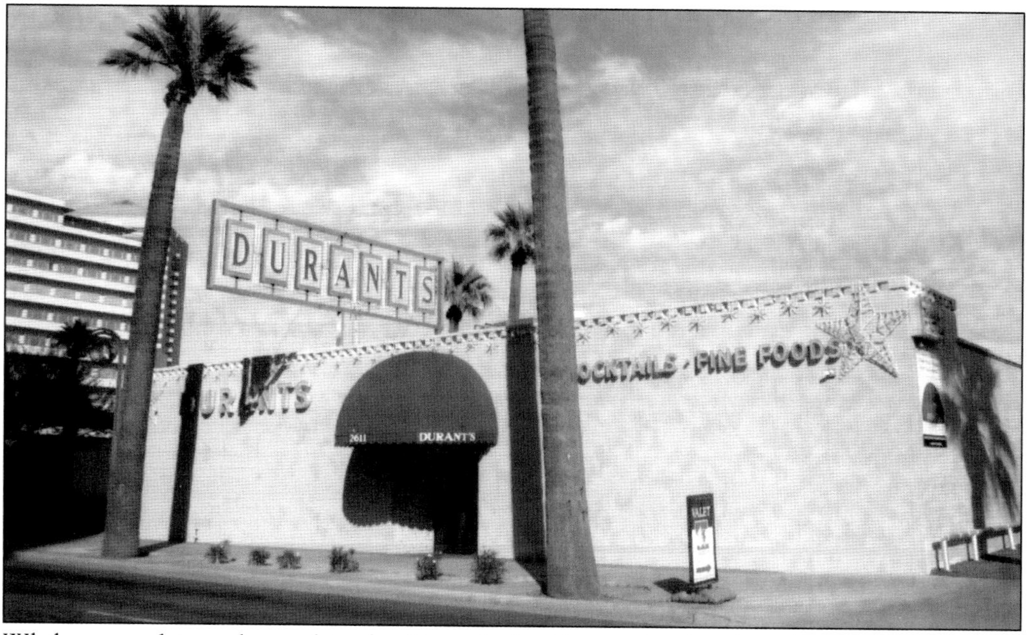

While many things changed in the Central Corridor in the decades after the war, Durant's restaurant, established by Jack Durant in 1950, remained a fixture. While the formal entrance is on Central Avenue, frequent customers enter from the rear entrance through the kitchen. Durant's has long been frequented by Phoenix movers and shakers who found its dark, quiet interiors conducive to conducting business. (Photograph by the author.)

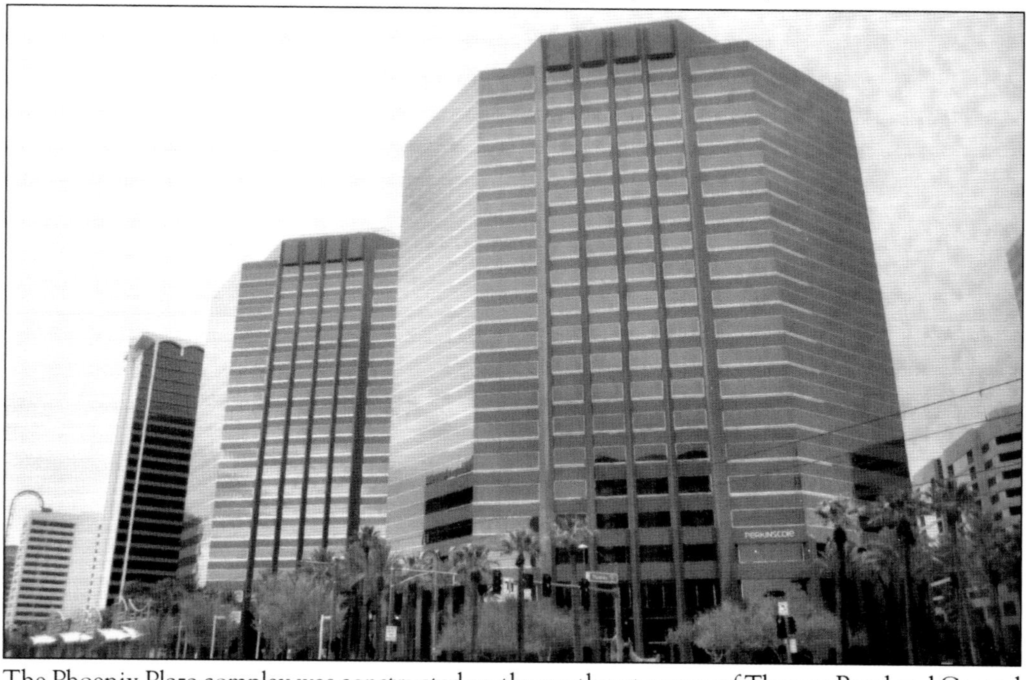

The Phoenix Plaza complex was constructed on the northeast corner of Thomas Road and Central Avenue between 1988 and 1990. Originally the site of Palm Lodge (page 32) and Bob's Big Boy (page 85), its four office and hotel towers cover over 10 acres. It was one of the last major office complexes constructed in Midtown. (Photograph by the author.)

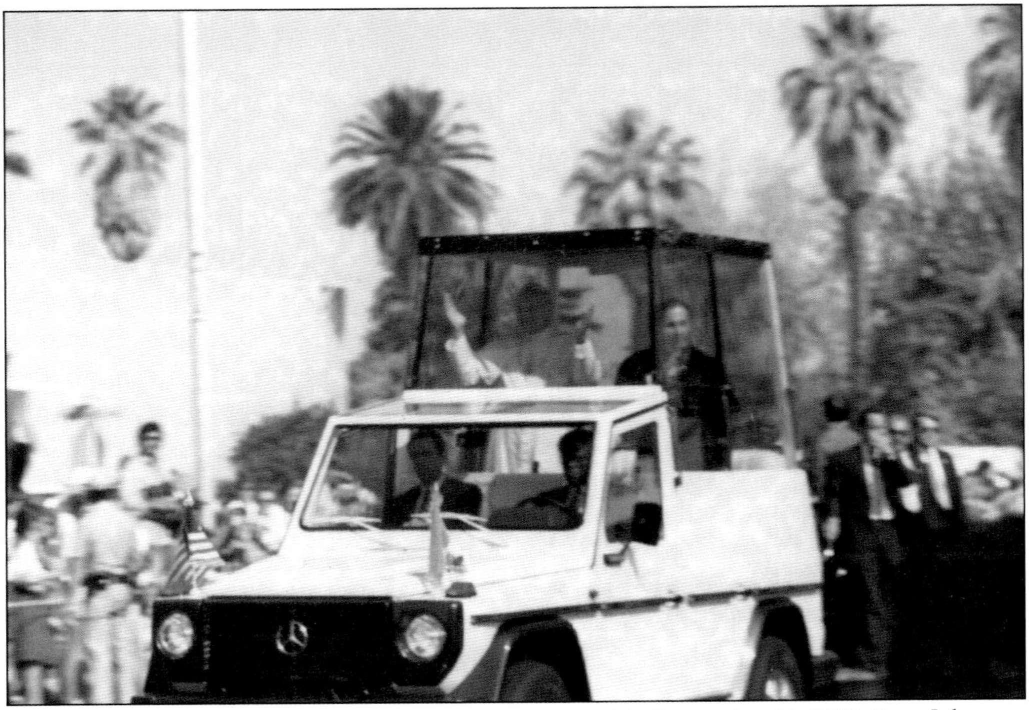

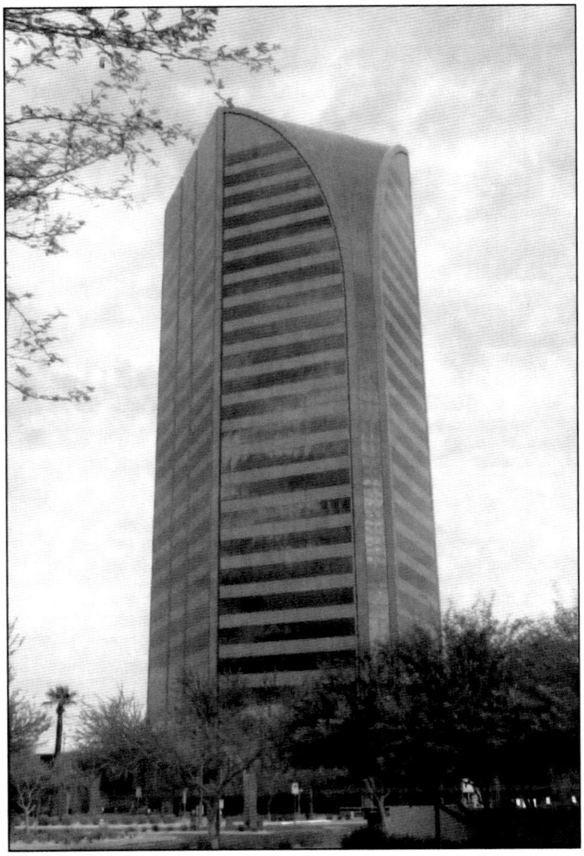

On September 14, 1987, Pope John Paul II visited Phoenix during a tour of the United States. He arrived in the morning and started the day with a visit to St. Joseph's Hospital. By mid-morning, he had begun a motorcade south on Central Avenue to St. Mary's Basilica downtown. This photograph shows the pope in his "Popemobile" on Central Avenue, just south of the Regency House. (Courtesy of Regency House Association.)

In 1991, the Dial Tower was completed on the site of the original O'Malley Building (page 103). Although the project was originally conceived with twin towers, the second one was never constructed. The second tower location is now a park. Located near the Phoenix Art Museum, Heard Museum, and other arts destinations, it was renamed the Central Arts Plaza in 2015. It was the last tower constructed in Midtown. (Photograph by the author.)

Five

Retreat and Renewal 1992–2015

After the boom years of the 1960s, major construction in Midtown slowed in the 1970s but continued into the 1980s. By the 1990s, however, the nexus of major commercial development had shifted to the Camelback Corridor, and downtown Phoenix was making a comeback. Many of the Midtown office towers constructed during the 1960s no longer attracted tenants, and their space went vacant. No longer economically viable, some of the 1950s and 1960s buildings were torn down. Park Central Mall, once teaming with shoppers, gradually lost its retail establishments in the early 1990s, and much of its space became office use. The construction of the Papago Freeway along the Moreland Corridor in the 1980s also disrupted Midtown activities and traffic. A savings and loan crisis in the early 1990s caused a major recession and further reduced the demand for new construction.

Despite the challenges, some positive things occurred that helped set the stage for a Midtown revival. While the Papago Freeway might have destroyed many historic buildings, the controversy it generated sparked a preservation movement in the 1970s. In 1984, the City of Phoenix, under the leadership of Mayor Terry Goddard, formed an ad hoc committee on historic preservation. The following year, the city established its Historic Preservation Office, Historic Preservation Commission, and legislation that provided overlay zoning and funding that could both protect and preserve historic buildings and neighborhoods. Over the years, a number of neighborhoods and buildings in Midtown were designated as historic and saved from demolition.

An increased interest in urban living, as well as the attractive historic neighborhoods and mid-century architecture, began drawing residents back into Midtown. Many saw definite advantages to living close to downtown, with its new sports and entertainment venues. An emerging and energetic arts district, along with major expansions of the Phoenix Art Museum and Heard Museum, also added to the attraction. A new central library rose beside the new freeway. Instead of being torn down, many existing buildings were updated or underwent adaptive reuse. At this writing, a number of multi-family and mixed-use projects are under construction in the Midtown area.

If the 1990s saw a decline for Midtown, the new century shifted to opportunity and revival.

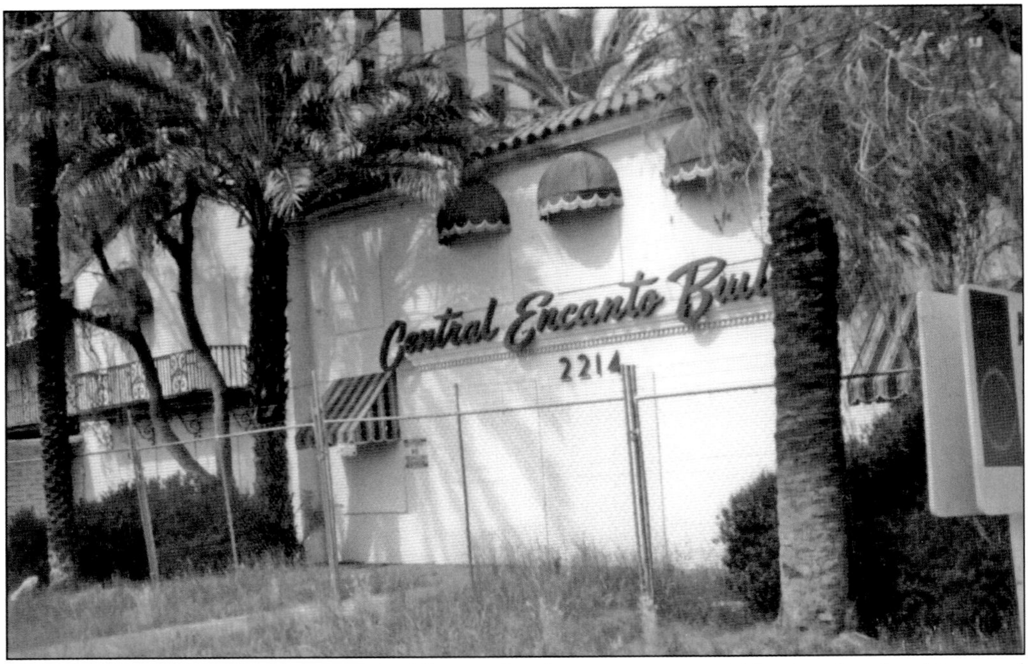

The Papago Freeway issue (pages 104–105) stimulated an interest in neighborhood and architectural preservation, which gained momentum in the 1970s and 1980s. When opened in 1939, apartments at the El Encanto building on the southwest corner of Central Avenue and Encanto Boulevard rented for as low as $85 and had tenant-controlled refrigeration air-conditioning. In the 1960s, it was converted to office space and closed in the 1980s. Severely damaged by fires in 1991, it was in a dilapidated condition, as shown above in 1992, and slated for demolition. Preservation activists recognized its historical value, as well as rehabilitation potential, and campaigned to save it. Below is a group of preservationists demonstrating in front of the El Encanto. Preservationist G.G. George, who campaigned vigorously to save residential neighborhoods from the Papago Freeway through Midtown, holds a sign that says "Save Our Heritage." (Both, courtesy of Encanto Citizens Association.)

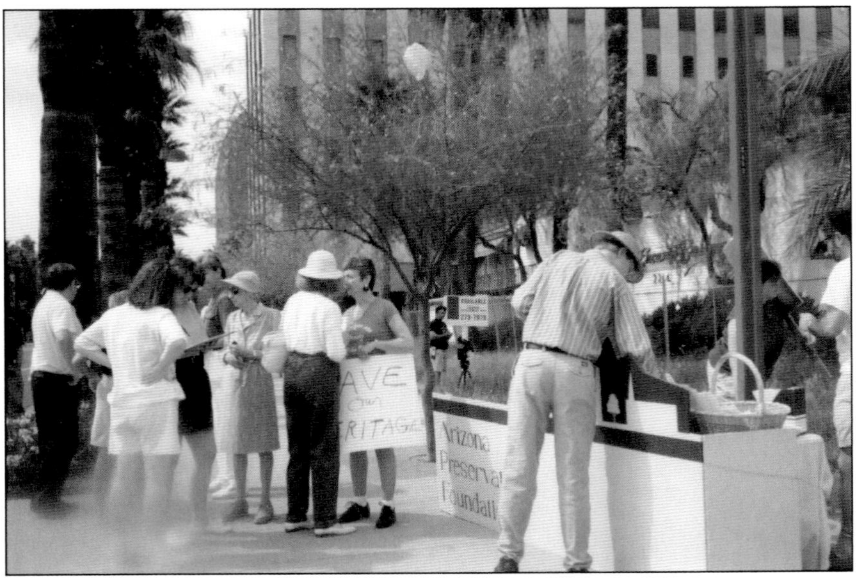

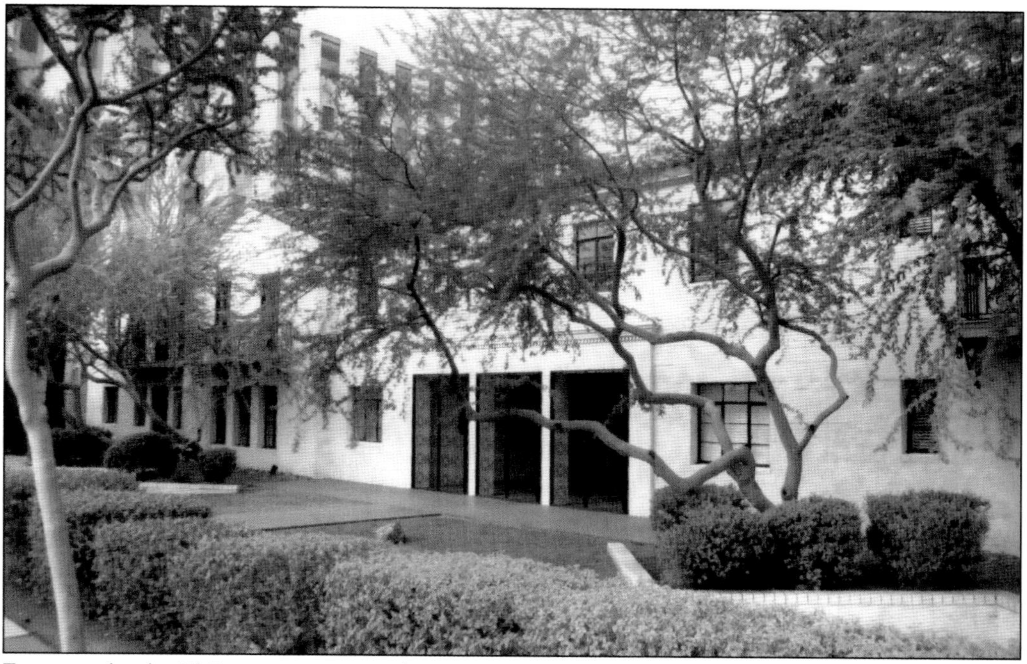

Fortunately, the El Encanto was saved by local businessman Greg Melikian and his family, who valued both the structure and the city's architectural heritage. Completely restored, the El Encanto is now an office building. (Photograph by the author.)

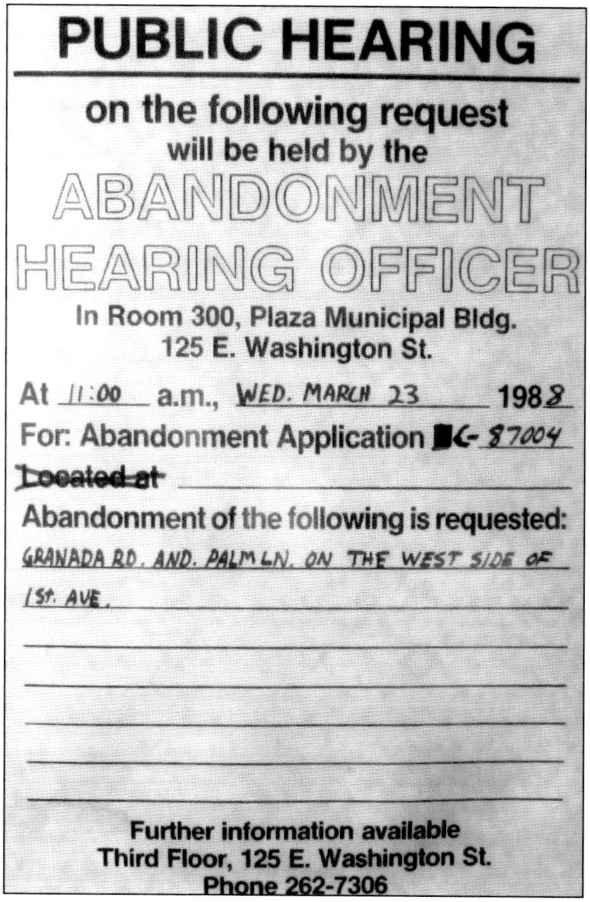

PUBLIC HEARING

on the following request
will be held by the

ABANDONMENT
HEARING OFFICER

In Room 300, Plaza Municipal Bldg.
125 E. Washington St.

At 11:00 a.m., WED. MARCH 23 1988

For: Abandonment Application C-87004

~~Located at~~

Abandonment of the following is requested:

GRANADA RD. AND. PALM LN. ON THE WEST SIDE OF 1st. AVE.

Further information available
Third Floor, 125 E. Washington St.
Phone 262-7306

Because of concern for cut-through traffic from Central Avenue due to high-rise construction, the Encanto Citizens Association and Willo Historic District led an effort to close Granada Road and Palm Lane west of First Avenue. In March 1988, the City of Phoenix granted the closures. In later years, access was gradually closed to all the streets west of Central Avenue between McDowell and Thomas Roads. (Courtesy of Encanto Citizens Association.)

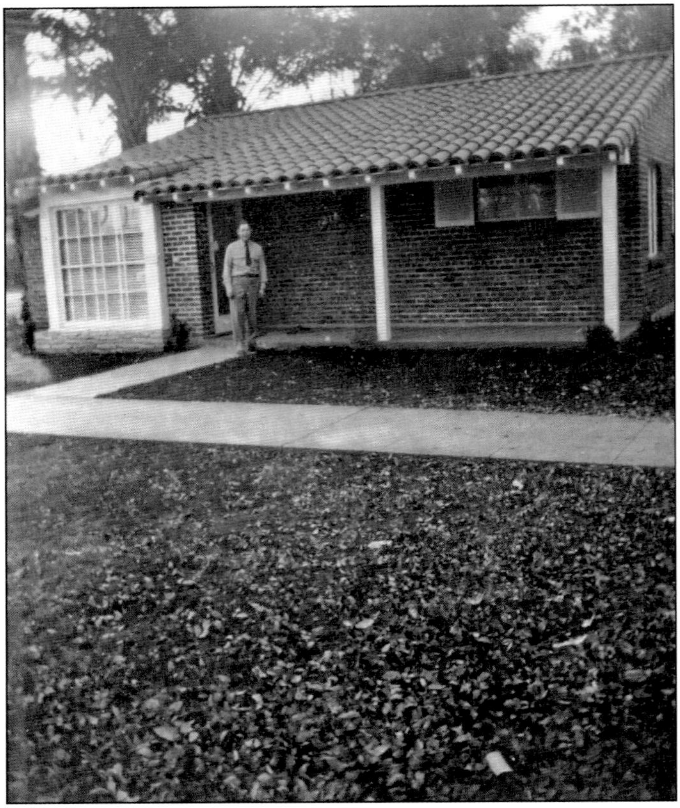

While the Papago Freeway replaced established neighborhoods and businesses, it also presented some opportunities. A park named for former Phoenix mayor Margaret Hance was constructed over the freeway between Third Street and Third Avenue. Among the historic structures saved was the Shackelford dentist office, shown here around 1947 with Dr. J. Gordon Shackelford, at the southwest corner of Central Avenue and Culver Street. It became the home of the Phoenix Trolley Museum. (Courtesy of the Shackelford family.)

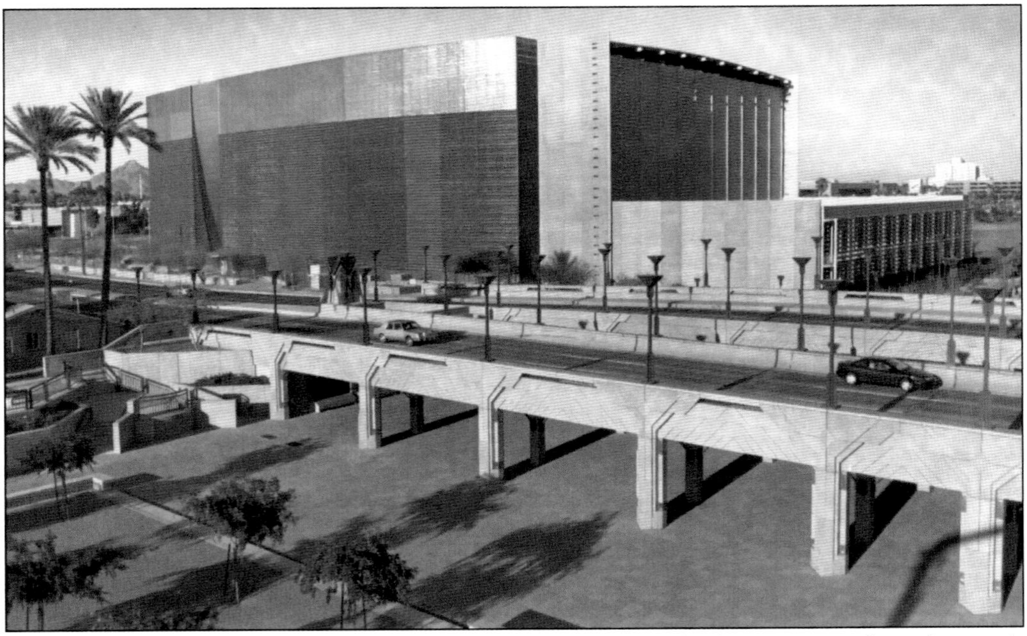

In 1995, the City of Phoenix opened the Burton Barr Central Library. Located on the north edge of Hance Park, it replaced the Phoenix Public Library at Central Avenue and McDowell Road (page 80). The old library became part of an expanded Phoenix Art Museum. (Courtesy of McClintock Collection, Arizona Room, Phoenix Public Library.)

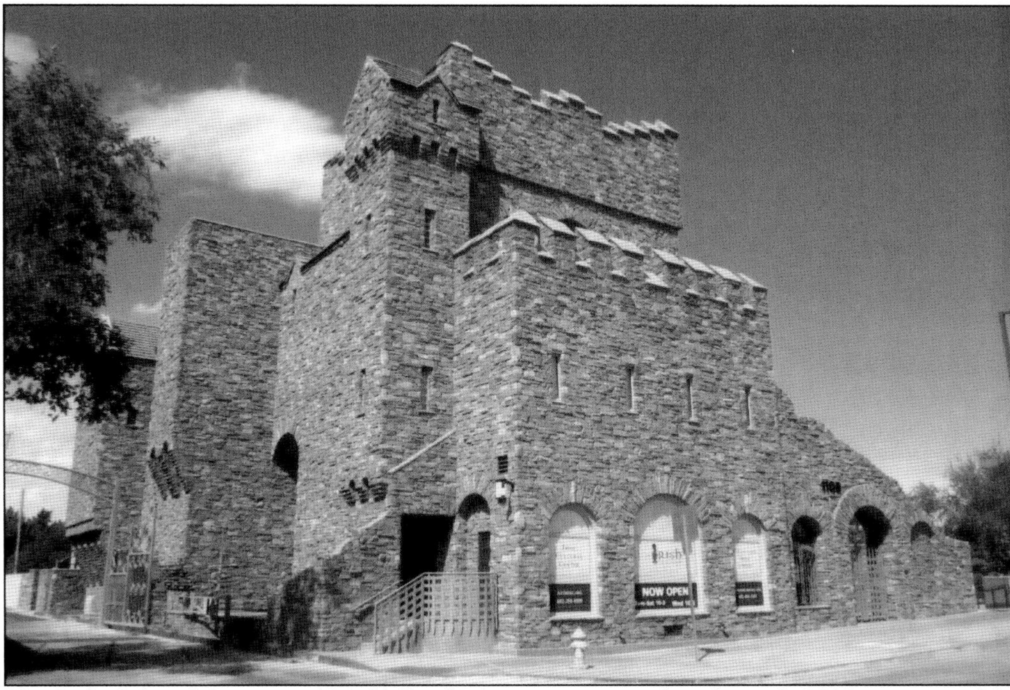

The Irish Cultural Center and McClelland Library, constructed in the early 2000s, are two of the cultural attractions at Hance Park. Located on the south side of the park, the center and library provide opportunities to learn about the Irish heritage through classes, lectures, music, art, festivals, and displays. This photograph shows the library building on Central Avenue. (Photograph by the author.)

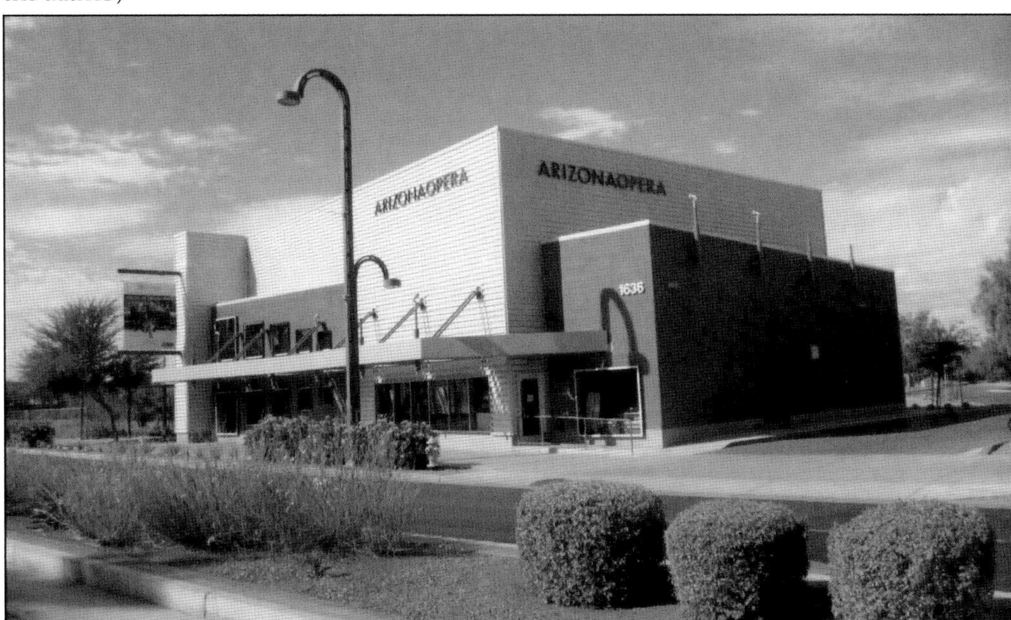

Just north of McDowell Road on the west side of Central Avenue stands the Arizona Opera headquarters. Originally an office furniture store for Walsh Brothers, the building underwent an extensive conversion designed by architect Robert Graham. (Photograph by the author.)

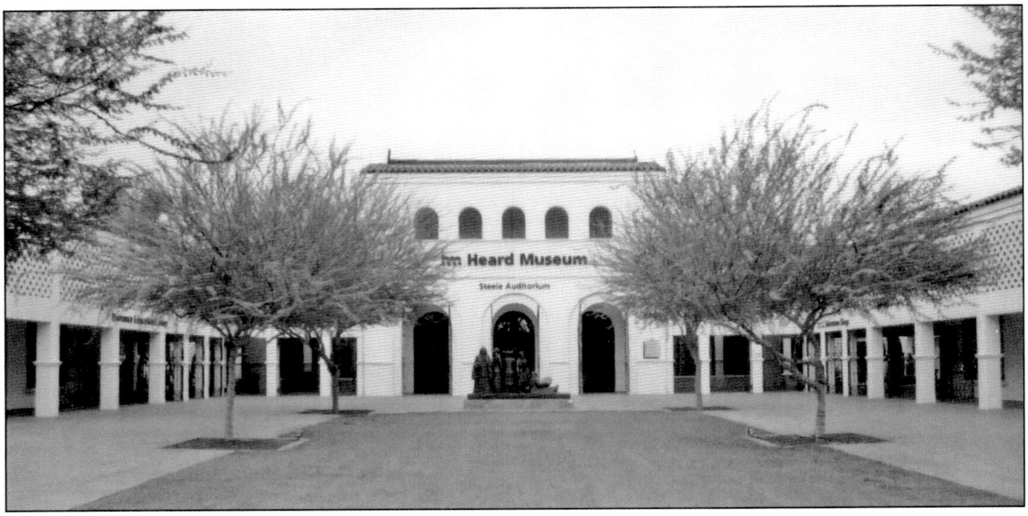

From its original building constructed by the Heard family on Monte Vista Road, the Heard Museum (page 60) grew into a major campus with galleries, exhibit rooms, classrooms, and performance space, as well as a library and archive that holds thousands of books, documents, and photographs. This photograph shows the museum from Central Avenue. It hosts several annual festivals and art shows, including the annual Museum Guild Indian Fair and Market. (Photograph by the author.)

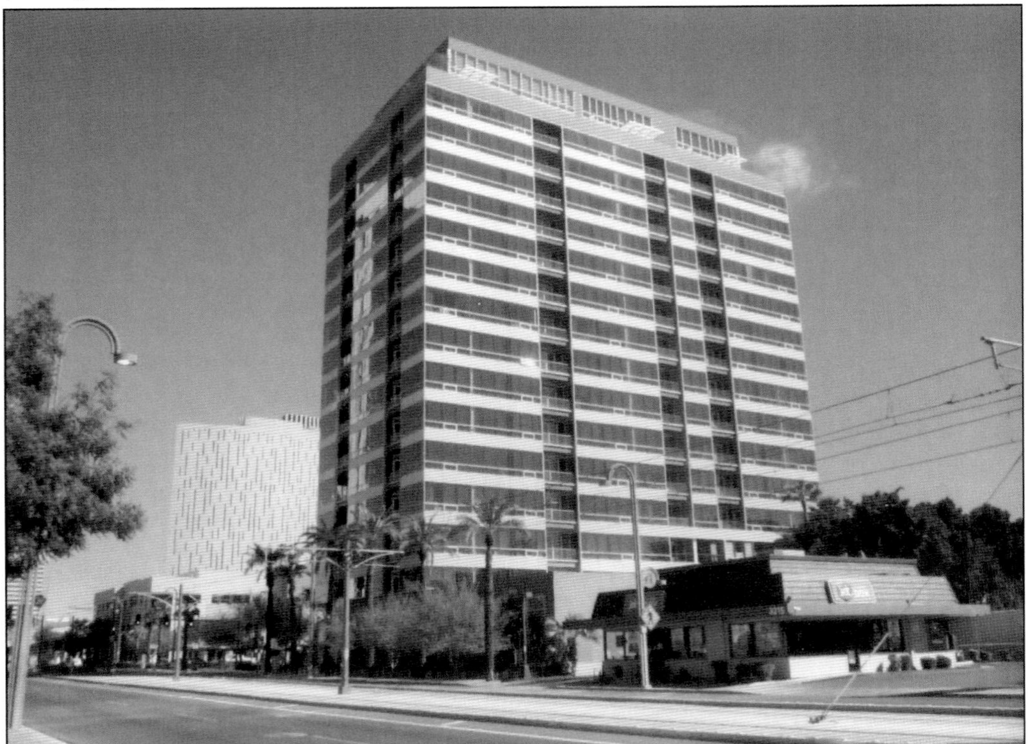

In the early 2000s, the Century Plaza office building at the southeast corner of Central and Lexington Avenues underwent a major adaptive reuse conversion into a condominium building. It is now called One Lexington. (Photograph by the author.)

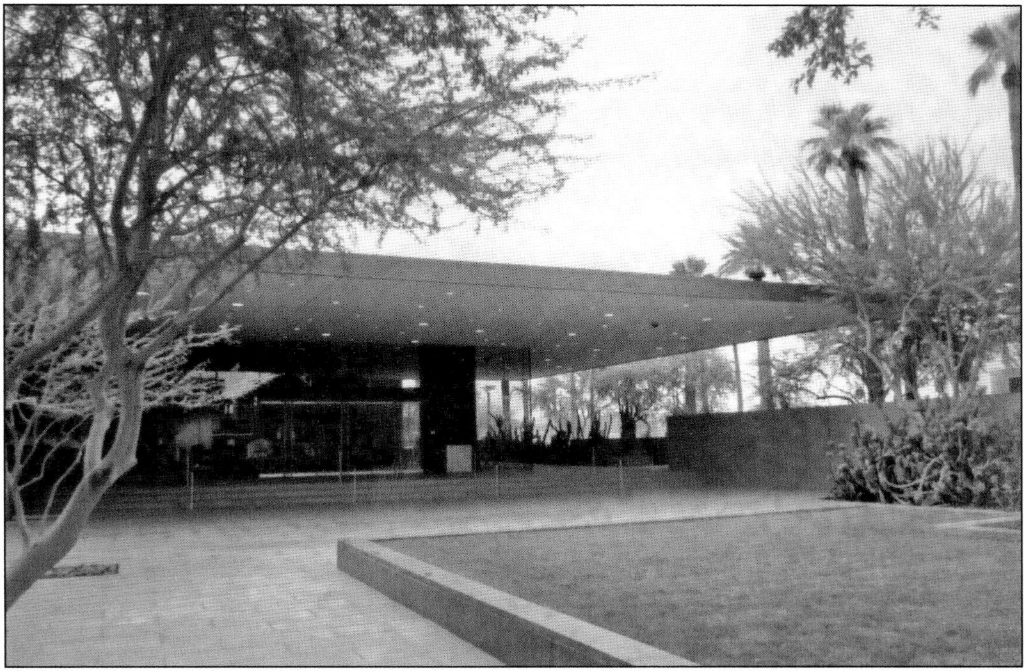

The Phoenix Art Museum had its roots in efforts of the Phoenix Women's Club to improve the quality of art in the community. Planned to occupy the civic center site at the northeast corner of McDowell Road and Central Avenue (page 8), the museum opened in 1948 in a house just east of Central Avenue on Coronado Road. In 1959, after a successful fund drive, the museum moved into a new building just north of the Phoenix Public Library. Over the decades, the museum grew with the addition of exhibition spaces, classrooms, a research library, and theater. Above is the main entrance; below is the second-level Contemporary Gallery. (Above, photograph by the author; below, courtesy of Douglas Sydnor, FAIA.)

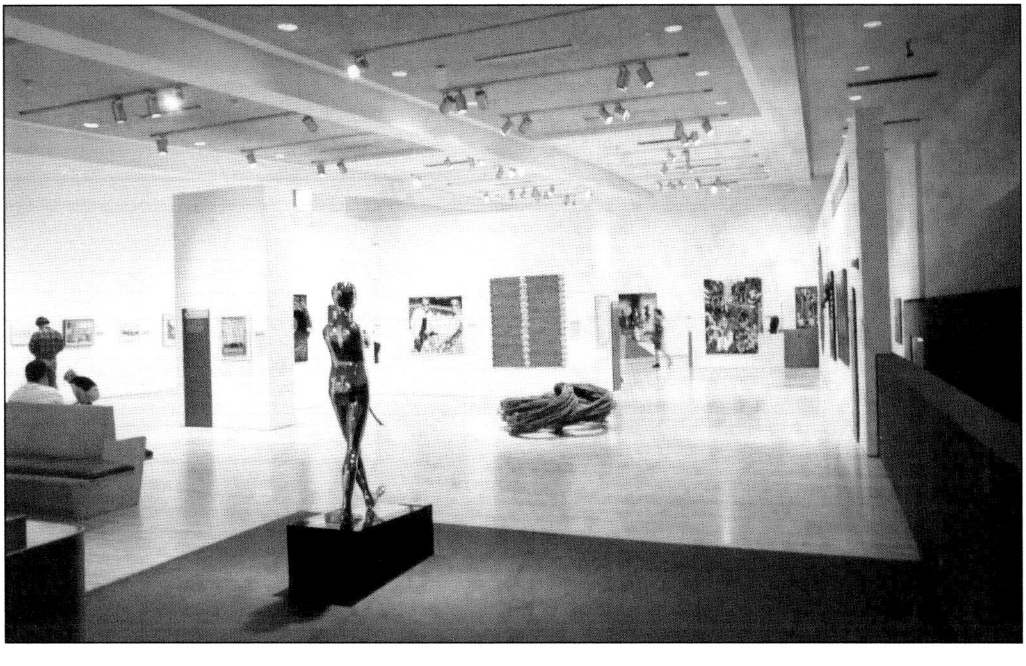

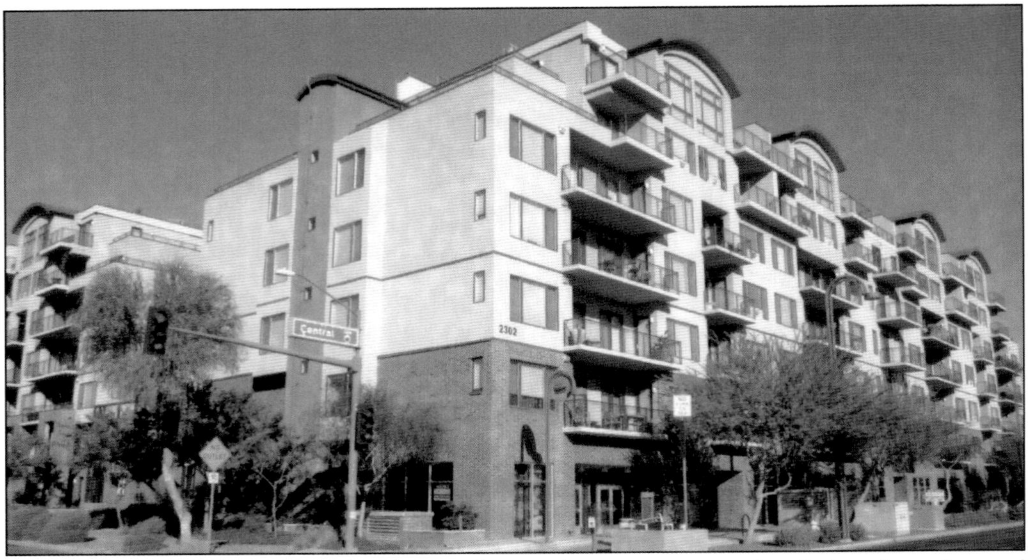

In the early 2000s, the revival of Midtown, along with an interest in urban living, drove demand for more apartments in the Central Corridor close to downtown and cultural amenities. In 2000, construction began on the Tapestry on Central condominiums, located at the northwest corner of Central Avenue and Encanto Boulevard, the site of the Dr. Craig home (page 40). (Photograph by the author.)

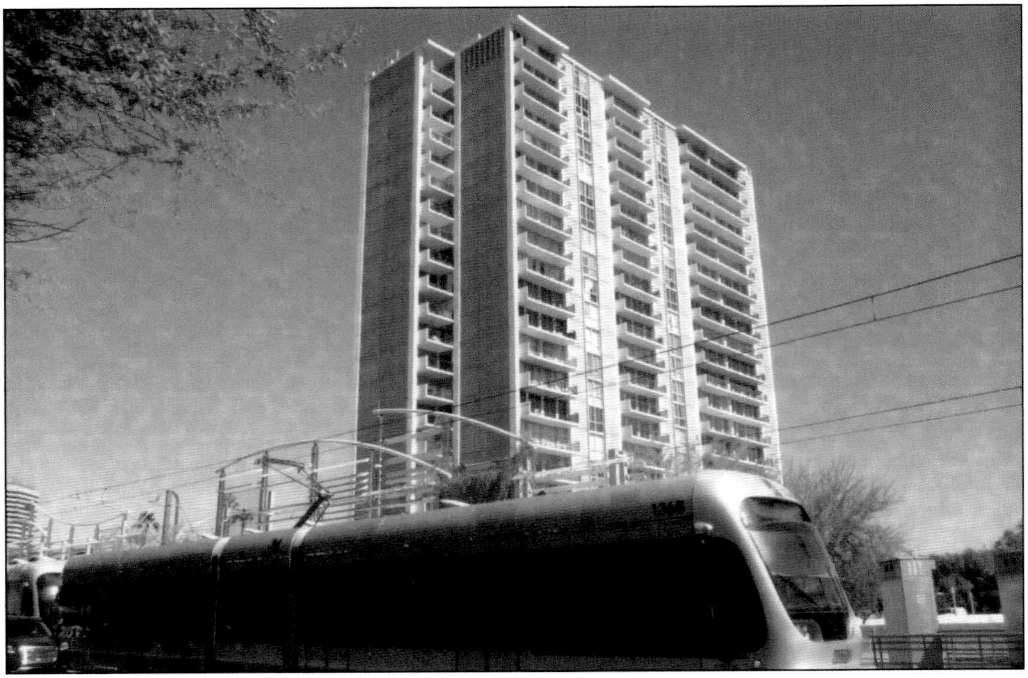

After the Phoenix Street Railway system went out of business in 1948, mass transit relied almost entirely on buses. In 1989, a plan to create an urban rail system with financing from a sales tax was soundly defeated by voters. By the late 1990s, public opinion had shifted. In 2000, voters approved a sales tax for expanded public transit, which included light rail. In December 2008, for the first time in 60 years, street rail once again ran on the streets of Midtown. (Photograph by the author.)

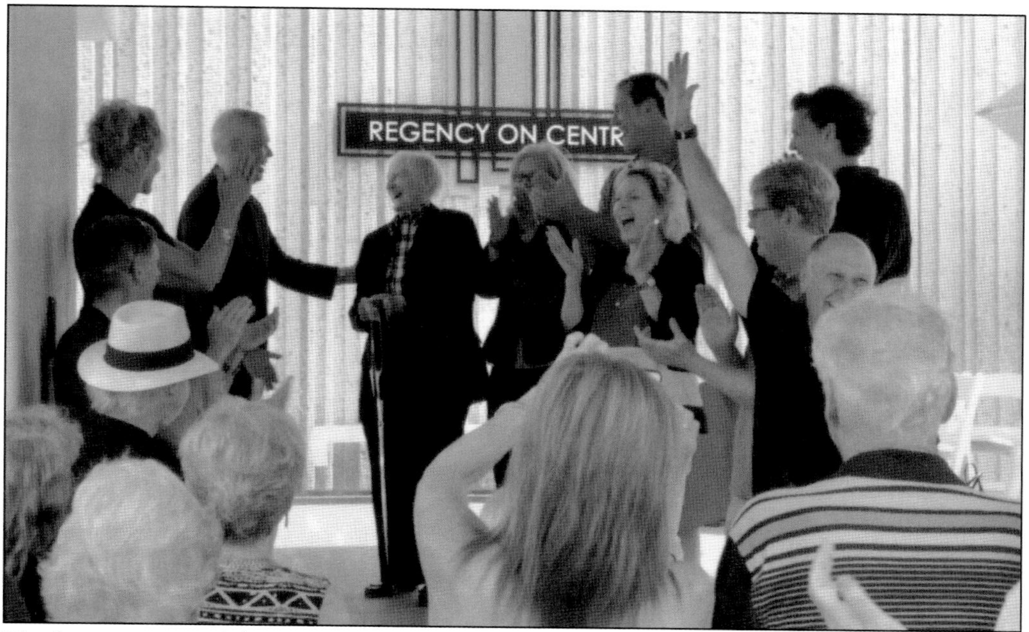

The homeowners of the Regency House (page 102) recently completed a multimillion-dollar renovation to preserve the structure. This photograph from November 1, 2014, shows George Schoneberger (in plaid shirt and jacket with scissors), the building's original architect, after cutting the ribbon to commemorate the project's completion as residents and local dignitaries look on. It was renamed Regency on Central. (Photograph by Brett Noe Productions.)

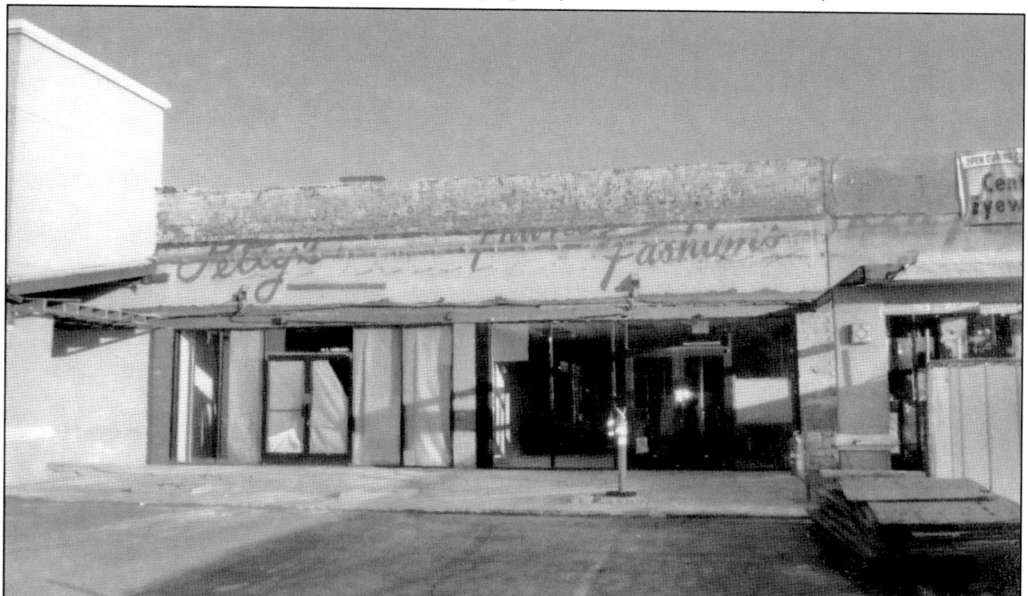

Over the years, Uptown Plaza (page 82) was modified and remodeled to fit the times and market demands for space and appearance. These "improvements" covered the original brick facade and canopies. In 2014, work began to restore the mid-century features from the original 1955 construction. This photograph from early 2015 shows the original facade revealed for the first time in decades, along with original stenciled wall signs from 1955. At this writing, work continues on the center. (Photograph by the author.)

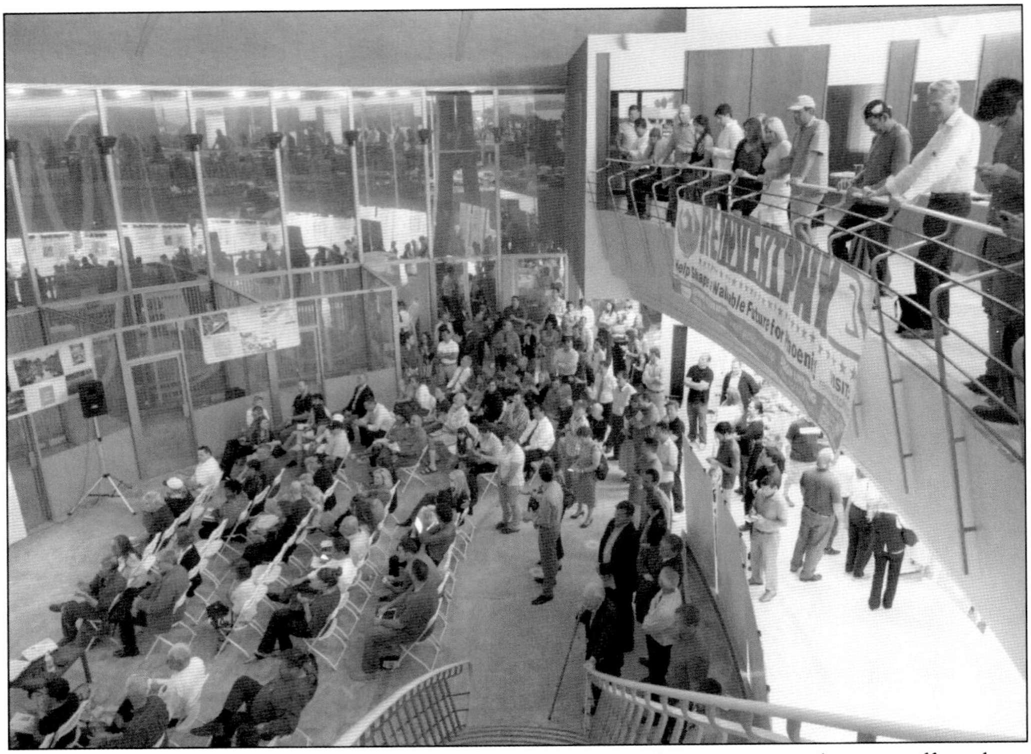

The City of Phoenix Planning and Development Department began a major planning effort along the light rail corridor in 2010 called ReinventPHX. Its objectives included promoting quality development, smart growth, civic engagement, and a return on the community's investment in light rail. The effort involved community input to create a new plan for the Midtown area. Above is a community meeting held in 2014 to view the initial planning proposals and obtain comments. Former Phoenix mayor John Driggs (page 109), with walking stick, can be seen at the bottom of the stairs. Below is a concept of how the area around Park Central could be expanded. (Both, courtesy of City of Phoenix Planning and Development Department.)

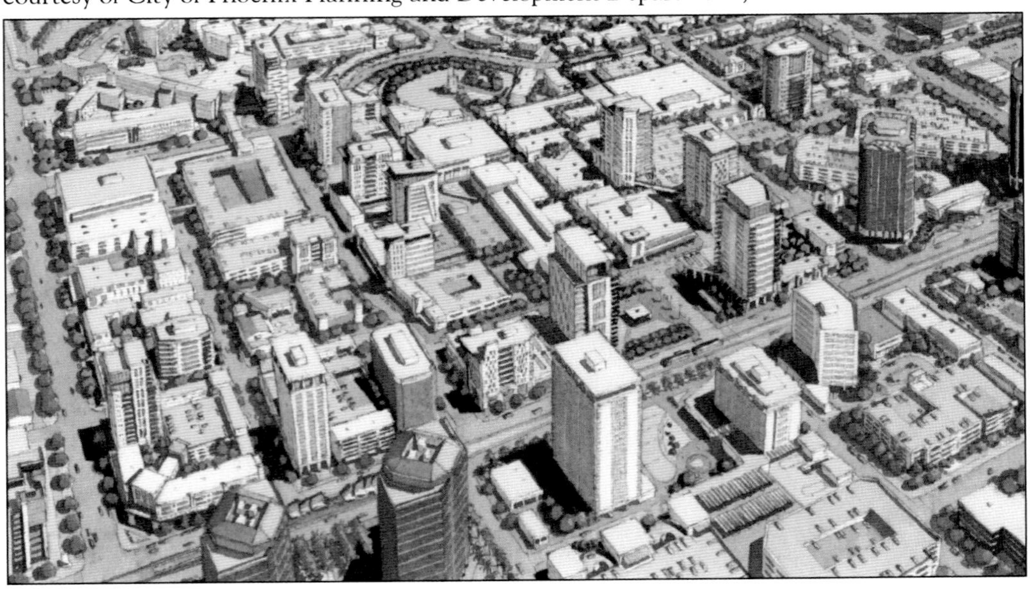

Bibliography

Anderson, J. Seth, Suad Mahmuljin, and Jim McPherson. *Downtown Phoenix*. Charleston, SC: Arcadia Publishing, 2011.
Bommersbach, Jana. *The Trunk Murderess: Winnie Ruth Judd*. New York, NY: Simon & Schuster, 1992.
Conrad, Leigh, and G.G. George. *Phoenix's Greater Encanto-Palmcroft Neighborhood*. Charleston, SC: Arcadia Publishing, 2014.
Fleming, Lawrence J. *Ride a Mile and Smile the While*. Phoenix, AZ: Swaine Publications, Inc., 1977.
Keyt, Clara. *The Development of Millionaire's Row: 1893–1971*. Phoenix, AZ: City of Phoenix Historic Preservation Office, Planning and Development Services, 2010.
Luckingham, Bradford. *Phoenix: The History of a Southwestern Metropolis*. Tucson, AZ: The University of Arizona Press, 1989.
McLaughlin, Dorothy, and Herb McLaughlin. *Phoenix 1870–1970 in Photographs*. Phoenix, AZ: Arizona Photographic Associates, 1970.
Melikian, Robert A. *Vanishing Phoenix*. Charleston, SC: Arcadia Publishing, 2010.
Ryden, Don W. *Midcentury Marvels: Commercial Architecture of Phoenix, 1945–1975*. Phoenix, AZ: City of Phoenix, 2010.
Sydnor, Douglas B. *Plugger: The Architecture of Reginald Sydnor*. Scottsdale, AZ: Douglas B. Sydnor, 2011.

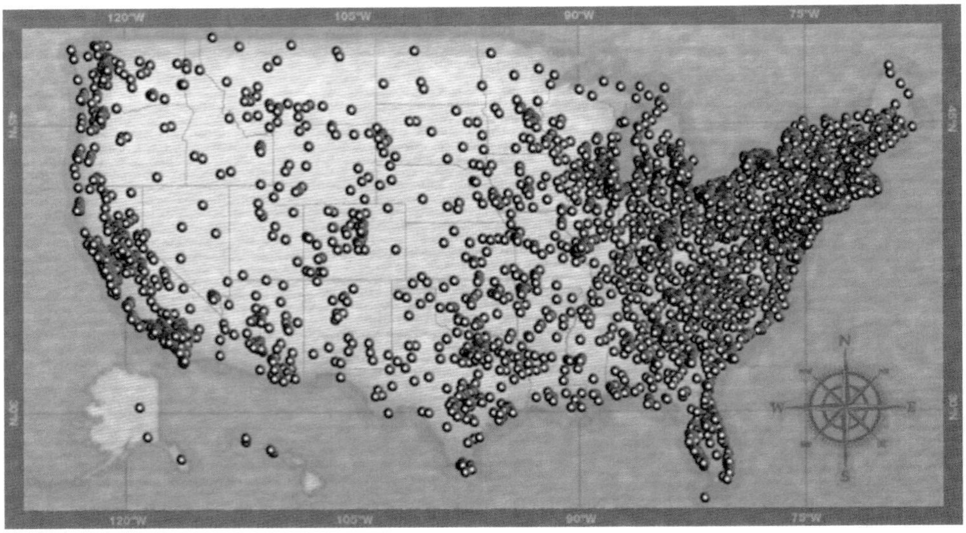